A History of
Christian Worship
An Outline
of Its Development and Forms

William D. Maxwell

Foreword by Robert G. Rayburn

Baker Book House
Grand Rapids, Michigan 49506

Copyright 1936 by
Oxford University Press

Paperback edition issued 1982
by Baker Book House
with permission of copyright owner

ISBN: 0-8010-6132-6

Printed in the United States of America

Formerly published under the title,
An Outline of Christian Worship:
Its Development and Forms

FOREWORD

I N many areas of the evangelical church today there is a genuine desire to improve the quality of corporate worship. Unfortunately in recent decades there has been little emphasis given among evangelicals to this all-important part of the Christian's individual and community life. Thus, many believers have grown up knowing little about the biblical teaching on worship or the rich heritage in worship that the Church has, not only from its early centuries but also from Reformation and later times as well.

The more liberal churches have for some years given special attention to the improvement of corporate worship, and many of them have experienced what has been called a "liturgical renewal." Unfortunately the term *liturgy* is to many evangelicals an offensive word. Undoubtedly they have not understood its basic meaning. They think of it in terms of rigidly prescribed orders of worship with no spontaneity and no extemporaneous prayer. They have missed the fact that every church has its liturgy. The only question is whether the liturgy is rich and meaningful or uncoordinated and meaningless.

With the renewed interest on the part of many pastors and their people in evangelical churches in enriching their corporate worship, it was good news indeed that Baker Book House was putting William D. Maxwell's *An Outline of Christian Worship* back into print. I know of no book which gives such a concise and yet complete history of the development of Christian worship from ancient times to the present day. Any pastor or Christian who is concerned with improving the corporate worship of his church should become familiar with the history of worship since the beginning of the Christian Church. Those in the Reformed churches should be especially interested in the Reformation and post-Reformation orders and forms of worship, the discussions of which occupy more than half of the space in this volume.

William D. Maxwell was a Canadian born in Ontario in

1901; he went to Edinburgh for graduate studies after his graduation in theology from Knox College in Toronto. He remained in Scotland and became a minister in the Church of Scotland (Presbyterian) pastoring a number of different churches. Maxwell made a lifetime study of Christian worship and published a number of books and articles on the subject. Even during his service as Senior Chaplain of the 15th Scottish Division in World War II he gave illuminating lectures to his fellow chaplains and to other Christians on this vital subject.

The careful reader of this book will find it a very well written introduction to a fascinating subject. It will certainly whet the appetite for more study in the same area.

Robert G. Rayburn
St. Louis, Missouri

PREFACE

THIS book is an attempt to give a concise outline of Christian worship and the forms it has taken from earliest times to the present. The aim has been practical, directed towards the clear delineation of basic facts and principles at a time when a quickened interest in worship is manifest throughout all communions of the Church.

A large proportion of the space is devoted to the worship of the Reformed Churches, particularly to the early liturgies of these Churches. This has been necessary because of the strange neglect shown towards these liturgies by British scholars, resulting in widespread misunderstanding of a most important period.

Public worship as here treated is restricted to the Sunday Morning worship of the Church, and that which has grown out of the Quire Offices.

A work such as this, to be of value, requires documentation, but it has seemed to me to be of first importance that this should be as unobtrusive as possible. Instead, therefore, of quoting works in the footnotes, numbers are used which refer to the bibliography given at the end, the Roman numerals referring to the section and the Arabic numerals to the particular work. If a text or compilation is referred to, the Roman numeral is replaced by the word 'Text'. The bibliography, though limited in the interests of economy and simplicity, will suffice to direct the reader to the principal liturgical texts and to such standard works as will, in their turn, open up the literature of the subject in all its branches.

My thanks are due in especial to the Reverend W. Napier Bell, M.A., for many wise and helpful suggestions, and for valuable assistance in reading both script and proof; also to the Reverend Millar Patrick, D.D., and the Reverend W. McMillan, Ph.D., D.D., for their advice and criticism, as also to Mr. J. C. Meikle, of the Oxford Press, for his great kindness in compiling the Index.

W. D. M.

PREFACE TO THIRD IMPRESSION

SINCE the second impression of this book, *The Book of Common Order*, 1940, which is the authorized standard of worship of the Church of Scotland, has appeared. Accordingly, the original matter of pp. 135–6 which described the interim rite of the re-united Church of Scotland as contained in *An Ordinal and Service Book for the Use of Presbyteries* has been replaced by a brief and scarcely adequate description and scheme of the rite now established in the Church of Scotland.

Did space permit, other alterations might properly have been made. In particular, as Dr. J. S. Whale has pointed out, I have omitted to mention the notable enrichment of worship contributed by the great English Hymn-writers of the 18th and 19th centuries, whose hymns became an integral part of Anglican, but especially Congregational and Methodist, and, later, Scottish worship. For this omission I apologize, and refer the reader to section *X* of the Bibliography for further enlightenment, and in especial to Bernard Lord Manning's valuable work, *The Hymns of Wesley and Watts* (London, 1942).   W.D.M.

NOTE TO FOURTH (1949) IMPRESSION

A few minor corrections only have been made (particularly on p. 63), together with a few additions to the Bibliography.
                                        W. D. M.

NOTE TO NINTH (1963) IMPRESSION

In the Bibliography, pp. 194–5, Section XII, 'Some Additional Books' has been extended by the inclusion of additional, mostly recent items.
                                        W. D. M.

CONTENTS

I

PRIMITIVE WORSHIP: ITS ORIGINS AND GROWTH

WORSHIP consists of our words and actions, the outward expression of our homage and adoration, when we are assembled in the presence of God. These words and actions are governed by two things: our knowledge of the God whom we worship, and the human resources we are able to bring to that worship.[1] Christian worship is distinct from all other worship because it is directed to the God and Father of our Lord Jesus Christ. Its development is unique because the Holy Spirit has been with and in the Church to counsel and guide it since the day of Pentecost. It is this that gives the historical approach to worship its peculiar validity and practical importance.

§ 1. Origins

The New Testament was committed to writing before Christian worship had fully developed, but it does not leave us without some clear witness. The Book of Acts portrays the early life of the Church, and the Epistles and Revelation add further details. Four things stand out. First, for a time at least Christians continued to worship in the synagogues and in the Temple. Secondly, they frequently shared a common meal known as the *Agapé* or Love Feast. Thirdly, usually at the conclusion of the *Agapé*, sometimes apart from it, they celebrated the eucharist in obedience to our Lord's command at the Last Supper.[2] Fourthly, this action was often followed by prophesying or speaking with tongues, an ecstatic exercise in which some were specially gifted, but

---

[1] For works on the theory of worship, see Bibliography I.
[2] See, e.g., I. 14, pp. 20–2 on the difference between the Last Supper and the eucharist. Whether our Lord actually used the words of command is really immaterial, see, e.g., III. 13, p. 127.

one that had to be most carefully controlled, as we see from St. Paul's admonitions concerning it. Comparatively early, approximately by the middle of the second century, the second and fourth elements disappeared from the main stream of Christian worship. We need not, accordingly, concern ourselves further with these, but confine our attention to the two permanent elements derived respectively from the Synagogue and the Upper Room.

From the beginning the reading and exposition of the Holy Scriptures in a setting of praise and prayer has been one of the essential elements in Christian worship. This is a direct inheritance from the Jewish Synagogue.

Our Lord Himself, 'as his custom was', had worshipped regularly in the synagogues; St. Paul always went first to the Synagogue when he came to a new city; and the Jewish Christians loved the Synagogue and its ways, where they had worshipped and been taught from early childhood. It was to be expected, therefore, that when the Christians were expelled from the synagogues their worship should follow similar lines and contain many of the same elements.

By contrast, the Temple worship left little mark upon Christian worship, and this principally for two reasons. First, the great majority of the Jews of the Dispersion had never seen the worship of the Temple, and, even in Palestine, the real home of Jewish worship at the time of our Lord was in the synagogues; while to the Gentile Christians the Temple and its worship meant little. Secondly, forty years after the death of our Lord, the Temple was destroyed by the Romans and never rebuilt; the synagogues remained.

The origin of the Synagogue is obscure, but it grew out of the Dispersion.[1] To preserve their distinctive life and give it continuity, the Jews required as a people to have constant access to their sacred books. Out of this need the

[1] Probably the chief contributing factor to the origin of the Synagogue was the Reform of Josiah; see Oesterley and Robinson, *Hebrew Religion*, London, 1930, p. 212.

institution of the Synagogue arose, until by our Lord's time one synagogue at least existed at the centre of every considerable community of Jews, from Persia to the westernmost boundaries of the Roman Empire.

The primary purpose of the Synagogue was to enable men to hear the Law read and expounded. The central act in its worship, therefore, was the reading of the Law, first in Hebrew, then in the common tongue accompanied by an exposition. Around this, singings and prayers naturally and inevitably gathered.

For the praise the old psalms were used and new psalms composed. The prayers were in such a form that all could take part in their recitation, and, though not committed to writing until probably the fourth or fifth century of our era, by the time of our Lord both their form and content appear to have been fixed and were handed down by oral tradition. By that time also readings from the Prophetic Books, added to the canon of Jewish Scripture two centuries earlier, were included in the Synagogue services. All this, Christianity inherited from the old Judaism.

But Christian worship was not a precise copy of the Synagogue worship. There was a new emphasis and content to accord with the new revelation and to express the new spirit. The Prophetic Books rather than the Law became the chief centre of interest. Soon, too, although more than a century passed before the canon was fixed, the Christian Scriptures began to take form, comprising letters and memoirs of the Apostles and others, collections of the sayings and acts of our Lord, and finally the Apocalypse. These new Scriptures early took precedence over the old, and the highest place was given to the Gospels, described by Origen as 'the crown of all Scripture'. The Christians continued to use the Psalms in their worship much as they had been used in the synagogues, but also composed hymns of their own. Their prayers, too, though related in form to those of the Synagogue so that it was possible for all to take part, soon underwent a separate development, until a new body of devotion appeared, fitted to express the worship of those who had come to know God as revealed in Jesus Christ.

To this the early Christians added another element derived directly from our Lord, the perpetuation in prayer and sacramental fellowship of the experience of the Upper Room. More than words could do, this holy action brought to mind all that our Lord had done, and made them supremely conscious of His living Presence with them. The experience was charged with power by the fact of the resurrection; and custom, in obedience to the Apostolic injunction, soon settled down in its choice of the first day of the week for the celebration of the Lord's Supper, with daybreak, the hour when He first discovered Himself to them, as the hour of worship. Not Friday, the day of His death, but Sunday, the day of His resurrection, was the Lord's day; and to that day belonged their highest act of worship, when they showed forth His death victoriously in the eucharist, while He Himself, their risen Lord, was present in their midst. They had no theory of our Lord's presence in the sacrament such as came to divide the Church in later days, but they knew it as a fact of spiritual experience, a vivid reality.

Putting together, then, the references to worship in the New Testament in the light of later history—a reasonable course since the history is continuous—we arrive at something like this towards the end of the first century:

First, that which grew out of the Synagogue: Scripture lections (1 Tim. iv. 13; 1 Thess. v. 27; Col. iv. 16); Psalms and hymns (1 Cor. xiv. 26; Eph. v. 19; Col. iii. 16); common prayers (Acts ii. 42; 1 Tim. ii. 1–2) and people's Amens (1 Cor. xiv. 16); a sermon or exposition (1 Cor. xiv. 26; Acts xx. 7); a confession of faith, not necessarily the formal recitation of a creed (1 Cor. xv. 1–4; 1 Tim. vi. 12); and perhaps almsgiving (1 Cor. xvi. 1–2; 2 Cor. ix. 10–13; Rom. xv. 26).

Secondly, commonly joined to the above, the Celebration of the Lord's Supper, derived from the experience of the Upper Room (1 Cor. x. 16, xi. 23; Matt. xxvi. 26–8; Mark xiv. 22–4; Luke xxii. 19–20). The Prayer of Consecration would include thanksgiving

(Luke xxii. 19; 1 Cor. xi. 23, xiv. 16; 1 Tim. ii. 1), remembrance of our Lord's death and resurrection (Acts ii. 42; Luke xxii. 19; 1 Cor. xi. 23, 25, 26), intercession (John xvii), and perhaps the recitation of the Lord's Prayer (Matt. vi. 9–13; Luke xi. 2–4). Probably there were singings in this part of the service, and the Kiss of Peace (Rom. xvi. 16; 1 Cor. xvi. 20; 1 Thess. v. 26; 1 Pet. v. 14). Men and women were separated as in the synagogues; the men were bareheaded and the women veiled (1 Cor. xi 6–7). The attitude of prayer was standing (Phil. i. 27; Eph. vi. 14; 1 Tim. ii. 8).

Thus Christian worship, as a distinctive, indigenous thing, arose from the fusion, in the crucible of Christian experience, of the Synagogue and the Upper Room. Thus fused, each completing and quickening the other, they became the norm of Christian worship. Christian worship found other forms of expression, but these belong to the circumference, not to the centre. The typical worship of the Church is to be found to this day in the union of the worship of the Synagogue and the sacramental experience of the Upper Room; and that union dates from New Testament times.

§ 2. *The* Kiddûsh *and the Last Supper*

The origin of the Last Supper itself is a question that may with profit be briefly discussed at this point. Until recently the traditional view was that the Last Supper was the Passover, celebrated by our Lord with His disciples for the last time on the night of His betrayal. But the evidence has been re-examined, and another view has been put forward, and is now commonly accepted as more nearly explaining the facts.

It may be summarized as follows. The Last Supper is held to derive from a simple repast shared weekly by small groups of male Jews, very often by a rabbi and his disciples. Its purpose was to prepare for the Sabbath or a festival, and it was religious in character. It consisted of religious discussion followed by a simple meal of common bread and wine mixed with water, the cup being passed from one to another, and prayer offered. This meal was known as the

Kiddûsh, and it was commonly observed in pious circles of the day, especially in Messianic circles. It is almost certain that our Lord and His disciples were accustomed to partake of this meal of fellowship on the eve of every Sabbath and festival: the 'last supper', therefore, was the last of these meals that they shared together.

There are many indications, as we examine the narratives, that we have here the origin of the Last Supper.

If the Passover had begun on 'the night on which He was betrayed', our Lord could not have been tried and executed that day, for it was against the law of the Jews to hold a trial or execution during the Passover. But the Last Supper took place, according to Jewish reckoning, on the same day as the trials and crucifixion. This alone is really sufficient to prove that it was a pre-Passover meal that our Lord shared with His disciples, and not the Passover proper; although, being closely associated with the Passover as a normal part of its celebration, it is not unnatural to find it called the 'Passover' in the narratives: it would be clear enough to a Jewish reader what was meant.

Further, the character of the Last Supper was fundamentally different from that of the Passover. The Passover was strictly a family festival; the *Kiddûsh* was always observed by a group of male friends. At the Passover the paschal lamb was offered; this is missing at the Last Supper, yet it was essential to the Passover. Unleavened bread ($\ddot{\alpha}\zeta\upsilon\mu\upsilon\varsigma$) was required for the Passover; but ordinary leavened bread ($\ddot{\alpha}\rho\tau\upsilon\varsigma$) was always used at the *Kiddûsh*, and all the narratives specifically state that ordinary bread was used at the Last Supper. Several cups were used at the Passover; at the Last Supper, as at the *Kiddûsh*, there was only one cup. At the Passover the passage narrating the exodus from Egypt was invariably read; there is no mention of this having been done at the Last Supper.

There is a further point relative to the subsequent history of the eucharist which may also be mentioned. From the beginning the Lord's Supper was celebrated frequently, a weekly celebration soon becoming the settled practice. The *Kiddûsh*, too, was observed weekly, but the Passover only yearly. Yet their subsequent practice clearly shows that the disciples understood from our Lord's words and actions that they were to celebrate the eucharist frequently; this would have been unlikely if the Last Supper had been the yearly Passover and not the weekly *Kiddûsh*.

In conclusion, it may be noted that at the *Kiddûsh* water was mixed with the wine in the ordinary eastern fashion; and this, apart from the Armenian Church, was the universal practice of the Church in celebrating the eucharist.

These points, taken separately and together, demonstrate conclusively that the Last Supper derives from the *Kiddûsh*.[1]

§ 3. *The Sub-Apostolic Age*

No liturgical texts belonging to this period have come down to us. Our sources of information are meagre, but they suffice to indicate the general trend of development, and show that the rites of the Church, though still in a fluid state, were fundamentally similar. Till *c.* A.D. 140 our only sources of importance are Clement of Rome's letter to the Corinthians (A.D. 96), Pliny's letter to the Emperor Trajan (A.D. 112), and the *Didaché* (*c.* A.D. 130–40).

Clement's letter[2] is an exhortation, not a liturgical document, but at one point it breaks out into words that may be traced in liturgies of two centuries later.[3] The prayer lacks order, but possesses a notable dignity and solemnity of phrase. Here is an extract:

'May the sealed number of the elect in the whole world be pre-

---

[1] See especially II. 1, 2, 3, and 9, III. 9, and III. 13, pp. 123 sqq. on the *Kiddûsh*. Against this view, see J. Mackinnon, *The Historic Jesus*, London, 1931, pp. 217 sqq., I. 6, pp. 44 sqq., and XII. 2, pp. 1 sqq.

[2] His *First Epistle to Corinthians*, lix–lxii. English trans. from Greek, as here quoted, in III. 5, pp. 51–3, except concluding doxology. See also Lightfoot, *Apostolic Fathers*.

[3] Parallels between Clement and liturgy of Book VIII of the *Apostolic Constitutions* detailed in III. 19, vol. i.

served intact by the Creator of all things, through His well-beloved
Son Jesus Christ, by whom He has called us from darkness to light.
. . . Thou hast opened the eyes of our hearts that we may know
Thee, . . . who abasest the insolence of the proud, who scatterest the
machinations of the people, who exaltest the humble and puttest
down the mighty. . . . O Master, be our help and succour. Be the
salvation of those who are in tribulation; take pity on the lowly, raise
up them that fall, reveal Thyself to those who are in need, heal the
ungodly, and restore those who have gone out of the Way. Appease
the hunger of the needy, deliver those who suffer in prison, heal the
sick, comfort the faint-hearted, that all people may know that Thou
art the only God, that Jesus Christ is Thy Servant, and that we are
Thy people and the sheep of Thy pasture. . . .

'. . . Thou, Lord, hast created the earth, Thou who remainest
faithful throughout all generations, just in Thy judgements, wonderful
in Thy might and majesty. . . . O pitiful and merciful God, forgive
us our faults, our injustices, our shortcomings, our transgressions, . . .
cleanse us by Thy truth and direct our steps, . . . and make Thy face
to shine upon us. . . . Give peace and concord . . . to all the dwellers
of the earth. . . .

'It is Thou, Lord, who hast given to our princes,[1] to those who
rule over us upon earth, the power of royalty, by the excellent and
unspeakable virtue of Thy might, in order that we may submit ourselves to them, and not put ourselves in opposition to Thy will.
Grant them, Lord, health, peace, concord, and stability, that they
may exercise unhindered the authority with which Thou hast entrusted them. . . . Direct their counsels, . . . so that exercising peace-
fully and mercifully the power Thou hast given them, they may
obtain Thy favour. . . . We praise Thee who art able to do these and
better things than these, through Jesus Christ the High Priest and
Guardian of our souls, through whom be glory and majesty to Thee,
both now and throughout all generations, for ever and ever. Amen.'

Scholars agree that this noble prayer cannot be regarded
as the reproduction of a fixed form, but it is a fine example
of the style of solemn prayer in use towards the end of the
first century, particularly in the celebrant's Great Intercession at the eucharist.

Earlier in the letter[2] there is an allusion to the *Sanctus*,

---

[1] Duchesne [III. 5, p. 52] says, 'Note the spirit in which the Christians
prayed for the emperor on the morrow of the fury of Domitian.'
[2] *Epistle* xxxiv. Cf. Isa. vi. 3, and Rev. iv. 8, 11.

'Holy, Holy, Holy, Lord of hosts, every creature is full of Thy glory,' which was probably even then a customary part of the eucharist. Reference is also made to the 'offering' of 'oblations',[1] which, though later a technical name for the offering of the sacred elements, here probably includes the offering of alms.

Pliny's letter to Trajan[2] is more informative, but its liturgical value is limited by the fact that the writer is not a Christian and is speaking only at second hand when he describes the worship of the Christians in Bithynia, where he was Governor. Two rites are mentioned, but precisely what these are must be left as uncertain. Both take place on a 'fixed day' (*stato die*), which it is generally agreed means Sunday.

The first rite is observed 'before daybreak', when a hymn is sung *secum invicem*[3] to Christ as God, and Christians bind themselves by a *sacramentum* to abstain from evil. They meet again later to eat food described as 'common and harmless', and this comprises the second rite.

Our next document, the *Didaché*,[4] though its exact date is uncertain, is generally believed to describe worship in Jewish Christian circles in the Sub-Apostolic Age. It does not belong to the central stream of development. It is of special interest, nevertheless, partly because it illustrates a practice closely related to the *Kiddûsh*,[5] but principally because it is an example of the combined eucharist and *Agapé*, in which the blessings of the bread and the cup are not only separate, but the cup is blessed before the bread. The prayers are brief, and are here quoted in full:

ix. 'As touching the eucharist, we give thanks in this manner. First over the cup.

'We give thanks to Thee, our Father, for the holy vine of David

[1] *Epistle* xl.
[2] A longer digest and references to full text in III. 6, pp. 16–17.
[3] This may refer to some form of antiphonal singing.
[4] The Greek text of the chapters quoted is given in III. 9, p. 231, and in Bigg and Maclean's edition, London, 1922. But see also XII. 2, pp. 171–5.
[5] See the parallel Jewish prayers given in Cabrol and Leclerq, *Monumenta Ecclesiae Liturgica*, I. i. 17–23.

Thy servant which Thou hast made known to us through Jesus Thy servant. To Thee be the glory for ever.

'Over the broken bread.

'We give thanks to Thee, our Father, for the life and knowledge which Thou hast made known to us through Jesus Thy servant. To Thee be glory for ever. As this broken bread was scattered over the mountains, and has been gathered together and made one, so may Thy Church be gathered from the ends of the earth into Thy kingdom; for Thine is the glory and the power through Jesus Christ for ever.

'Let no one eat or drink of your eucharist but those baptized in the Name of the Lord, for it was concerning this that the Lord said, "Do not give that which is holy to the dogs".

x. 'When you have been filled, give thanks thus:

'We give thanks to Thee, holy Father, for Thy holy Name, which Thou hast caused to dwell in our hearts, and for the knowledge, faith, and immortality which Thou hast made known to us through Jesus Thy servant. To Thee be glory for ever. Thou, O Lord, Ruler of the universe, hast made all things for the sake of Thy Name, hast given meat and drink to all for their enjoyment that they might give thanks to Thee; but to us Thou hast given spiritual meat and drink, and eternal life through Jesus Thy servant. Before all things we give Thee thanks, for Thou art mighty. To Thee be glory for ever. Remember, O Lord, Thy Church, to deliver it from all evil and to perfect it in Thy love; and gather it that Thou hast sanctified from the four winds of heaven into Thy kingdom which Thou hast prepared for it, for Thine is the power and the glory for ever.

'May grace (Coptic version: "the Lord") come, and this world pass away. Hosanna to the God (Coptic: "the house") of David.

'If any one be holy, let him come; if any one be not, let him repent.

'Maranatha. Amen.

'Then suffer the prophets to give thanks (or, as it may be translated, "to continue the eucharist") as they wish (τοῖς δὲ προφήταις ἐπιτρέπετε εὐχαριστεῖν, ὅσα θέλουσιν).'

Wednesday and Friday are mentioned as fast days, and chapter xiv makes it clear that Sunday was the normal day fixed for the celebration of the Lord's Supper:

xiv. 'Every Lord's day, when you have assembled together, break bread and give thanks, after having confessed your sins so that your sacrifice may be pure.'

§ 4. The Second Century

Justin Martyr's well-known account of the Sunday worship at Rome, written in his *Apology* to the Emperor Antoninus Pius, *c.* A.D. 140, brings us back to the main stream. Justin gives only a broad outline, but it is sufficient to give us a clear idea of the worship of the time; and writing as he does from Rome some seventy years after the death of St. Paul, we may be sure that the worship he describes is not far removed from Apostolic practice. The most important passages follow.[1]

There is, first, a description of a celebration of the eucharist after a baptism.

'Our prayers being ended, we salute one another with a kiss. Then bread, and a cup of wine mixed with water (κρᾶμα), are brought to him who presides (ὁ προεστώς) over the brethren. He, taking them, offers praise and glory to the Father of all through the Name of the Son and the Holy Spirit, and gives thanks (εὐχαριστίαν) at great length for that we have been counted worthy to receive these gifts from God; and when he finishes the prayers and thanksgivings all the people present cry aloud, Amen. Amen in the Hebrew tongue means, So be it.

'After the President has given thanks and all the people have said Amen, those among us who are called deacons give to all present, sharing it among them, the bread and wine mixed with water over which thanks have been given (ὁ εὐχαριστηθεὶς ἄρτος, κτλ.), and carry it also to those who are absent. And this food is called eucharist (εὐχαριστία) by us, of which it is not right for any one to partake save only he who believes that the things taught by us are true, and is washed with the washing that is for the forgiveness of sins and regeneration, and so lives as Christ commanded us.'

Justin further states that these things are received, not 'as common bread and drink', but as 'the body and blood' of Christ, and that this is in accord with the Gospels, in which the express commands of our Lord are handed down. He adds also that this Christian rite has no

---

[1] *First Apology*, lxv–lxvii. Other passages from his writings confirm the details mentioned in these accounts.

connexion with Mithraism, but rather that the reverse is true:

'The evil demons, imitating this [our rite], have taught that the same should be done in the mysteries of Mithras; for you know, or may learn, that in the mysteries of initiation the bread and a cup of water are set forth with a certain form of words.'

Next, Justin describes the Sunday service as normally celebrated.

'On the day called the Feast of the Sun, all who live in towns or in the country assemble in one place, and the memoirs of the Apostles or the writings of the Prophets are read as time permits. Then, when the reader has ended, the President instructs and encourages the people to practise the truths contained in the Scripture lections. Thereafter, we all stand up and offer prayers together; and, as I mentioned before, when we have concluded this prayer, bread and wine and water are brought.

'Then the President likewise offers up prayers and thanksgivings according to his ability, and the people cry aloud saying Amen. Each one then receives a portion and share of the elements over which thanks have been given; and which are also carried and ministered by the deacons to those absent.'

Justin ends his description by a mention of the gifts collected from wealthy persons; these are given into the keeping of the President to use as he approves for the support of widows and orphans, and the assistance of prisoners and aid of strangers on their travels. He states, in conclusion, that the Christian day of worship is the first day of the week because it commemorates the Creation and the Lord's Resurrection.

From these and other passages in Justin's works the liturgy, as celebrated about the middle of the second century, may be thus reconstructed:

The Liturgy of the Word

Lections from the Prophets, and the Epistles and Gospels (called 'Memoirs of the Apostles')
Instruction and exhortation based upon the lections
Common prayers, apparently in litany form
Psalms and hymns also probably had a place

The Liturgy of the Upper Room[1]

Kiss of Peace
Offertory: Collection of gifts for poor
    Bringing in of the Elements
Prayer of Consecration:[2]
    Thanksgiving for creation, providence, and redemption
    Memorial of Passion (later known as Anamnesis)
    Oblation of gifts with self-oblation
    Invocation of the Word and Holy Spirit to bless the gifts of
      bread and wine (later known as the Epiclesis)[3]
    Intercessions
    People's Amen
Fraction
Communion
Dismissal

In this early worship it will be observed that the balance was kept between the sacramental and Scriptural elements: both the reading of the Scriptures with instruction and the consecration and reception of the bread and wine were integral parts of the rite. Without either it was incomplete.

Apart from psalmody and hymnody, prayer takes two forms: that which is offered by the celebrant 'according to his ability', and to which all respond saying Amen; and that which is said 'by all together', implying a litany form. Thus we have the solemn prayer of consecration said by the celebrant alone, and a litany of some kind in which all join.

· The celebrant, as his designation indicates,[4] led the worship standing behind the Holy Table and facing the people. This position of the celebrant is supported later by the arrangement of the early basilicas,[5] and is referred to technically as the basilican posture.

[1] Throughout I have preferred to use names that indicate their origin for these divisions common to all liturgies. In the East the usual designation was *Proanaphora* and *Anaphora*; in the West, *Missa catechumenorum* and *Missa fidelium*

[2] Based upon Linton's reconstruction in Text 1, p. 15. He probably errs in including the Words of Institution in the prayer, for there is no contemporary evidence to support this view.

[3] On origin of the Epiclesis, see II. 1, pp. 205–30, and III. 20, and review in *Theology* (S.P.C.K.), Sept. 1935, by E. C. Ratcliffe.

[4] See p. 11 above.   [5] See p. 28 below; also IX. 1, p. 86, and III. 7, p. 100.

Consecration is by prayer, not by formula; and the elements consist of leavened bread and wine mixed with water. The people are communicated by the deacons.

In conclusion, no other form of worship but the eucharist is mentioned by Justin. It is not until Tertullian's time (c. 200) that we hear definitely of Vigils, a midnight service preparatory to the eucharist, derived probably from a yearly 'watching' held on Easter eve; St. Cyprian's evidence thirty years later is the earliest for the observance of days commemorating martyrs.

§ 5. *The Third and Fourth Centuries*

The sources now become too extensive to examine in detail, and only the main course of development can be followed. The most important evidence comes from the writings of Clement of Alexandria (d. c. 220), Tertullian (d. c. 240), Origen (d. 251), a book of prayers belonging to an Egyptian bishop, Sarapion of Thmuis (c. 340), consecrated by St. Athanasius, and from the catechetical lectures of Cyril of Jerusalem delivered there in 347.[1] The church order of Hippolytus also provides interesting evidence, but this is reserved for separate discussion.[2]

All these writers, except Sarapion and Hippolytus, are reticent when they deal with the Prayer of Consecration and the Liturgy of the Upper Room. Christians were at this time under suspicion and subject to sporadic persecution; accordingly, they kept their 'mysteries' secret, revealing them only to the initiate. This secrecy, observed from shortly after Justin's death until the death of Constantine, was known as the *disciplina arcani*. Nevertheless, many new and important details emerge in their writings; and, since these are not usually quoted as novelties, it is probable that

---

[1] The references need not be given in detail here; the most important will be conveniently found in Text 2, pp. 20–5, or in Fortescue, III. 6, pp. 28–53. For Sarapion's Prayer Book see English translation in Text 3, and Brightman's article in *Jour. of Theol. Studies*, i. 88–113.

[2] See pp. 21–5 below.

many of them had been long embedded in Christian practice, although the precise date of their origin is obscure.

Cyprian, for example, is the first to mention the *Sursum corda*, which appears hereafter as the introduction to the Prayer of Consecration in every known liturgy. We find also at this time definite mention of the Salutation, so called because it was the usual greeting between Christians when they met. Christians are the family of God; it was natural, therefore, that the bishop or presiding presbyter should so greet the people at the beginning of each service. Soon it came to preface every bidding to prayer, including the *Sursum corda*, and the following becomes a common dialogue:

Salutation. Minister: The Lord be with you.
    or, Peace be with you.
    or, The grace of the Lord Jesus Christ, the love of God, and the communion of the Holy Ghost be with you all.
    People: And with thy spirit.

Sursum corda. Minister: Lift up your hearts.
    People: We lift them up unto the Lord.
    Minister: Let us give thanks unto the Lord.
    People: It is meet and right so to do.

The *Sanctus* has been mentioned already,[1] but now it appears in a form that came to be widely used:

Holy, Holy, Holy, Lord God Almighty,
Heaven and earth are full of thy glory;
Glory be to Thee, O Lord.

Other responses mentioned are the *Kyrie eleison* ('Lord have mercy'), the normal response in the litanies, together with the 'Thanks be to God', and the Amens. Mention is

[1] See p. 8 above. It is to be distinguished from the *Trisagion*,
    Holy God, Holy and Mighty, Holy and Immortal,
    Have mercy upon us,
which we meet later as a constant feature in most Eastern and Gallican liturgies. It is used in the Roman only on Good Friday, at the Mass of the Presanctified.

made also of the Lord's Prayer, following the Prayer of Consecration.

The ceremonial was simple; all things were done decently and in order. Prayers were said standing or kneeling, the arms outstretched with palms outwards, or folded upon the breast. The lections were read from a rostrum or rostrums situated where the readers could be easily heard, and the sermon was preached from the sanctuary steps. The people stood for the Gospel, as if hearing a proclamation from their king.[1] The gifts and alms were collected at the offertory, and the elements prepared. At communion the celebrant received first, setting the example to the people, then the other clergy in order of their rank, the 'religious', the men, and the women.

Gradually further signs of respect came to be made by clergy and people alike. This was particularly noticeable at two points where the Incarnation was specially emphasized: when the Gospel book was carried from the Holy Table to the place where the Gospel was read, and when the elements were brought to the Holy Table. Ceremony soon grew round these acts. It was natural that devotion should express itself not only in words. but in reverent, dramatic action.

The number of clergy taking part depended upon the number available in the local church; the celebrant might be a bishop or presbyter, and the practice of concelebration was not unusual, when a bishop and his presbyters, or several presbyters together, recited the liturgy in unison. The deacons performed a variety of functions. The chief deacon directed the people during the worship, and recited some litanies. Other deacons kept order, guarded the doors, took the collection, and presented the elements at the offertory, read the Gospel and assisted in com-

---

[1] Cureton's *Ancient Syriac Documents*, p. 27: 'At the conclusion of all the Scriptures let the Gospel be read, as the seal of all the Scriptures; and let the people listen to it standing up on their feet, because it is the glad tidings of the salvation of all men.' (So-called Canons of Addai, 3rd cent.).

municating the people. Lesser ministers acted as readers, thurifers, &c.

The worship was still in a fluid state, but the typical structure of the liturgy as celebrated in the late third or early fourth century in a metropolitan church would approximate to this:

The Liturgy of the Word

Lections: Law, Prophets, Epistles, Acts, Gospels, Letters from
    bishops
Psalms sung by cantors between the lections
Alleluias
Sermon or sermons
Deacon's litany for catechumens and penitents
Dismissal of all but the faithful

The Liturgy of the Upper Room

Deacon's litany for the faithful, with diptychs (lists of names) of
    living and dead
Kiss of peace
Offertory: Collection of alms
           Presentation of elements
           Preparation of elements and admixture of water to wine
Sursum corda
Consecration Prayer:
  Preface: Thanksgiving and adoration for creation, &c.
  Sanctus
  Thanksgiving for redemption
  Words of Institution
  Anamnesis
  Epiclesis
  Great Intercession for living and dead
Lord's Prayer
Fraction
Elevation—'Holy things to the holy'—and Delivery
Communion of all in both kinds, each communicant replying Amen;
    during reception Psalms xliii and xxxiv were sung by cantors
Post-communion Thanksgiving
Deacon's litany and celebrant's brief Intercession
Reservation of bread only, for sick and absent
Dismissal

With this structure before us, we may see how it works out as a living rite.

The service begins when the clergy have taken their places behind the Holy Table in the sanctuary, a semicircular apse with raised platform. After private prayers, the lections begin, their number and length not yet fixed; the last is always a Gospel, read by a deacon. Cantors, standing outside the sanctuary, usually on the steps of a rostrum, lead the singing between the lections. Then the bishop preaches, followed by one or more presbyters. The instruction ended, the deacon leads litanies for the catechumens and others not of the faithful, who are then dismissed, while door-keepers watch the doors that none may enter. Thus the Liturgy of the Word concludes.

The Liturgy of the Upper Room begins with the deacon's litany for the faithful, in which he remembers the living and the dead. Then the Kiss of Peace is given by all, probably accompanied by some form of words such as, 'The peace of the Lord be with you.' The Offertory, which follows, consists of the collection of the alms, presentation and preparation of the elements, during which psalms are sung.

A curtain has meanwhile been drawn to veil the sanctuary, though this was not universally in use, and the bishop, saluting the people, calls them to prayer with the *Sursum corda*, and begins the Prayer of Consecration, his presbyters joining with him if concelebration is the custom. After he has recited the Lord's Prayer, he breaks the bread; then, elevating the bread and the cup, he cries, 'Holy things to the holy', and the people reply, 'There is one holy, one Lord Jesus Christ', after which they come forward to communicate, receiving in the order before noted. The children also are communicated, infants receiving from the cup only. Meanwhile psalms are sung, and the service is concluded by a brief thanksgiving and intercession by the bishop, sometimes preceded by a deacon's litany; when the bishop's prayer is ended the deacon dismisses the people.

We see how the liturgy has grown. Although fixed forms, except in the dialogue, do not yet appear, both in structure and in content there is a notable similarity throughout Christendom.

It is not difficult to understand how a traditional form of words, action, and structure came into being. People who do the same thing frequently, fall into the habit of doing it in the same way, especially if there is no reason for change. Unnecessary change involves disturbance, confusion, uncertainty, and resultant disorder. Forms of words tend to become traditional, and young presbyters would copy their bishop. Moreover, the smaller churches would naturally look to the mother church of the district or province for their pattern, and would mould their worship upon it. Also between the great cities, linked by the Roman roads, there would be constant intercourse; and this would help to establish a certain uniformity. Some of the details would, of course, differ in certain localities, and the length of the parts would vary according to local use. Yet the similarities were greater than the differences, and from this fluid rite all the liturgies of Christendom are derived.

The services were probably about three hours in length, and the prayers correspondingly long, but the worship throughout was responsive and co-operative in character.

The deacons' litanies were biddings to prayer, followed at frequent intervals by the people's response, *Kyrie eleison*. The Prayer of Consecration was unbroken by responses except at the *Sanctus*, in which all the people joined.

As an example of the consecration prayer of the period we have that of Bishop Sarapion. It represents Egyptian use about the middle of the third century, and the influence of the *Didaché* or common parent rite can be detected. The prayer lacks literary grace and cohesion, and is dominated by the Alexandrian conception of the Logos. This latter probably accounts for the curious preface, where thanksgiving for creation and providence is transformed into adoration of the Logos, and for the omission of the invocation of the Holy Spirit in the epiclesis and the lack of an anamnesis. Yet this prayer is a valuable example, discovered less than fifty years ago, of the type of consecration prayer which existed before the liturgy was fixed. To indicate its structure clearly, the prayer is here divided into its parts, with titles in italics.[1] After the *Sursum corda*, it begins:

Preface: thanksgiving and adoration

It is meet and right to praise, to hymn, to glorify Thee, the unbegotten Father of the only-begotten Jesus Christ. We praise Thee, O unbegotten God, who art unsearchable, ineffable, incomprehensible by any created substance. We praise Thee who art known of Thy Son, the only-begotten One, who through Him art spoken of and interpreted and made manifest to created nature. . . . We praise Thee, O unseen Father, Provider of immortality. Thou art the Fount of life, . . . light, . . . all grace and truth, O Lover of men, O Lover of the poor, who reconcilest Thyself to all, and drawest all to Thyself through the advent of Thy only beloved Son. We beseech Thee to make us living men. Give us a spirit of truth, that we may know Thee the true God, and Him whom Thou hast sent, Jesus Christ. Give us Thy Holy Spirit, that we may be able to tell forth and announce Thy unspeakable mysteries. May the Lord Jesus Christ speak in us and the Holy Spirit hymn Thee through us. For Thou art far above all rule and authority and power and dominion and every name that is named, not only in this world but also in that which is to come. Beside Thee stand thousand and myriad myriads of angels, archangels, thrones, dominions, principalities, powers; by Thee stand the two most honourable six-winged seraphim, with two wings covering the face, and with two the feet, and with two flying, and crying, Holy; with whom also receive our cry of Holy, as we say

Holy, Holy, Holy, Lord God of hosts,
Heaven and earth are full of Thy glory.

Oblation and institution

Full is the heaven, full also is the earth of Thy excellent glory, Lord of hosts. Fill also this sacrifice with Thy power and participation: for to Thee have we offered this living sacrifice, this bloodless oblation. To Thee have we offered this bread, the likeness of the body of the only-begotten One.

This bread is the likeness of the holy body, because the Lord Jesus Christ, in the night in which He was betrayed, took bread, and brake it, and gave to His disciples, saying, Take ye and eat, this is My body which is being broken for you for remission of sins. Wherefore, we also making the likeness of the death have offered the bread, and

---

[1] Both text and divisions are from Text 3, with slight alterations. For Greek text see III. 9, pp. 186–7.

beseech Thee through this sacrifice, O God of truth, to be reconciled to us all and to be merciful; and, as this bread was scattered on the top of the mountains, and, gathered together, came to be one, so also gather Thy holy Church out of every nation and every country and city and village and house, and make one living catholic Church.

We have offered the cup also, the likeness of the blood, because the Lord Jesus Christ, taking a cup after supper, said to His disciples, Take ye, drink ye, this is the new covenant, My blood, which is being shed for you for remission of sins. Wherefore, we have also offered the cup, presenting a likeness of the blood.

Epiclesis

O God of truth, let Thy holy Word come upon this bread, that the bread may become the body of the Word, and upon this cup that the cup may become the blood of the Truth; and make all who communicate to receive a medicine of life for the healing of every sickness and the strengthening of all advancement and virtue, not for condemnation, O God of truth, and not for censure and reproach. For we have invoked Thee, the Unbegotten, through the Only-Begotten in Thy Holy Spirit.

Intercessions

Let this people receive mercy; let them be counted worthy of advancement; let angels be sent forth as companions of the people for bringing to naught the evil one and for the establishment of Thy Church. We intercede also on behalf of all who have been laid to rest, whose memorial we make. [*Here the names were recited.*] Sanctify these souls, for Thou knowest all. Sanctify all who are laid to rest in the Lord, and number them all with Thy holy hosts, and give them a place and mansion in Thy kingdom.

Receive also this eucharist of Thy people, and bless those who have offered the offerings and thanksgivings; and grant health and soundness and cheerfulness, and all advancement of soul and body to this whole people; through the only-begotten Jesus Christ in the Holy Spirit, as it was and is and shall be unto generations of generations and to all the ages of the ages. Amen.

§ 6. *The Church Order of Hippolytus* (*Third Century*)

Opinions have differed about the date, place, and importance of the so-called 'Egyptian Church Order', but it is now generally agreed that it was originally a Greek document entitled *The Apostolic Tradition*, compiled by Hippolytus of Rome in the second quarter of the third century. The Greek text is lost, but we possess a complete Ethiopic translation derived through the Coptic, and also fragments of Latin, Coptic, and Arabic translations.[1] Thus Duchesne rightly warns us, since the text exists only in versions, that 'when we come to details we must be cautious, since later editors of this class of composition are always prone to allow their ideas and tastes to modify the directions found in the document which serves as the basis of their work'.

For our purposes, the relevant part of the Hippolytan Order is the Consecration Prayer used at the eucharist when a bishop was consecrated. It was not a fixed prayer, but the model that is indicated appears to contain much traditional phraseology. As Hippolytus says, 'It is not necessary for him to recite the same words, but, according to his own ability, so each one is to give thanks.'

Lietzmann rightly regards this document as of great importance, but appears to claim too much for it when he declares it to be 'the model of all liturgies known to us from that time to the present day'.[2] Gavin[3] approves this point of view, but adds nothing to the argument. We may agree with Duchesne that 'its author must have drawn his inspiration from Roman use'. It is pure conjecture, however, to say that it is *fully* representative of Roman liturgical usage in the third century, and it is safer to attribute the lack of such Jewish yet widespread elements as the *Sanctus* and the thanksgiving for creation and providence, to the eccentricity of the author or reviser, than to declare this lack to be evidence for the primitive usage at Rome. Some Anglican and Roman scholars, writing recently, seem inclined to overvalue the Hippolytan Canon, no doubt partly because

[1] Critical and best edition in English in Text 4; another English translation of Consecration Prayer in II. 4, pp. 148–69; and in Text 2. That quoted here is Duchesne's, III. 5, pp. 524 sqq., where he also gives the Latin version. I have made one or two emendations of slight importance. See also III. 9, pp. 14, 158 sqq., 174 sqq.
[2] III. 9, p. 261.   [3] III. 8, pp. 97 sqq.

it is an early third-century witness displaying several of the same weaknesses found in the present Anglican and Roman Consecration Prayers, and partly out of enthusiasm at finding an early western source of such interest. But Brilioth's is probably a fair estimate:

'On the whole, the evidence seems to me to indicate that the formula of Hippolytus represents, not the type of congregational service in use towards the end of the second century, but the work of an individual who deviated from the traditional form[1] under the influence of a Pauline theology, and of a reaction against the Jewish elements in the liturgy, and thus took the passion and atonement as his dominant ideas; and that, with regard to the subject-matter of the eucharistic prayer, the Clementine liturgy is really more primitive than Hippolytus.'[2]

The following is a translation of the Prayer of Consecration. It has the quality of terseness which from the beginning characterized Western, and particularly Roman, prayer. The division into parts is my own; the order of the parts is significant.

After the Kiss of Peace the deacons present the bread and wine at the Holy Table, and the bishop, laying his hands upon the gifts, begins the eucharistic prayer, accompanied by the presbyters who concelebrate[3] with him: the salutation and *Sursum corda* precede the prayer which begins with Thanksgiving for Redemption.

'We give thanks to Thee, O God, through Thy beloved Servant (*puer* from παῖς = Fr. *garçon* = servant) Jesus Christ, whom Thou didst send to us in the last days, a Saviour and Redeemer and

---

[1] Hippolytus was, in fact, a schismatic.

[2] III. 14, pp. 25-6. The 'Clementine liturgy' is that in Book VIII of the *Apostolic Constitutions*, to which we turn in the next chapter. It would have been more accurate to say that the subject-matter of the Clementine eucharistic prayer is more representative than the Hippolytan of widespread primitive practice.

[3] Concelebration is ancient in its origin, and is still frequently met with in the Eastern Churches, especially at solemn festivals. It was the normal method of celebration in the ancient Celtic Church, and widespread in the other Gallican Churches, still surviving at Lyons on Holy Thursday. It also survives in the Roman rite at the consecration of bishops and the ordination of priests; but is permissible at any time. It is not unknown at clerical 'retreats' and pontifical masses. See III. 7, pp. 922, 91, 740. See also pp. 16 and 18 above.

Messenger of Thy will, who is Thine inseparable Word, well-pleasing unto Thee, and through whom Thou didst make all things. Thou didst send Him from heaven into a virgin's womb, who, being conceived, was incarnate and shown to be Thy Son (*filius*), born of the Holy Spirit and a virgin; who, fulfilling Thy will, and acquiring for Thee a holy people, stretched out His hands when He suffered that He might free from suffering those who had believed on Thee;

Words of Institution

'Who, also, when He was of His own free will betrayed to suffering that He might destroy death, break the fetters of the devil, tread hell underfoot, illumine the righteous, fix the boundary, and manifest His resurrection, taking bread and giving thanks to Thee, said, Take ye, eat ye, this is My body, which is broken for you. After the same manner, He took the cup, saying, This is My blood, which is shed for you; as oft as ye do this, ye make My memorial.

Oblation and Epiclesis

'Wherefore, mindful of His death and resurrection, we offer unto Thee this bread and cup, giving Thee thanks that Thou hast counted us worthy to stand before Thee and to minister unto Thee.

'And we beseech Thee, that Thou wouldst send Thy Holy Spirit upon this oblation of Thy holy Church; that, uniting them into one, Thou mayest grant to all Thy holy ones who receive that their faith may be confirmed in truth in the fulfilment of the Holy Spirit, that we may laud and glorify Thee; through Thy Servant (*puerum*) Jesus Christ, through whom be glory and honour unto Thee, Father, Son, and Holy Spirit, in Thy holy Church, both now and for evermore.

'*And the people shall say*: As it was, is, and ever shall be, world without end, and for evermore. Amen.'

Then follows a series of three brief prayers by the bishop for worthy reception and the true benefits thereof, the deacon directing the people. Then the elevation follows, with this dialogue:

'*The deacon shall say*: Let us attend.

And the bishop: Holy things to the holy.

And the people shall say: One holy Father, one holy Son, one is the Holy Spirit.

The bishop shall say: The Lord be with you all.

And the people shall say: And with thy spirit.'

[The people then come forward to receive, after which the service concludes with a prayer and blessing. The rubrics are not clear, but probably the first prayer was said by a presbyter, and the second, the blessing, given by the bishop.]

Presbyter's prayer

'God Almighty, the Father of the Lord and our Saviour Jesus Christ, we give Thee thanks, because Thou hast imparted to us the reception of Thy holy Mystery: let it not be for guilt or condemnation, but for the renewal of soul and body and spirit; through, &c.

'*And the people shall say*: Amen.

And the presbyter shall say: The Lord be with you.

And the people shall say: And with thy spirit.'

Bishop's blessing, given with outstretched hand

'Eternal God Almighty, the Father of the Lord and our Saviour Jesus Christ, bless Thy servants and Thy handmaids; protect, help, and prosper them by the power of Thine archangel. Keep and confirm in them Thy fear by Thy greatness; provide that they shall both think what is Thine and believe what is Thine and will what is Thine; grant to them peace without sin and anger; through, &c.

'*And the people shall say:* Amen.

And the bishop shall say: The Lord be with you all.

And the people shall say: And with thy spirit.

And the deacon shall say: Go in peace.'

II

LITURGICAL FORMS IN THE EAST

§ 1. *The so-called Clementine Liturgy, contained in Book VIII of the 'Apostolic Constitutions', c.* A.D. 380

THE first complete liturgy preserved to modern times is that contained in Book VIII of the *Apostolic Constitutions*, belonging approximately to the year A.D. 380. By this time the Imperial ban upon Christianity had been lifted, and the *disciplina arcani*, accordingly, was relaxed.

There has been considerable speculation about this so-called Clementine Liturgy, and some scholars have maintained that it was never a living rite but simply a private compilation. That it was a private compilation is true, for, in the form in which it has come down to us, it is from the pen of the same person that edited the *Epistles of Ignatius*, adding to the seven authentic letters six others of his own. Similarly, parts of this liturgy in style and doctrine bear evidence of his hand. A particular instance of this occurs in his vast expansion of the preface of the Consecration Prayer. But there can also be no doubt that the liturgy as a whole is based upon a living rite of the period, and that it certainly represents the actual worship of the Syrian Church, particularly in the city of Antioch, about A.D. 350–80; and further, that it may be taken as exemplifying the parent-rite of all the Eastern liturgies.

As a contemporary witness to fourth-century worship its value is unique, for it is not a service book that has been in continuous use, subject to change and revision. Embedded in 'a manual of ecclesiastical life' which had been lost for centuries, it comes to us unaltered.

Besides the liturgy in Book VIII[1] there is also the

---

[1] Greek text in Text 5, pp. 3 sqq. with discussions of authorship, &c., on pp. xvii sqq., ibid. His conclusions should be compared with Lietzmann's

summary of a similar rite in Book II,[1] which may be derived from a somewhat earlier source. But since in the main it confirms the 'Clementine Liturgy', we may here take the two together.

This is the general scheme of the worship:

The Liturgy of the Word

[Prayers: Litanies, &c.?]

Lections from Law, Prophets, Epistles, Acts, Gospels, interspersed with psalms sung by cantors

Sermons

Dismissal of catechumens, &c.; four classes in all, after a separate deacon's litany and bishop's prayer of blessing has been said for each class

Liturgy of the Upper Room

Deacon's litany and bishop's prayer for the faithful

Salutation and response

Kiss of Peace, with words and response

Offertory: Ceremonial washing of bishop's and presbyters' hands
         Presentation of elements at Holy Table by deacons
         Vesting of celebrant in a 'splendid vestment'
         'Fencing' of Table by chief deacon

Sursum corda, preceded by salutation

Consecration Prayer:
    Preface: Thanksgiving for Creation and Providence (very long)
    Sanctus
    Thanksgiving for Redemption
    Anamnesis: Words of Institution
              Memorial and Oblation
    Epiclesis
    Great Intercession

[Lord's Prayer?]

Deacon's litany and bishop's prayer

in III. 9, pp. 122 sqq., notably the latter's contention that it represents a living rite, p. 133, ibid. English translation with further discussions in II. 6, pp. 258 sqq., an important book for this whole period, but some of its conclusions should be reconsidered in the light of later research; and in Text 2. On the whole manual see De Lacy O'Leary, *Apostolic Constitutions*, London, 1906.

[1] Greek in Text 5, pp. 28–30; translation in Text 2, pp. 74–7, from which most of the excerpts given here are taken.

Elevation: 'Holy things, &c.', with response
  Gloria in excelsis (Luke ii. 14 only)
  Benedictus qui venit (Matt. xxi. 9, and the words, 'God
   is the Lord, and hath appeared unto us')
Delivery: 'The Body of Christ'; 'The Blood of Christ: the cup of
  life'
Communion, while Psalm xxxiv is sung
Deacon's Exhortation and Bidding
Bishop's post-communion, thanksgiving, and intercession
Bishop's prayer of blessing
Dismissal of people by deacon

A quotation from Book II shows how the congregation
was disposed:

'When thou assemblest the Church of God, do thou, O bishop,
like the captain of a great ship with all understanding command the
assemblies to be made, giving directions to the deacons, as to sailors,
to assign their places unto the brethren, as to embarking soldiers,
with all care and reverence.

'And, in the first place, let the building[1] be oblong, pointing
towards the east, having at the east sacristies at both sides, like a ship.
And let the bishop's throne be in the centre [i.e. of the apse at the
east end], and let the seats of the presbyters be on both sides of him,
and let the deacons stand by, well equipped in light raiment. For
they are like sailors and overseers of the rowers on each side of the
ship. By their care, let the laymen be seated on one side, with all
quietness and good order. And let the women be seated apart, and
keep silent.'

Precisely how the service began is uncertain; there may
have been preliminary singings and litanies as in the later
liturgies, but the first thing mentioned in our texts is the
lections. These seem to have been both numerous and long,
and were drawn from each section of the Bible in this order:
the Law, historical books, Job and the Wisdom books, the
Prophets, Acts, Epistles, and Gospels.

'Let the lections be read two by two', Book II directs, 'and afterwards let another sing hymns of David, and the people sing in reply

---

[1] The building described is a basilica with apse. In this book it is not
possible to deal with church architecture, but a brief bibliography is given
in Section IX.

at the ends of the verses.[1]. . . And after that, let a deacon or a presbyter read the Gospels. . . . And when the Gospel is read, let all . . . stand with much silence, for it is written, "Be silent and hear, O Israel", and again, "Stand thou here, and hear".'

The lections are followed by the sermons:

'Next, let the presbyters exhort the people, one at a time, but not all of them; and last of all the bishop,' as becomes the captain of a ship,' directs Book II. Book VIII mentions a salutation before the sermon: 'Let him who is ordained bishop salute the Church, saying The grace of our Lord Jesus Christ, and the love of God, and the communion of the Holy Ghost, be with you all. And let all answer, And with thy spirit.'

When the sermons were ended, all not entitled to take part in the Liturgy of the Faithful were dismissed by the deacon. Of these, four classes are mentioned: the catechumens, those possessed of evil spirits, those candidates for baptism undergoing advanced instruction, and those under discipline. At the deacon's bidding, each class stood up in turn[3] and joined with him in a litany, after which in each case they bowed to receive the bishop's prayer of blessing and were then dismissed by the deacon. To each clause of the litanies all made the reply, *Kyrie eleison*, and a charmingly intimate touch is found in the rubric, 'more especially let the little children answer'. It is a homely picture, the children 'standing by under the charge of their fathers and mothers' and taking their part in the worship of the Church. So the Liturgy of the Word concludes.

Now only the faithful remain, and the deacons carefully

[1] A method known as the *Psalmus responsorius* to be sharply distinguished from the later antiphonal psalmody sung alternately by two choirs. Cf. III. 5, p. 58, and his excellent description of the 'Clementine rite', pp. 57–64, part of which is quoted on a later page.

[2] A common practice as we know from contemporary evidence of *Peregrinatio* of Egeria, describing worship in Jerusalem: 'Here it is the custom of all the presbyters who are present, for as many of them as wish to preach, and after them the bishop preaches'. Text of *Peregrinatio* in III. 5, App. 5.

[3] But see II. 5, p. 101. His view that only the catechumens stood does not appear to be what is conveyed by the rubrics and the text. The point is somewhat obscure.

scrutinize their ranks to see that all are in their proper place and order, with mothers in charge of children standing apart. Others guard the doors that none may leave or enter; and others 'walk about and observe the men and women, so that there be no disturbance, and that none may nod, whisper, or sleep'. Book II adds 'for it is right to stand wisely and soberly and watchfully, with the hearing attentive to the Word of the Lord'.

The Liturgy of the Faithful begins with a comprehensive deacon's litany for 'the peace and welfare of the world', 'the holy Catholic and Apostolic Church', the diocese and all bishops, presbyters, ministers and rulers, the fruits of the earth, all in sickness, prison or exile, the children, and all men. The bishop's prayer summarizes and concludes the litany; then the Peace is given:

'Let the deacon say: Let us attend.

Let the bishop salute the Church and say: The peace of God be with you all.

And let the people answer: And with thy spirit.

And let the deacon say to all: Salute ye one another with a holy kiss.

And let the clergy salute the bishop, and the laymen the laymen, and the women the women.'

The offertory follows. A deacon provides water for the bishop and presbyters to wash their hands ceremonially, as 'a symbol of the purity of souls dedicated to God'; and the chief deacon 'fences' the Table, forbidding any 'who are not of the faithful', or 'who have aught against any', or who 'are in hypocrisy' to remain, bidding all 'with fear and trembling to stand upright before the Lord to offer'.

'After which let the deacons bring the gifts to the bishop at the Holy Table. And let the presbyters stand on his right hand and on his left, as disciples standing by a teacher.'

The bishop meanwhile prays in silence, then putting on 'a splendid vestment', and standing at the Holy Table facing the people, he makes the sign of the cross on his forehead, and salutes the people with the apostolic Grace. Then calling

them to prayer with the *Sursum corda*, he begins the solemn
Consecration Prayer:

'It is truly meet and right, before all things to glorify Thee who
art the living God, who art before the beginning of created things, of
whom the whole family in heaven and earth is named; who alone art
unbegotten, without beginning. . . .'

Duchesne's fine description of this great prayer may be
quoted:

'The eucharistic prayer goes on, starting from the majesty of the
unapproachable God, passing in review all His benefits conferred
upon His creatures, enumerating all the wonders of nature and grace,
appealing to the great types of the ancient covenant, and concluding
at length by a return to the mysterious sanctuary, in which the
Divinity rests in the midst of spirits, where the Cherubim and
Seraphim sing together the eternal hymn. . . .

'At this point the whole congregation raise their voices [in the
Sanctus], joining with the choir of angels in their hymn, "Holy, Holy,
Holy, . . ."

'The hymn being ended, there is once more silence, and the bishop
then proceeds with the eucharistic prayer which has been interrupted:
"Yea, truly Thou art holy . . .", and he commemorates the work of
Redemption, the incarnation of the Word, and His earthly life and
passion. At this moment the improvisation of the celebrant follows
closely the Gospel account of the Last Supper, and the mysterious
words spoken for the first time by Jesus on the eve of His death are
repeated at the Holy Table. Thereupon the bishop, taking as his text
the last words, "Do this in memory of Me", expands them, recalling
to memory [in the anamnesis] the passion of the Son of God, His
death, resurrection, ascension, and the hope of His glorious return,
declaring that it is truly in keeping with Christ's command, and in
commemorating these events that the congregation offers to God this
eucharistic bread and wine. Finally, he prays the Lord to regard the
oblation with favour, and [in the epiclesis] to cause to descend upon
it the virtue of His Holy Spirit, in order that it may be made the body
and blood of Christ, the spiritual food of His faithful people, and the
pledge of their immortality.'

And now the bishop goes on to the Great Intercession,
joining it to the eucharistic prayer as a natural sequence:

'We pray thee, O Lord, for Thy holy Church spread from one end
of the world to the other, . . . that Thou wouldst keep it unshaken

and untroubled . . ., and for myself, who am nothing, now offering
to Thee, . . . for the deacons and for all the clergy . . ., for the king, . . .
and those in authority, the army, for the saints in all ages who have
pleased Thee, . . . whose names Thou knowest . . ., for this people, . . .
the virgins, . . . widows, . . . women in labour, . . . and for the babes,
. . . for this city, . . . the sick, those in bitter slavery, in exile, in prison,
. . . those that hate and persecute us for Thy Name's sake, those who
wander, . . . the catechumens, those possessed of demons, the penitents, . . . for seasonable weather, the fruits of the earth, . . . the absent.
For unto Thee is due all glory, worship, and thanksgiving, honour,
and adoration, to the Father, and to the Son and to the Holy Ghost,
both now and ever unto all perpetual and endless ages of ages.'

The people say Amen; and in common usage the Lord's
Prayer may have followed.[1] The bishop then salutes the
people, and they reply; after which the deacon leads them
in a brief litany, the bishop concluding with a brief prayer,
the people saying Amen.

The deacon then cries, 'Let us attend!', and the bishop,
elevating the Bread and the Cup in the sight of the people,
says aloud, 'Holy things to the holy', to which the people
answer, 'There is one Holy, one Lord Jesus Christ; unto
the glory of God the Father, blessed for ever. Amen.'

Then the angels' hymn, 'Glory to God in the highest',
was sung in its Scriptural form, followed by the 'Hosanna'
and *Benedictus qui venit*, in this form:

> 'Hosanna to the Son of David.
> Blessed is He that cometh in the Name of the Lord.
> God is the Lord, and hath appeared unto us.
> Hosanna in the highest!'

Meanwhile, or immediately afterwards, the fraction took
place, followed by the delivery and communion:

'And after this, let the bishop communicate, then the presbyters,
deacons, subdeacons, readers, singers, ascetics, and of the women the
deaconesses, virgins, and widows; afterwards the children; and then
all the people in order, with reverence and piety, without disturbance.'

The bishop ministered the Bread and a deacon the Cup,

[1] See earlier practice described on pp. 16 and 17 above, and the almost
unanimous witness of later practice.

the people, all of whom communicated, coming forward to the steps of the apse or sanctuary to receive. During communion there was said or sung Psalm xxxiv, where the words, 'O taste and see that the Lord is good', have special significance. Afterwards 'the deacons take what remains and carry it into the sacristy'.

When the singing has ceased, the deacon bids the people to thanksgiving, leading them in a bidding prayer:

'Unto Him who hath vouchsafed unto us to be the participators in His holy Mysteries, . . . that they may be . . . to our salvation, for the benefit of soul and body, . . . for remission of sins, and for life in the world to come.'

He then says, 'Let us rise', and the bishop epitomizes the whole action in a brief thanksgiving, supplication, and intercession. Afterwards, at the deacon's bidding, the people bow their heads as the bishop says a final prayer of blessing, concluding with an ascription of praise. The service has ended, and the deacon says, 'Ye are dismissed in peace.'

What is here portrayed is common worship; it is not a drama that may be watched but not shared, nor do we encounter the modern sacerdotalism of the single voice. All participate, the centre of the action being at the Holy Table. Throughout there is a strong sense of the Real Presence. Judged by modern standards, the worship was lengthy, but it must not be forgotten that the Eastern genius expressed itself most effectively in elaboration. Moreover, if lengthy, this worship did not halt or drag; there was unbroken progress towards a grand culmination. That culmination was consecration and communion; and after it had been reached the service quickly ended.

We may observe the important place given in this corporate worship to the Holy Scriptures. Not only are the responses, psalms, and hymns drawn from the Scriptures, but the lections and their exposition are an integral part of the rite. So a didactic element is provided which is essential to intelligent participation in the holy Mysteries. This was characteristic of the worship of the early Church.

§ 2. *Kindred Eastern Rites of the Fifth and Sixth Centuries*

It is not possible in a work of this scope to examine in detail the many Eastern rites derived from or closely associated with the fourth-century rite contained in the *Apostolic Constitutions*. Nor is it necessary for our purpose; for if we understand the rite of the fourth century, we are in a position to understand all the later Eastern rites. Certain changes took place in the next two centuries, and there were differences between the families and individuals of the Eastern rites, but all were built upon the same foundation as the rite we have just studied, and resembled it closely. After the seventh century all the Eastern rites had become fixed, and since that time practically no change has taken place.

The simplest and most convenient classification of the rites of Christendom is under the names of the three great patriarchates, Antioch (Syria), Alexandria, and Rome. This does not imply that the rites so classified necessarily had their origin in the cities named, but only that the rites of one class belong to one family, with so many common characteristics as to suggest a common origin.

I. ANTIOCH.

1. The *Apostolic Constitutions*, Books II and VIII
2. The Byzantine rite (Constantinople)
   (a) Liturgy of St. Basil
   (b) Liturgy of St. Chrysostom
3. The Jerusalem rite
   (a) Liturgy of St. James
   (b) All other Syrian rites
   (c) The Persian rites (Nestorian)

The rite[1] in the *Apostolic Constitutions* is based upon the

---

[1] 'Its importance is shown to be neither more nor less than can be claimed for the sources which it has embodied.' II. 5, p. 97.

parent rite of this Antiochene group. The first to become
fixed was the Liturgy of St. Basil, which is still used in
the Eastern Orthodox Churches during part of Lent, at the
midnight celebrations on Christmas and Epiphany, and on
St. Basil's day, January 1st.

The Liturgy of St. Chrysostom, a shortened form of St.
Basil's, is the rite now normally in use throughout the
Orthodox Churches. On Good Friday the bread and wine
are not consecrated, but the Liturgy of the Pre-Sanctified,
attributed to St. Gregory Dialogos, is used, the elements
having been previously consecrated. This is practically
St. Chrysostom's rite with all that relates to consecration
omitted. It is also in use on certain week-days during
Lent, except Saturdays. Translated into Old Slavonic,
these are the liturgies in use in the Russian Church.

The Liturgy of St. James, or the Jacobite Liturgy, was
the first fixed rite of the Patriarchate of Jerusalem. It is
named from our Lord's brother, the first bishop of Jerusalem, but dates from the fifth century. From it are derived
all the other Syrian rites, including the Nestorian.[1]

II. ALEXANDRIA.

1. Sarapion
2. The Liturgy of St. Mark
3. All other Egyptian and Ethiopic rites

We have dealt already with what is known of Sarapion's
rite, a primitive and local variation of the Alexandrian fluid
rite. After the rite became fixed the regular use of Alexandria and Egypt was the Liturgy of St. Mark (Greek). This
rite is still used in its Coptic form under the name of St.

[1] Greek texts of these liturgies, or, if original is not Greek, in English
translation in Text 5; English translations of St. Basil's, St. Chrysostom's,
and St. James's in Text 6. Modern service book of Eastern Orthodox Church
in Text 7, and liturgy alone in Text 8; inexpensive editions in Texts 9 and 10.
Russian and Armenian translated into English in Texts 11 and 13. Translations of Consecration Prayers of Antiochene Group in Text 1. Texts 5 and 6
also give fuller details of the individual rites comprising the great families
than are given above.

Cyril, on the Friday before Palm Sunday. Its place was early taken by St. Basil's (Coptic), now the normal use in the Coptic Church, Egyptian in the Liturgy of the Word but Antiochene in the Liturgy of the Faithful. St. Gregory's, the other Coptic rite, is also Antiochene in the Liturgy of the Faithful; it is of greater length than St. Basil's, and is used only at the midnight celebration at Christmas, and at Epiphany and Easter. The Ethiopic liturgies are also derived from St. Basil; and the one most frequently used shows that it has been influenced by the Hippolytan church order. The Ethiopic liturgies are ruder in form and they differ in the Liturgy of the Faithful.[1]

III. ROME.

1. The early Roman rite
2. The Gallican rites (All the non-Roman Western rites)
3. The Lutheran, Reformed, and Anglican rites

These are mentioned here only to complete the classification under the great Patriarchates. Later chapters will be devoted to their history and exposition.

This classification is intended to indicate only broadly the families into which the great liturgies fall; a more detailed classification will be found in most of the texts mentioned. Fortescue explains briefly how these parent-rites became fixed:

'The way in which this came about must have been something like this. In various centres the old vaguer rite crystallized into different forms. Insistence on one part at one place, on another at another, different parts shortened or enlarged, slight rearrangements of the order, caused for some practical reason, bring about different types of liturgy. The influence of these centres causes their customs to be followed in the country round and in the dependent dioceses. We see that three of the parent-types are those of the old patriarchal cities. It was natural that the bishops of these patriarchates should

[1] On the whole see Text 5, pp. lxiii–lxxvi, and pp. 113–244. St. Mark is translated in Text 6; and the Coptic rite in its modern form is translated in Text 12. Translations of the Consecration Prayers of the Alexandrian group are in Text 1, pp. 84–107; for the Ethiopic see Text 14.

imitate their chief in his liturgical practices. So from these centres new types spread. But they are still more or less fluid types of liturgy. Even within the area of each there was room for some difference. The prayers are still to a great extent said extempore. Our first period, then, introduces us to four [Fortescue classifies the Roman and Gallican liturgies separately] general types of liturgy, the parents of all the others in Christendom. The next stage is absolute uniformity. The prayers are written down and read from a book. This naturally puts an end to any variety within the domain of each rite. But meanwhile, before final uniformity is reached, each of these parent-types goes through the same development as did the original parent of all. Again, within the same type there are differences. Outlying churches evolve peculiarities of their own; sometimes changes, shortening of parts that seem too long, the addition of some new ceremony or the expansion of an old one, are made deliberately. So we have the derived liturgies, each the daughter of one of the four great parents, obviously belonging to its family, and yet no longer to be considered the same rite. These, too, are written down; so we have the many liturgies now used, which however are not disconnected novelties, but may all be classified as either one of the original four, or derived from one of them.'[1]

§ 3. Developments in Ritual and Ceremonial in the East after the Fourth Century

Before leaving the Eastern liturgies we may note briefly and in a general way certain of the principal changes that took place, after the fourth century, in the words and action of the worship.

The service of the prothesis, a private preparation of the clergy, appears. It consisted of prayers said while the ministers vested and prepared the elements, each prayer relating to the mystical meaning of what was being done. This service usually took place in the sacristy as the people were assembling, and meanwhile another minister censed the people preparatory to worship.

A more important addition, probably earlier than the fourth century, with its origins lying far back in the Synagogue services, was a preparation before the reading of the

[1] III. 6, pp. 77-8.

Holy Scriptures. It usually consisted of various prayers and singings, mingling praise, penitence, adoration, and supplication, the dominant feature being the deacon's litanies. After the fourth century this preparation, in some form, is a constant feature in all the liturgies.

About this time the lections tended to be fixed.[1] Their number was gradually reduced normally to two, an Epistle and Gospel, but at certain seasons a passage from the Old Testament or from the Acts or the Revelation was included in place of or in addition to the Epistle. There were other exceptions, such as in the Coptic rite which retained four lections from the New Testament, and in the Armenian where an Old Testament lection is a constant feature as well as the Epistle and Gospel.

In the East the Creed found a place in the liturgy earlier than in the West.[2] From the sixth century onwards it appears in the Liturgy of the Faithful, closely associated with the Offertory or Communion. Creeds were from an early period used at baptisms, and it is not surprising that they soon became an integral part of public worship.

Turning from the words to the acts, we find that, during and after the fourth century, the ceremonial ceased to be merely utilitarian and acquired a mystical significance, becoming in consequence more elaborate.

This appears, for example, in the development of the sanctuary screen,[3] dividing the apse from the nave. At first, the only division consisted of steps, but at a fairly early period a curtain was introduced, which could be drawn at the more solemn parts of the service. After the fourth century this curtain became a screen, and, except in Egypt and

---

[1] For fourth-century usage see II. 5, pp. 198 sqq. That described above is slightly later.

[2] 'The introduction of the Creed into the eucharist was first made by Peter the Fuller, monophysite Patriarch of Antioch (476–88). . . . The first mention of the introduction of the Creed into the liturgy in the West is a canon of the Council of Toledo in 589.' F. J. Badcock, *The History of the Creeds*. London, 1930, p. 188. For the Byzantine rite see p. 34 above and p. 53 below.

[3] The earliest form of screen was a lattice or rail, κάγκελλος or κιγκλίς.

Cappadocia, this screen became solid. It was formally decorated by raised pictures of our Lord, the Virgin, the Evangelists, Apostles, and saints. These pictures were known as icons, and the screen the iconostasis. In the iconostasis there were three doors, the centre one opposite the Holy Table being called the Royal Door. Across or above this door a veil could be drawn in order doubly to screen the sanctuary at the consecration.

The shutting off of the sanctuary increased the importance of the deacon, whose function it was to act as a link between celebrant and people. While the holy mystery was celebrated within the sanctuary, the chief deacon stood, for the most part, outside the iconostasis, directing the people's prayers and keeping them abreast of the action within.

The prayers were no longer said throughout in a clear voice, but most of the celebrant's prayers were recited in a subdued tone, the voice being raised (the ecphonesis) at certain points to indicate that a prayer had been concluded. Many of the celebrant's prayers were said during singings or deacon's litanies: in Eastern worship there were many concomitant parts which in modern texts are usually shown by parallel columns.

From the fifth century onwards it also became increasingly unusual for the people to communicate every Sunday. But worship in the East, though highly dramatized, yet remained a common action in which all took an active part. The office of the deacon ensured this, entrusted as he was with the direction of the people's acts and words.

Music,[1] now that persecution had ceased and the Church was in peace, was given opportunity to develop. At first there had been only one or two cantors, but now choirs came to be formed and, as the music became more elaborate and difficult, the choir came to represent the people, voicing most of their responses. The general effect was to provide

[1] There is no attempt in this book to deal at length with the music of the Church, but a short bibliography is given in Section X.

a glorious setting of praise and supplication for the whole action, so that throughout the worship the voice of the singers was seldom silent. Sometimes the choir was hidden from sight behind the screen as in the Russian Church; sometimes they took their place in the nave under the dome as in the Greek Church. And, even if the music became too diversified and elaborate for the people to take an active part in it, it was of such compelling beauty as to incite the worshipper to spiritual adoration.

After the fourth century the ceremonial became more pronounced at the Gospel and Offertory. Devotion had already tended to express itself in action at these points, but now it took definite and colourful form; and because the processions passed through the doors of the sanctuary screen, they came to be known respectively as the Little and Great Entrance.

The Little Entrance occurred at the Gospel during the anthem, *Trisagion*. The other lection was read from an ambo in the nave, or even from within the sanctuary, for the screen was no barrier to the voice. But when the Gospel was about to be read, the deacon, bearing the Gospel Book, and accompanied by the celebrant and a procession of ministers and acolytes bearing crosses, lights, and incense, came through the north door of the iconostasis and passed down to the centre of the church, where amid censing and prayer the Book was ceremonially blessed and kissed. The procession then returned through the Royal Door to the Holy Table, and, the door still remaining open, the deacon read or sang the Gospel. The Gospel ended, the doors were closed.

The Great Entrance took place at the Offertory during the anthem, Psalm xxiv. 7-10, to which was added in 574 the Hymn of the Cherubim. A more imposing procession than before was formed in the sanctuary; this time all the ministers took part, the acolytes bearing lights, the thurifers incense, and the other ministers carrying the instruments of the Passion, the cross, the spear, the scourge, and the thorns. As at the Little Entrance, the procession passed through the north door of the iconostasis, the celebrant bearing the Cup, and the deacon the paten upon his head. Both Cup and paten were veiled. When the procession returned from the church to the sanctuary amid clouds of incense, it entered the Royal Door, which was then shut and veiled, remaining so until the celebrant and his ministers had communicated. Then the doors were flung open as celebrant and deacon came through the Royal Door to give communion to the people.

A change, too, took place after the fourth century in the method of giving communion. The primitive practice had been to give communion in both kinds separately, the people receiving the Bread from the celebrant, who placed it in their crossed hands, and the Cup from the deacon. But a new practice began to prevail, which became the normal method of giving communion in the East. It is known as communion by intinction: the Bread is dipped in the Wine, and then administered by means of a spoon. The Fraction was highly elaborated in the Eastern rites, where it always remained a separate action, not embedded in the Consecration Prayer when the Words of Institution are recited, as in the Anglican rite.

In the East piety came to invest every action with a mystical significance. These actions often had their origin in practical necessity, but gradually a highly imaginative devotional meaning was attached to them. A brief quotation from Frere[1] serves to illustrate this:

'The entry of the Gospel, brought in with great procession and preceded by lights, shows the coming of the Saviour into the world: the Book is regarded as representing the presence of the incarnate

[1] III. 17, p. 54. This is the best general treatment of ceremonial in the eucharist. On religious symbolism see I. 1, vol. ii. See also Jenner, *Christian Symbolism*, London, 1910, containing a good bibliography; and J. R. Allen, *Christian Symb. in G B. and Ireland*, London, 1887. The standard is D. Detzel, *Christliche Ikonographie*, 8 vols., Freiburg, 1894.

Lord. The *Trisagion* of the congregation corresponds to the *Gloria in excelsis* of the angels; the *prokeimenon*, or respond, to the prophecies of the Old Testament; the Epistle with the apostolic witness. The *Alleluia* gives the attestation of David; and the Reading of the Gospel is the climax of the first cycle.

'In the second, the Lord is symbolized by the gifts of bread and wine. The Holy Table is the sepulchre of Christ; the corporal is the linen cloth enwrapping His body. The veil of the paten is the kerchief round His head. The larger veil, or *Aer*, which covers both paten and chalice, is the stone with which St. Joseph closed His Sepulchre. The Great Entrance is the Way of the Cross; the laying of the paten and chalice on the altar is the burial. The consecration corresponds to the Resurrection; and this symbolism is worked out fully through the Anaphora. In later days there was a still further development of this symbolism.'

To the modern mind much of this symbolism may seem unreal, but it was not so to the Eastern mind; and it provided a means of contact with the living Lord which for many was more real and went deeper than any mere words could have done, serving to open up vast reaches of devotion and rapture. Symbolism is meaningless only to the uninstructed or unimaginative mind.

Such worship was more emotional than intellectual, and, where the sermon was allowed to fade into insignificance, the emotional element over-predominated. Yet there is little in this worship, when properly understood, to offend against reason; and Christianity has always made most enduring progress by an appeal both rational and emotional. The intellectual appeal must be there to give the emotional stability and permanence, but it dare not be exclusive. Elaborate symbolism in Christian worship is not to be mistaken for gaudy and formal display; to the instructed worshipper each action and symbol is pregnant with meaning. The Puritan John Bunyan properly insisted that there is an Eye-gate as well as an Ear-gate to the City of Mansoul. Christian worship at its best provides a way for man's whole being and nature to approach God, and opens many channels of grace through which God draws nigh to man.

In conclusion, we may observe that, in spite of the sense of the mysterious which pervaded Eastern worship, there was seldom any reluctance to translate the liturgy into the language of the community using it. Thus we find the Eastern liturgies not only in Greek, but in Syriac, Coptic, Ethiopic, Persian, Slavonic, Latin, and other tongues, the most recent change being to translate the Old Slavonic of the Russian Church into Rumanian. This is in harmony with one of the basic principles of Christian worship as a corporate act of the whole community. To be truly corporate, worship must be intelligible to all who take part in it. We now turn to the history of worship in the West.

III

LITURGICAL FORMS IN THE WEST

c. A.D. 500–1570

THE Western rites, like those of the East, developed from the fluid rite of the Primitive Church, and the groundwork is the same. Both derived ultimately from the Synagogue and the Upper Room, and fell into two divisions, the Liturgy of the Word and the Liturgy of the Faithful.

The main parts within this structure were also similar, but they developed on different lines. Notably there is the fact that, in the West, and particularly in the early Roman rite, brevity and sobriety of expression were distinguishing marks as opposed to the diffuseness and flamboyancy of the East; and while in the East the liturgy was fixed throughout the year, no part changing from Sunday to Sunday except the lections, and not necessarily these, in the West from earliest times there were many variable parts known by the general name of *propria* or 'propers'.

These propers were: the introit, i.e. a psalm, or parts of psalms, sung antiphonally at the entrance of the clergy; the collect;[1] the lections; the gradual, a psalm sung between the lections, so named because it was sung at the *gradus* or steps of the altar,[2] sanctuary, or ambo; the secrets, collects said at the end of the offertory; the offertory psalm or anthem, commonly called the offertory; the proper preface, a short variable section of the preface of the consecration prayer, containing a special thanksgiving according to the season; the communion psalm, commonly called the communion; and the post-communions, collects said immediately before the dismissal. Other parts also varied on occasion, especially

---

[1] For description of the collect as a form of prayer see pp. 176–9 below.
[2] In the West the Holy Table was described from early times as the *altare*, i.e. *alta ara*, or 'high altar'.

in the Gallican rites, but these are the principal propers of the Western rites.

The history of worship in the West may be divided more or less arbitrarily into three periods.

The first is from A.D. 50 to 500, when worship in the West was passing through the fluid stage to fixed forms. For three centuries Greek was the vernacular of Christendom, but by the fourth century it had been displaced by Latin as the liturgical language; and towards the end of the fourth century local Latin rites began to emerge as fixed forms. Information about Western worship is extremely fragmentary during this period, our main sources of knowledge being Justin Martyr's account and the Hippolytan church order. By the sixth century, however, evidence of two main rites existing side by side begins to emerge, and documents appear which testify to the order and content of these rites.

The second period is roughly from A.D. 500 to 900. It begins with two Western parent-rites existing side by side: the Roman rite, at first only the local use of the city of Rome; and the Gallican rite, which spread over the rest of Europe and varied considerably according to local use. It ends with the ascendancy of the Roman rite. During this period the two rites influenced each other continually until the ninth century, when, the Roman See having increased in power and authority, the Gallican rites were suppressed under Pepin and Charlemagne. With few exceptions, among which may be noted the rite of the Celtic Church, the Gallican rites dropped out of use, and even where they remained they were in highly Romanized versions. On the other hand, the Roman rite of the tenth century was not that of the fourth or fifth century, but one considerably altered by Gallican influence and containing much Gallican material.

The third period is from approximately A.D. 900 to 1520, the period of the ascendency of the Roman rite. During this time the rite was not absolutely fixed, but varied considerably in different dioceses and provinces, while minor changes were continually taking place. Of these changes the variations in ceremonial and emphasis were more important than those in the text. The Canon (*Canon actionis*, the rule of the action), that part of the Consecration Prayer which follows the Preface, has remained practically unchanged since the sixth century, but the rite as a whole did not assume its present fixed form until 1570. The date 1520 marks approximately the appearance of the earliest Lutheran masses in Germany; these were, at the outset, translations and paraphrases of the Roman liturgy with, however, a change of doctrinal emphasis brought about by important modifications of the traditional ceremonial, and significant revisions and omissions in the text.

§ 1. *The Gallican Rites*

The origin of the Gallican rites is obscure, but most liturgists now agree that they derive from the fluid rite of the Primitive Church, and represent the natural development of the liturgy among the more barbaric peoples beyond Rome. It is to be expected, therefore, that we should find rites more colourful, elaborate, and flamboyant than the local Roman rite; and this proves to be so.

Since the earliest texts of the Gallican rites date only from the seventh century, it is not possible to state precisely what the earlier forms were. Further, the liturgy in the West took fixed and definite form many centuries later than in the East. Indeed, as Lietzmann writes,

'Free liturgical composition obtained in the West into Merovingian times [sixth century]. New prayers were constantly being formulated. . . . The ideal appeared at times to be to compose for each Sunday and festival its own liturgy. We find this tendency in Rome and Milan as well as in Gaul and Spain. In Rome, though not suppressed, it tended to confine itself to the formation of a kernel of prayers which did not vary, and of which the Prayer of Consecration was the core.'[1]

[1] III. 9, p. 262.

This serves to indicate how varied the Gallican rite was in its local expression, and how difficult it is to describe it, save only generally and representatively. This difficulty is further complicated by the comparative lack of texts. Indeed, there is only one collection, *Libellus missarum*, which seems to be free from Roman influence. It was discovered in a palimpsest at Karlsruhe less than a century ago. Cabrol, who has submitted it to a searching scrutiny, declares it to be a Gallican missal of the seventh century, and French in its origin.

In addition to this palimpsest there are two imperfect Gallican sacramentaries, dating from the late seventh or early eighth century, known as the *Missale Gothicum* and *Missale Gallicanum vetus*. These also are from France, but contain many Roman elements. Even more Roman is the *Missale Francorum*, a quarter of a century later. In the ninth and tenth centuries more texts[1] appear, but by this time it is difficult to distinguish between the Gallican and the Roman. The Mozarabic rites in Spain and the Ambrosian rite of Milan[2] were also members of the Gallican family, but space forbids an examination of them. The Celtic rites will be briefly considered separately.

A further source of information which should not be disregarded, though its value has probably been over-estimated by Duchesne, is a letter[3] bearing the name of St. Germain of Paris (d. 576). It is, however, by another hand, and

---

[1] Texts of the Gallican rite: excellent bibliography in Leclercq's article 'Gallicane', *Dictionnaire d'archéologie chrétienne et de liturgie*, VI. i. 474–591; also Migne, *Patrologia Lat.* liii, lxii, lxxiv, lxxviii; and in Texts 15 and 16, pp. 283 sqq.; representative Consecration Prayers in Text 1, pp. 110–23.

[2] Mozarabic texts: best bibliography in *Dict. d'archéol.*, &c., Cabrol's article 'Mozarabe'; Alcuin Club Tracts, xv, London, 1924; and Jenner's article 'Moz. Rite', in *Catholic Encyc.* x. 611–23. Ambrosian texts: Lejau's article 'Ambrosien', *Dict. d'archéol.*, &c. i. 1373–1442; also English translation of modern rite in Text 17.

[3] Migne, *Patrologia Lat.* lxxii, relevant parts quoted in III. 5, pp. 189–227, accompanied by a description of the later Gallican rite, but as celebrated later than Duchesne suggests. See also important article by Wilmart, 'Germain de Paris', in the *Dictionnaire d'Archéologie chrétienne et de liturgie*.

the writer lived probably a century and a half later. It has therefore only a secondary interest for us as describing a local French rite of the late seventh or early eighth century.

A notable feature of the Gallican rite was the place it appears to have given to the people in worship. There were many responses and musical parts. The deacon also seems to a large extent to have retained his primitive function of directing the devotions of the people, leading in litanies, and ministering the Cup at communion. In the West sanctuary screens rarely hid the Holy Table; the deacon, therefore, was not so prominent as in the East, but in the Gallican rite he never became a mere assistant of the celebrant, as in the Roman. It seems probable that the Lord's Prayer was recited by all, or at least by all the ministers.

The Gallican prayers lacked the austerity of the Roman and were more prolix; it is not difficult to distinguish in the modern Roman rite a collect Gallican in origin from one purely Roman.[1] The Gallican rite as a whole was more sensuous, symbolical, and dramatic than the Roman rite of the same period, and much lengthier. It abounded in propers, and was by far the most flexible rite known. Its ceremonial was elaborate and splendid, and its use of incense copious. As in the Roman rite, the two principal actions were the entry of the clergy and the reading of the Gospel. Later the Great Entrance became a feature of some Gallican rites, but this was an importation from the East. Concelebration appears to have been frequent, particularly in the Celtic Church, where it was normal.[2] This had the advantage of largely excluding private masses.

[1] See III. 21, where several examples of early Roman collects and prefaces are collated with Gallican prayers. Probably the classical severity of the Roman prayers is due to the great conserver, Pope Leo the Great (d. 461); see III. 22, p. 56.

[2] See p. 16 above; also III. 6, p. 187; III. 5, p. 175, n. 2. Warren, in III. 12, pp. 128–30, errs when he contends that this practice was exclusively Celtic.

The Gallican rite of the late seventh century, as celebrated in France, would be approximately of the following scheme:

The Liturgy of the Word

Ingressa or *Officium*
Celebrant's salutation: *Dominus sit semper vobiscum*, and response
Kyries
Benedictus (Luke i. 68–79) or *Gloria in excelsis*
Collect
Prophecy or Old Testament Lection
Lection from Acts or Epistles
Benedictus es ('Blessed art thou, O Lord God of our fathers') or
 Benedicite
Gospel (Procession with lights, and *Gloria tibi, Domine*)
Chant—*Tersanctus* or *Kyries*
Sermon or Homily
Deacon's litany
Dismissal of catechumens

The Liturgy of the Upper Room

Offertory: Collection and preparation of elements
 Admixture (of water with wine)
 Psalm sung throughout antiphonally
 (Prayer of the Veil) (Litany of the Faithful)
Reading of diptychs
Collect after the names
Kiss of Peace, and collect for peace
Salutation and *Sursum corda*
Prayer of Consecration:
 Contestatio or *Immolatio* (i.e. Preface. Long, diffuse, varied,
 always a proper)
 Sanctus
 Collect (*Collectio post sanctus* to connect *Sanctus* with Words of
 Institution—really the Anamnesis)
 Words of Institution
 Post mysteria (Collect as Epiclesis)
Fraction (into nine pieces in form of cross):
 Collect: *post secreta*
 Antiphon sung meanwhile
 Commixture (of bread and wine) also takes place here
Lord's Prayer (with protocol and embolism)[1]

---

[1] The 'protocol' consisted of words of introduction, and the 'embolism'

Celebrant blesses people
Delivery and Communion (while Psalm xxxiv, *Ad accedentes*, is sung)
Prayer of Thanksgiving or post-communion collect
Deacon dismisses people: *Missa acta est*, or *In pace*, or other
    formula

As we see from the scheme, the liturgy began with the singing of an antiphon, a psalm, or versicles and responses sung alternately by two choirs, during which the clergy entered in solemn procession, censed by thurifers. The celebrant took his place at the altar in the basilican posture, his ministers disposed about him; and, the *Ingressa* ended, he saluted the people with the formula, *Dominus sit semper vobiscum*, the people replying, *Et cum spiritu tuo*. Then the *Kyries* were sung in Greek, followed by the *Benedictus*; by the seventh century the *Gloria in excelsis* was sometimes substituted, but the *Benedictus* was native to the rite. Collects followed, and a lection from the Old Testament which might be followed by a chant, and another lection from the Acts or the Epistles. The hymns from Daniel (LXX) next found a place, usually the *Benedictus es*, sometimes the *Benedicite*. Then came a procession with the Gospel Book, with lights and incense, after which the Gospel was read by the deacon. This was followed by the *Tersanctus* (Latin translation of the *Trisagion*), and a sermon or homily based upon the Gospel. Then a deacon's litany, so closely akin to the Eastern litanies that it was little more than a translation. To each clause the people responded with the Latin paraphrase of the *Kyrie eleison*: *Precamur te Domine, miserere* ('Have mercy, O Lord, we beseech Thee'). After the litany, the celebrant said a collect, and the deacon dismissed all who were not of the faithful.

At the Offertory, while the elements were being made ready and the water mixed with the wine, a psalm was sung antiphonally; then the elements were unveiled while a prayer of the veil was said. In the older use a litany of the

was a brief prayer based upon the last words of the Lord's Prayer, *Libera nos a malo*. It is frequently referred to as the *Libera nos*.

faithful may have been said also at this point. Then the diptychs were read, and the celebrant said a *collectio post nomina*, and the Kiss of Peace was given, followed by another collect *ad pacem*. Now, saluting the people, the celebrant called them to prayer with the *Sursum corda*.

The Prayer of Consecration began with a long preface known as the *contestatio* or *immolatio*, which, though not so long as the Eastern prefaces, greatly exceeded the Roman in length, and varied frequently. It was concluded by the *Sanctus*, sung by the people. A collect, the *post sanctus*, usually of the nature of an anamnesis, connected the *Sanctus* with the Words of Institution, and a collect *post mysteria*, in reality the epiclesis, completed the consecration, the prayer concluding with an ascription to the Trinity. In some Gallican rites intercessions followed, but whether these belonged to the Gallican rite proper is uncertain.

The Fraction, executed elaborately, accompanied by a collect *post secreta*, came next while an antiphon, the *confractorium*, was sung or the *Benedictus qui venit*; and the commixture or immixture of the Bread and Wine took place at this point. After this, the Lord's Prayer was said, introduced by a protocol and concluded by an embolism. The celebrant then blessed the people, and the delivery and communion followed, the deacon ministering the Cup. Meanwhile Psalm xxxiv. 8 was sung; and after communion a prayer of thanksgiving or a collect was said, and the deacon dismissed the people with the usual formula.

Members also of the Gallican family were the Celtic rites. Of these in the early ages little is known, but the theory, once seriously put forward, that they are descended directly from the fluid rite of the East through Ephesus cannot be entertained.[1] In structure and content the Celtic rites are unmistakably Gallican, not Eastern.

---

[1] This view was based upon the anonymous and erroneous *Cursus Scottorum*, a document of the eighth century; see for details, III. 12, pp. 30–62.

While there are many comparatively early fragments, the two chief sources[1] for the Celtic rites are the late seventh-century Bangor Antiphonary, a collection of collects, hymns, canticles, versicles, and responses used in the monastery where St. Columbanus is said to have begun his monastic career; and the Stowe Missal, also monastic, belonging to the early tenth century. Further information comes from such fragments as that of Karlsruhe, an early ninth-century manuscript containing three masses. The *Bobbio Missal*,[2] a seventh-century manuscript, is also considered by some, notably by E. Bishop, to be 'an example of the kind of book in vogue in the second age of the Irish Saints'.

Taking these sources together, and following principally the Stowe Missal, we may obtain a general view of the Celtic rite in the early tenth century. It still retained at this time many Gallican features, and indeed was predominantly Gallican; but Roman influence had begun to make itself felt from the seventh century onwards, when the Roman Easter was accepted in Southern Ireland. The dominance of the Roman rite comes much later, and may be dated approximately from the time of Queen Margaret of Scotland, towards the end of the eleventh century. Thereafter, the Sarum rite[3] gradually gained the ascendancy.

Before the service began, while the ministers vested and the elements were prepared, a private preparation was made by the clergy consisting of a confession of sins, litany of the saints, and various collects. The rite proper began with the introit.

This work is valuable, but many of its conclusions are out of date, and must be accepted with reserve in the light of modern research. See also *Dict. d'archéol.*, &c. II. ii. 2990–1.

[1] Full and detailed information of all the texts, too numerous to mention here, is given in Gougaud's important article, 'Liturgies celtiques', in *Dict. d'archéol.*, &c. II. ii. 2969–3032; see also Jenner, 'Celtic Rite', in *Catholic Encyc.* iii. 496 sqq. For the Stowe Missal see Text 18, also III. 12. Irish litanies in Text 19.

[2] In Mabillon, *Lit. Rom. Vet.* ii, and in Text 15.

[3] See p. 145 below.

Liturgy of the Word

Introit (not mentioned in missal, but in tracts. Probably sung from Psalter)
Salutation
Collect (St. Peter's in iii. kal. Julias)
Imnus Angelicus (i.e. the *Gloria in excelsis*, which may have been preceded by the *Tersanctus* or *Trisagion*)
Collects (several, including that of the day)
Lection from Old Testament or Apocalypse
Epistle
Collects
Psalm sung antiphonally, followed by collects
Alleluia, with more collects
Deacon's litany, concluded by collects
Chalice half-unveiled, while Ps. cxli. 2 was sung thrice
Chant, *Veni, Domine, sanctificator, omnipotens, et benedic hoc sacrificium preparatum tibi*, sung thrice
Gospel
Chant, nature of which is obscure
Collects *super evangelium*
Creed (that introduced into Byzantine rite by the Patriarch Timotheus, A.D. 511[1])

Liturgy of the Upper Room

Offertory: Full unveiling of elements
  Ps. lxxxv. 7, *Ostende nobis*, meanwhile sung thrice
  Offering of paten and chalice together with elevation
  Diptychs read, followed by a collect *post nomina*
Sursum corda (no salutation)
Prayer of Consecration:
  Preface (peculiar to this rite—Stowe)
  Proper Preface inserted—rubric in vernacular
  Sanctus (sometimes *Benedictus qui venit* followed—Roman)
  Post-sanctus collect (akin to Mozarabic for Christmas day)
  Canon (closely similar to Roman,[2] with a few unimportant Gallican peculiarities, and with many Celtic saints; The *Te igitur* is preceded by the words: *Canon dominicus papae Gilasi*)
Fraction, with Confession of Faith and Alleluias. The Fraction was elaborate, normally divided into 5 to 13 pieces in form of a cross. At Christmas, Easter, and Pentecost into 65 pieces. Priest assisted celebrant, hence *confraction*.

[1] See also p. 38 above.   [2] See pp. 60–3 below.

Lord's Prayer with protocol and embolism

The Kiss of Peace (formula similar to Mozarabic)

Celebrant's Blessing of people

Commixture, Delivery, Communion: deacon ministering Cup

   During celebrant's Communion, *Ecce Agnus Dei* sung

   During people's, antiphons from psalms, &c.

Post-communion thanksgiving, *Gratia tibi agimus*

Deacon's litany in some earlier rites

Deacon dismisses people: *Missa acta est. In pace*

In view of the previous description of a Gallican rite it is unnecessary to describe the manner of celebration in detail: the important differences appear in the above scheme. The *Benedicite* occurs in the documents, and may have been sung after the Prophecy or Old Testament lection. There is no evidence that incense was used. The position of the celebrant at this time was *ante altare*, that is, facing the altar with his back to the people. Concelebration was widely practised. At Iona, for example, it was the rule, it being the prerogative of bishops only or very eminent priests to celebrate alone.[1] Originally, apart from the preface, the Prayer of Consecration seems to have been brief—a short series of collects as in earlier Gallican rites—and was said audibly. The celebrant's blessing was given in the Eastern manner, the first, second, and fourth fingers extended, the third closed down upon the thumb-tip. Later the Roman mode was adopted, the thumb, first, and second fingers extended, the third and fourth fingers bent.[2] A peculiarity of the Celtic rites was the great number of collects, and also the position of the litany before the Gospel. The services appear to have been always choral until the period of the Roman ascendancy.

§ 2. *The Roman Rite*

The origin, and the development of the Roman rite prior to the sixth century, are clouded in obscurity. Until the

---

[1] III. 12, pp. 128–30. See p. 48 above.

[2] Note similarity to the hand of Sabazius; see *The Labyrinth*, ed. by Hooke, London, 1935, Oesterley's essay on Sabazius.

third century the rite was in Greek, and during this time we have a description and fragment in Justin Martyr's account and in the Hippolytan church order. These, however, are not merely descriptions of the local Roman use, but are rather related to the early fluid use of the Church in the first three centuries; and during the time Hippolytus was writing he was in schism. Early in the fourth century or even in the third century, it would appear, the rite began to take form in Latin; at this time also Constantine set the Church free from persecution and gave it a legal status. The eucharist was now celebrated publicly, and this brought about important changes, investing the primitive service with greater solemnity and splendour of ceremonial. This, however, is conjecture rather than history, for a lacuna exists between the early fourth and late sixth centuries. The only document of importance dates from about the middle of this period, and has been, without adequate reason, attributed to St. Ambrose. It is known as the *de Sacramentis*,[1] and in it part of the Canon is quoted, sufficient to indicate that the Roman Canon had begun to take fixed form at this time.

The *Leonine Sacramentary*[2] also contains fourth- and fifth-century material, although it is a later compilation. A sacramentary contained the celebrant's prayers said at mass,[3] ordinations, and other services, but omitted the other parts of the mass and the Canon. Thus it was composed of collects, prefaces, secrets, and post-communions proper to each Sunday and other days. Two other important sacramentaries may also be mentioned. The first is the so-called *Gelasian Sacramentary*,[4] from Gelasius I, pope

---

[1] Text in Migne, *Pat. Lat.* xvi. 417–64, particularly 462–4. Also the relevant portions are quoted in III. 6, pp. 130–1, and in II. 5, pp. 166–9, who, following Duchesne, III. 5, assigns it to so early a date as about the beginning of the fifth century. See also XII. 1, pp. 141 sqq.

[2] See Text 20; also article 'Léonien' by Cabrol in *Dict. d'archéol.*

[3] 'Mass' has no doctrinal significance, being derived simply from the words of dismissal in the West (Rom. *Ite, missa est*; Gall. *Missa acta est. Missa* is late Latin for *missio*).

[4] See Text 21; also Cabrol's article 'Gélasien', in *Dict. d'archéol.*

from 492 to 496. It is probably based upon Gelasius' work, but in the form in which it has come down to us the document may be as late as the eighth century, so containing additions and alterations. The Canon, however, may be taken substantially as that obtaining in Rome in the sixth century. The second is the *Gregorian Sacramentary*,[1] so named from Gregory the Great, pope from 590 to 604. This, certainly, is based upon Gregory's reforms, but in the form known to us is considerably later. From the ninth century to the fifteenth, texts are more numerous, and especially valuable are the *Ordines romani*,[2] detailed descriptions of the ceremonial of the mass.

We may now describe in some detail the Roman mass as it was celebrated about a century before the time of Gregory the Great.[3] It will be found to be the simplest of all rites, terse, austere, rigid in its economy of words, structure, and ceremonies.

Liturgy of the Word

Introit by two choirs as clergy enter
Kyries
Celebrant's salutation
Collect(s)
Prophecy or Old Testament lection
Antiphonal chant
Epistle
Gradual (Psalm sung originally by one voice)
Alleluia
Gospel, with lights, incense, responses
Dismissal of those not communicating (*Greg. Dialog.* i. ii. 23)

[1] Text of two ninth-century manuscripts in Text 22; on oldest fragments of early eighth-century manuscript, see Wilmart's article, 'Un missel grégorien ancien', in *Revue Bénédictine* (1909), xxvi. 281–300; others representing fusion with Gallican rite, in Migne, *Pat. Lat.* lxxviii. 25–240; see also Cabrol's article 'Grégorien' in *Dict. d'archéol.*
[2] First *ordo* in Text 23; also with some other *Ordines*, in III. 5, pp. 456–84. A good account with bibliography of texts also in Thurston's article 'Ordines romani', in the *Catholic Encyc.* A complete edition with notes is still wanting.
[3] This description is based mainly upon E. Bishop's valuable essay, in III. 21, and Cabrol's essay in III. 7, pp. 520–4; see also III. 11, chap. 8.

Liturgy of the Upper Room

Offertory: Collection of elements, spreading of corporal on altar, preparation of elements for communion, offering of gifts, admixture, psalm sung meanwhile

Salutation and *Sursum corda*

Prayer of Consecration:
Preface
Proper Preface
Sanctus
Canon (see pp. 60–3 for text)

Kiss of Peace

Fraction

Lord's Prayer with protocol and embolism

Communion, celebrant first, then people (Psalm sung meanwhile)

Post-communion collect (Thanksgiving)

Dismissal by deacon

The musical parts were rendered by trained singers, and the responses led by the deacons. A part of Bishop's description will show us the rite as actually celebrated:

'Nothing can possibly be more simple than the composition . . . of the early Roman Mass, say, about the middle of the fifth century. The singing of a psalm, the introit, by the choir at the beginning on the entry of the clergy; a prayer, or collect, said by the celebrant; followed by readings from the Bible, separated by a psalm sung by the choir which we call the gradual. After the collection of the offerings of bread and wine from the people, during which the choir sings another psalm, our offertory, the celebrant reads a second collect having reference to the offered gifts, which collect we call the secret. Next comes, as an introduction to the great action of the sacrifice, what we call the preface, said by the celebrant, and followed by a solemn choral song of praise to God, the *Sanctus*. Then follows the great act of sacrifice itself, embodying the consecration, namely, the prayer called the Canon. As a preparation for the communion of the priest and people, the celebrant says the Lord's Prayer, adding a few words which are, as it were, the echo of that holy prayer, our *Libera nos, quaesumus*. Then comes the communion of the people, during which a psalm is sung by the choir, which we call the communion. Finally, the celebrant says a third collect, our post-communion, and the assembly is dismissed. It is to be observed that these collects are extremely short; three or four lines, as we have them in our missal to-day. What can be more simple? It is the mass reduced to its least possible expression.'

Bishop's account does not mention the *Kyries*, which were probably sung at this time, a remnant of the deacon's litany which had recently disappeared at Rome. We know, also, that they were given ingenious variety by Gregory the Great, for it was he who changed the second *Kyrie* to *Christe*, and made them a little hymn of three, reading thus: *Kyrie eleison, Christe eleison, Kyrie eleison*. The lection from the Old Testament also found a place at this time, but during the fifth century it disappeared from the Roman rite, except during Holy Week, when many of the ancient characteristics are retained.[1] At this period the *Alleluia* was sung perhaps only at Easter, but it soon became a constant part of the rite. The dismissal of the catechumens had also disappeared, but in its place there is the curious dismissal of those who do not intend to communicate. By this time, all the faithful did not communicate every Sunday, as they had done at an earlier period. The position of the Lord's Prayer was changed by Gregory the Great, who placed it at the end of the Canon. The *Agnus Dei* was not introduced until the late seventh century, when Pope Sergius (687–701) ordered it to be sung during the celebrant's communion.

Turning to the ceremonial, the same characteristic of simplicity and economy is displayed. Elevation[2] at the Words of Institution, with all the ceremonial that gathered round it, was absent, as were bell-ringings, censing, lights, genuflexions. All these were later importations, partly from Gallican sources, but also the result of doctrinal development. Decency and order were rigorously guarded throughout, but at only two places was there elaborate ceremonial, namely, at the entry of the celebrant, and at the singing of the Gospel. In the early rite the celebrant stood behind the

---

[1] The Services for Holy Week may be bought separately for a few pence: in these is preserved the heart of the Roman rite.

[2] On the history of elevation in the liturgy, East and West, see the valuable and illuminating study, III. 16.

altar, facing the people; and in Rome, particularly, the early basilicas were so orientated that the celebrant, adopting the basilican posture, faced the East. The relics of saints were placed in a vault in front of the altar, and this prevented the celebrant from standing there. Later, what is technically known as the Eastward position became general, i.e. the celebrant stood in front of the altar with his back to the people and the altar occupied the place where the bishop's throne formerly stood. But even as late as the *Ordo romanus primus*, the celebrant still stands behind the altar, facing the people; and the Canon is said audibly, though curtains may have been drawn to make the action 'secret'.[1] The basilican posture is retained at St. Peter's when the Pope celebrates,[2] and has been recently restored by some Benedictines.

In conclusion, we may again quote Bishop:

'Those very things which in the popular mind are considered distinctive of Romanism, and which go to make up in the main what people call the sensuousness of the Roman rite, form precisely the element in it which is not originally Roman at all, but has been gradually borrowed, adopted in the course of the ages. The genius of the native Roman rite is marked by simplicity, practicality, a great sobriety and self-control, gravity, and dignity. But there it stops. Rome had a receptive, but not a creative imagination. The two chief characteristics of the Roman rite, then, are these: soberness and sense.'

Before proceeding to study the later development of the rite, we must examine the Canon. Its origin presents difficulty; and, in its present form, which dates at least from the sixth century since when it has been essentially unchanged, it is both a dislocation and a fragment, and is of inferior composition and style. Gregory the Great mentions that it was compiled by a 'scholasticus', and he did not esteem it unduly. It is clearly a compilation, parts of it being certainly as early as the fourth century. On looking more closely at its text,[3]

[1] See III. 13, p. 137.   [2] IX. 1, p. 86.
[3] Text finally fixed in 1570, here quoted, may be examined in any missal. With this may be compared the early text of late sixth and ninth centuries in parallel columns, in III. 7, pp. 516–18. See also III. 21, pp. 83–91.

we find that it falls into several sections, each of them being designated by the words with which it begins. The Consecration Prayer[1] opens with the *Vere dignum*, or Preface,

'Vere dignum et justum est, aequum et salutare, nos tibi semper, et ubique gratias agere: Domine sancte, Pater omnipotens, aeterne Deus. . . .[2] . . . per Christum Dominum nostrum. Per quem majestatem tuam laudant Angeli, adorant Dominationes, tremunt Potestates. Coeli, coelorumque virtutes, ac beata Seraphim, socia exsultatione concelebrant. Cum quibus et nostras voces, ut admitti jubeas, deprecamur, supplici confessione dicentes:'

The *Sanctus* follows, recited by the celebrant in a low voice, and at high mass sung by the choir as he proceeds secretly with the *Benedictus qui venit* and the Canon. The *Benedictus qui venit* with *Hosanna* stands next in the text after the *Sanctus*, but at high mass it is not taken up by the choir until the elevation is reached.

The Canon opens with the *Te igitur*,[3] a prayer for the acceptance of the gifts and offerings here offered for the whole Church, with a petition for the peace and unity of the Church, and for the Pope and the diocesan remembered by name. The *Memento Domine* is an intercession for certain persons named and for all present,

'pro quibus tibi offerimus, vel qui tibi offerunt hoc sacrificium laudis, pro se, suisque omnibus, pro redemptione animarum suarum, pro spe salutis et incolumitatis suae; tibique reddunt vota sua aeterno Deo, vivo et vero.'

The next prayer is the *Communicantes*,[4] which consists

---

[1] I have not ventured to translate the Canon; it seems advisable to present it in the original Latin so that the reader may form his own conclusions regarding the style and grammar. If a translation of a sort is desired it may be found in any missal or bought in booklet form from Burns, Oates, and Washbourne, London, at a cost of twopence. The best Latin-English edition is Cabrol's, published in London by Herder.

[2] Here follows the proper preface; Rome has thirteen.

[3] To what *igitur* refers is unknown; see III. 6, pp. 323–45 on the Canon. Is this prayer an epiclesis?—see III. 9, pp. 117–21.

[4] Here again we are confronted with grammatical difficulties. This prayer varies slightly five times yearly.

chiefly of the recitation of the names of the Virgin Mary, the Apostles, and sundry saints and martyrs, concluding with the petition,

'quorum meritis precibusque concedas, ut in omnibus protectionis tuae muniamur auxilio. Per eumdem Christum Dominum nostrum. Amen.'

The *Hanc igitur*[1] concludes the intercessions for the living:

'Hanc igitur oblationem servitutis nostrae, sed et cunctae familiae tuae, quaesumus Domine, ut placatus accipias, diesque nostros in tua pace disponas, atque ab aeterna damnatione nos eripi, et in electorum tuorum jubeas grege numerari. Per Christum Dominum nostrum. Amen.'

The consecration proper now begins with *Quam oblationem*:[2]

'Quam oblationem tu, Deus, in omnibus, quaesumus, benedictam, adscriptam, ratam, rationabilem, acceptabilemque facere digneris: ut nobis Corpus et Sanguis fiat dilectissimi Filii tui Domini nostri Jesu Christi.'

At this point the Words of Institution[3] are recited; they fall into two paragraphs, *Qui pridie*[4] and *Simili modo*:

'Qui pridie quam pateretur, accepit panem in sanctas ac venerabiles manus suas, et elevatis oculis in coelum, ad te Deum Patrem suum omnipotentem, tibi gratias agens, benedixit, fregit, deditque discipulis suis, dicens: Accipite, et manducate ex hoc omnes. Hoc est enim Corpus meum.

'Simili modo postquam coenatum est, accipiens et hunc praeclarum

---

[1] Fortescue (III. 6) says of it, 'Perhaps the most difficult prayer in the mass'. It is varied four times yearly by the insertion of an additional clause.

[2] 'Certainly an invocation', writes Fortescue, 'but not of the Holy Ghost.' What the five epithets 'benedictam, &c.' mean is not known, save that the first 'benedictam facere' clearly means 'to bless' (II. 5, p. 188), though many have ventured guesses. Rietschel says they are unintelligible. See III. 6, p. 334.

[3] In nearly all liturgies devotion has embellished the Words of Institution; see, e.g., Text 6, pp. 193–247, where the Words of Institution are quoted from eighty-two rites.

[4] The Roman formula appears always to have been 'on the day before' rather than the formula common to the Scriptures and all other liturgies, 'on the night in which'. Some Gallican texts have the Roman formula, but this is not now regarded as an originally Gallican feature.

Calicem in sanctas ac venerabiles manus suas, item tibi gratias agens, benedixit, deditque discipulis suis, dicens: Accipite et bibite ex eo omnes: Hic est enim Calix Sanguinis mei, novi et aeterni testamenti; mysterium fidei: qui pro vobis et pro multis effundetur in remissionem peccatorum. Haec quotiescumque feceritis in mei memoriam facietis.'

Unde et memores, the Roman anamnesis, follows:

'Unde et memores Domine, nos servi tui, sed et plebs tua sancta, ejusdem Christi Filii tui Domini nostri, tam beatae passionis, necnon et ab inferis resurrectionis, sed et in coelos gloriosae ascensionis: offerimus praeclarae majestati tuae de tuis donis ac datis, hostiam puram, hostiam sanctam, hostiam immaculatam, Panem sanctum vitae aeternae, et Calicem salutis perpetuae.'

The *Supra quae*,[1] which follows, is a prayer that what has been offered may be acceptable unto God as were the 'munera' of Abel and the 'sacrificium' of Abraham and Melchizedek. Then the celebrant continues in the *Supplices te*:

'Supplices te rogamus, omnipotens Deus: jube haec perferri per manus sancti Angeli tui in sublime altare tuum, in conspectu divinae majestatis tuae: ut quotquot ex hac altaris participatione, sancrosanctum Filii tui Corpus et Sanguinem sumpserimus, omni benedictione coelesti et gratia repleamur. Per eumdem Christum, &c. Amen.'

Then follow intercessions for the dead, *Memento etiam*,[2] and the *Nobis quoque*, a prayer for association with the Apostles and martyrs, the names of the latter being given at length, the whole concluding with this petition and grand doxology:

'. . . intra quorum nos consortium, non aestimator meriti, sed veniae, quaesumus, largitor admitte. Per Christum Dominum nostrum.

'Per quem haec omnia, Domine, semper bona creas, sanctificas, vivificas, benedicis et praestas nobis.

---

[1] Some have found in *Supra quae* and *Supplices te* an ancient Roman epiclesis; others have found it in the oblation *Veni sanctificatur*. It is probably a vain search. See III. 5, p. 181; III. 11, p. 385; III. 6, pp. 348–54, 334; and II. 4, pp. 115–17. See also the important Appendix 2 of XII. 2.

[2] 'Intercession for the dead was no regular or essential part of the Sunday Mass at Rome before the ninth century'. II. 5, pp. 184, 189.

'Per ipsum, et cum ipso, et in ipso, est tibi Deo Patri omnipotenti, in unitate Spiritus sancti, omnis honor et gloria. Per omnia saecula saeculorum. Amen.'

It is evident how hospitable the Roman Canon is to a particular idea of sacrifice peculiar to later Roman theology. The intention is to re-enact validly what Christ did by anticipation at the Last Supper. The method followed is to use, as nearly as possible, our Lord's own words and actions. Thus the theology of a later period, based upon current philosophical conceptions of 'substance' and 'accident', came to describe the bread and wine as being 'transubstantiated' into the Body and Blood. This is not a magical change wrought by man; it is a miracle accomplished by God, as the prayer for ratification, *Quam oblationem*, makes clear. Consecration is succeeded by sacrifice, when the 'Holy Victim' (*hostia*) is offered in *Unde et memores*, together with the prayer for acceptance, *Supplices te*, beseeching that what has been done on earth may be confirmed in heaven. This conception came to be grossly misunderstood during the Middle Ages, but what we have described is the primary intention in the 'Sacrifice of the Mass'. As Burkitt[1] points out:

'It may be that "transubstantiation" is incredible; it is certain that many superstitious ideas had come to be connected with the Mass by the beginning of the sixteenth century, and it may be these were inevitable. But before we can appreciate the Reformed worship, or condemn the unreformed service, it is necessary to have a clear idea of the structure of that service and of the principles underlying it.'

During the Middle Ages there were, as there are now, several ways of celebrating mass, and it is the principal of these ways which requires to be noted if the later development of the rite is to be understood.

The typical manner of celebration is called pontifical high mass, a sung mass[2] at which the celebrant is a bishop,

[1] See his valuable brief exposition in III. 22, pp. 41–52. Transubstantiation was officially defined in 1215 by the Fourth Lateran Council.
[2] For parts sung at high mass see pp. 69–71 below.

assisted by several clergy. An inevitable and early variant of this is high mass, i.e. a sung mass celebrated by a priest, assisted by a deacon, subdeacon, and servers. High mass required the services of a highly trained choir to sing the choral parts.

But often neither choir nor assistant ministers were available. Thus there arose the custom of low mass. At low mass the celebrant took on himself as far as possible the functions of the three ministers, and he was assisted by one or more servers. This involved a considerable abridgement in the ceremonial, and, since there was no choir, mass was not sung but said, mostly inaudibly, save those parts sung at high mass and the preparatory prayers, which were said aloud. By the sixteenth century low mass had become the popular service, as it still is in the Roman Church. It also became unusual after the ninth century to communicate at high mass, and communion was given to the people only at low mass; and this is still the general practice.

Sometimes, however, there might be a choir but no ministers to assist the celebrant. Thus another way of celebrating was devised, known as *missa cantata*. This is really a low mass, except that the mass is not said but sung. This service has become popular in England in modern times. The people do not ordinarily communicate at a *missa cantata*.[1]

Another type of celebration must be mentioned here. It is that known as *missa sicca* or dry mass.[2] It consisted of a low mass said without consecration of the elements, which were absent, and without communion. Thus the parts relevant to communion were omitted. This service had its origin in the West in the Middle Ages, and it may be compared with the Liturgy of the Pre-Sanctified in the East as

---

[1] Within these main divisions are many variations impossible to mention here. A full account of the ceremonial at all celebrations of the mass will be found in Part II of III. 18. See also pp. 69–71 below.

[2] A most important and valuable study of the *missa sicca* is contained in III. 23.

said during Lent and a somewhat similar service on Good Friday in the West.[1] Dry mass is important to our study because it proves to be not unlike the Ante-Communion in the Anglican Church and the Sunday Morning Service of the Reformed Churches, as will appear later.

It is not possible in a brief study to trace in detail the development of the Roman rite between the sixth and sixteenth centuries,[2] but certain facts must be noted.

The ceremonial of the rite lost its early austerity. This was partly owing to Gallican influence, and partly to the fact that 'in the later middle ages popular devotion attached enormous importance to seeing the Blessed Sacrament at the elevation. This became the ritual centre of the Mass.'[3] The culmination of the service was therefore held to be the supposed 'moment' of consecration, and many thought it sufficient to be present only at that point. The mass became more and more a spectacle, the rite itself being for the most part inaudible. Attention was focused almost wholly on the visible action.

Communion of the people had become increasingly infrequent after Constantine's time, in spite of protests voiced at Church Councils.[4] By the sixth century the minimum requirement was that the laity should communicate at Christmas, Easter, and Pentecost; but this was in 1215 reduced to Easter. The Cup was also withdrawn about this time, or earlier.

Certain changes were made in the text of the liturgy. The chief was the introduction of the Nicene Creed at Rome in the eleventh century. Also, many private prayers of the celebrant, which differed according to local use, found a

[1] These services are, of course, different in kind from the *missa sicca*; at them the elements are present, having been consecrated at a previous celebration.

[2] For a full description see III. 6, pp. 172–208; and until Charlemagne's time, III. 5, pp. 161–88.

[3] III. 6, p. 341. No doubt by 'ritual centre' Fortescue means 'ceremonial centre'. See his whole treatment of elevation, ibid , pp. 337–45. Date about twelfth and thirteenth centuries.

[4] See III. 8, p. 328 for references.

place at various points of the rite, particularly at the introit, Gospel, and offertory. These were made uniform in 157c

A little vernacular service, known as the Prone[1] and said from the pulpit, also became popular, particularly in France and Germany. In practice it was inserted into the mass after the Gospel. It was composed usually of bidding prayers, the Epistle and Gospel, the Creed, sermon, exhortation, and the Lord's Prayer, or sometimes a lengthy paraphrase of it.

Latin had gradually become restricted to the use of scholarship and diplomacy, and was not understood by the people, who used the vernaculars. But it was retained, except in the Prone, as the language of the liturgy. This inevitably hindered the participation of the people in the worship of the Church, which had become associated with an atmosphere of unhealthy mystery. To-day missals are provided for the people, with the Latin text and a vernacular translation in parallel columns, and the ceremonial is sufficiently described in vernacular rubrics. No such provision was or could be made before the sixteenth century. Service books were available only for the clergy or highly placed personages, and these books were most complicated. Also, the increasing elaboration of the music had not only reduced the psalmody to a few skillfully selected verses, but excluded active participation by the people. Further, the deacon, who had been a link with the people in the early fluid rite, and had remained so in the Eastern, and to a large extent in the Gallican rites, early became in the Roman rite a mere assistant of the celebrant.

As the ceremonial grew more elaborate it was invested with a mystical meaning, so that people following the action

---

[1] Described in Text 24, vol. ii, pp. 1020–45; see also vol. i, pp. cxlvi–cxlviii. He errs in supposing that the Reformed Services of Strasbourg, Geneva, and Scotland are derived from the Prone: see V. 7, pp. 17–47, 66–76 for textual evidence to the contrary. The Prone, of course, was not fixed by papal authority, and did not appear in the text of the mass.

might find it a guide for their devotion. Amalarius of Metz in the ninth century was the chief expositor of the symbolical meaning of the mass, and to this day his work provides the basis of most of the popular expositions. Brilioth[1] summarizes this teaching thus:

'The main idea was that the liturgy itself should be used so as to bring to remembrance the passion of Christ; the first part of the mass, however, deals with the history of Christ before his entry into Jerusalem. Some confusion of the order of events is inevitable. While the introit symbolizes generally the coming of Christ and his ministry, the *Gloria* shows the joy in heaven after his resurrection; and when the bishop sits down on his throne, there is symbolized the session of Christ at his Father's right hand. The Epistle, gradual, and Gospel signify the proclaiming of the Old and New Covenants and Christ's own preaching. The salutation before the Offertory is the greeting of the crowd at the triumphal entry. When the priest offers the oblation, Amalarius sees the entry of Christ into the temple to offer himself to the Father. In the *Sanctus* he is greeted with the people's praise; the first part of the Canon recalls the beginning of the passion and the disciples' flight. The remainder of the service symbolizes the death of the Lord, the centurion's confession, the taking down of the body, the burial, the resurrection, the appearance at Emmaus, and lastly the Ascension.'

Another point to be noted is the great increase in the number of masses said. As Fortescue[2] points out, 'the older system of assistance and communion or concelebration was replaced in the early Middle Ages by a separate mass said apart by each priest. . . . Each mass as a propitiatory sacrifice has a definite value before God; therefore two masses are worth twice as much as one.' With quantity as its criterion, piety logically demanded a maximum of celebrations.

Masses were also said to achieve definite ends. As early

---

[1] See III. 15, p. 83. See also III. 17, pp. 59–154. Modern popular expositions of the mass may be bought at the doors of most Roman churches for a few pence. Such teaching did not begin with Amalarius: it is at least as old as the third century. But Amalarius gave it a new prominence and popularity that increased during the Middle Ages.

[2] III. 6, p. 187.

as Hippolytus we hear of special masses for the dead, but in the Middle Ages these were increased out of all reckoning. As each mass was held to have value as an act of merit, it was now seriously computed how many were required to bring a soul through purgatory to paradise, and to what extent a mass could alleviate the pangs of a soul condemned to eternal punishment. There were masses for success in temporal affairs: for one going on a journey, for recovery from sickness, for the capture of thieves and the return of stolen goods, for rain or fair weather, for the release of captives; and here again the number required to achieve the object was solemnly determined. Masses were said even to bring about the death of persons; these were condemned and forbidden by the Synod of Toledo in 694.[1] Private masses became, as Heiler says, a cancer feeding upon the soul of the Church.[2]

By the ninth century the demand for private masses was so great that many priests were required. This had its effect upon the design of churches. Where several priests were attached to one church, the high altar was insufficient for each to say mass daily. So side chapels and chantries were formed, collegiate churches were founded for the purpose, and altars were placed in the bays of the naves of the cathedrals and abbey churches. This multiplicity of altars was peculiar to the West; in the East there was commonly only one Holy Table in each church.

The Roman mass attained uniformity shortly after the Council of Trent, the revision being completed in 1570.[3] Before that date there were various unimportant provincial and diocesan variations, consisting principally of differences in ceremonial and the celebrant's private prayers. The rite

---

[1] III. 6, p. 187.   [2] See I. 3, p. 71.
[3] Issued by Pius V's Bull, *Quo primum*. The Missal was entitled, *Missale Romanum ex decreto ss. Concilii Tridentini restitutum*. A far-reaching (but not doctrinal) revision and rearrangement of the Roman service books took place at this time. The changes made since have been few and unimportant; see III. 6, pp. 208–13.

of 1570 may therefore be taken as the typical rite of the Western Church towards the end of the medieval period. Thus the scheme of high mass given below, if compared with the scheme on p. 56, will indicate the main changes that have taken place since the sixth century. Those parts of the rite which accompany a main action are placed under it.

After a short preparation called the *Asperges*, mass begins:

The Liturgy of the Word

Introit and ⎫
Kyrie eleison (ninefold) ⎬ sung by choir
    Entry of ministers
    Private preparation of ministers at altar steps (said secretly):
        Invocation, *In nomine Patris* . . .
        Ps. xliii, with *v.* 4 as antiphon, and *Gloria*
        Ps. cxxiv. 8.
        Confiteor and *Misereatur* of celebrant to ministers
        Confiteor and *Misereatur* of ministers to celebrant
        Versicles and responses from psalms
        Collects *Aufer a nobis* and *Oramus te*
        Blessing of incense, and censing of altar and ministers
Gloria in excelsis said secretly by celebrant and sung by choir
Salutation and collects of the day, after which celebrant says the
        the Epistle and gradual silently
Epistle, sung by subdeacon; response, *Deo gratias*
Gradual sung by choir
Tract or Sequence (if any) sung by choir, while are said
    Prayers and Preparation for the Gospel:
        Munda cor meum ⎫
        Jube Domine benedicere ⎪
        Dominus sit in corde tuo ⎪
        Salutation, announcement of Gospel, and ⎬ by celebrant
           ministers' response, *Gloria tibi Domine* ⎪
        Gospel recited in low tone ⎪
        Response by ministers, *Laus tibi Christe* ⎭
    The same repeated, except for celebrant's blessing added, by
        deacon
Gospel, with lights and incense, sung by deacon, and responses
    sung by ministers

Preacher goes to pulpit:
    Intimations
    Bidding Prayers
    Epistle and Gospel read in vernacular
    Sermon
Nicene Creed sung as *Gloria in excelsis*
Salutation and bidding to prayer, but no prayer

The Liturgy of the Upper Room

Offertory: Psalm verses sung throughout while celebrant proceeds
    secretly
Offering of bread: collect, *Suscipe sancte Pater*
Admixture of water to wine: collect, *Deus qui humanae*
Offering of chalice: collect, *Offerimus tibi*
Prayers, *In spiritu humilitatis* and *Veni sanctificator*
Blessing of incense: *Per intercessionem*
Censing of elements: *Incensum istud*
Censing of altar, saying Ps. cxli. 2–4
Censing of ministers
Washing of celebrant's hands, while he recites the *Lavabo*,
    Ps. xxv. 6–12, with *Gloria*
Oblation, *Suscipe sancta Trinitas*, *Orate fratres* (said audibly),
    and *Suscipiat Dominus*
Secrets (collects corresponding to those of the day)
Salutation and *Sursum corda* (sung)
Prayer of Consecration:
    Preface and Proper Preface—sung by celebrant (then *Sanctus*
        and *Benedictus* said audibly)
    Sanctus, sung by choir while the celebrant proceeds with the
        Canon, said silently (except for raising of the voice at *Nobis
        quoque*), bell rung to announce beginning
    Elevation, with bells and incense at Words of Institution and
        singing of *Benedictus qui venit*
    Canon concludes with ecphonesis
Lord's Prayer sung by celebrant, with protocol and embolism
Pax and Fraction and Commixture
Agnus Dei said by celebrant, then sung by choir
Celebrant's Communion (while *Agnus Dei* is sung):
    Collect, *Domine Jesu Christe*
    Kiss of Peace to clergy
    Collects, *Domine Jesu Christe fili Dei vivi* and *Perceptio corporis tui*
        and Centurion's words, *Domine non sum dignus* (said audibly)

He receives the Bread, saying Words of Delivery
Thanksgiving, Ps. cxvi. 12–13
He receives the Cup, saying Words of Delivery
(Communion of the people, in one kind, with *Ecce Agnus Dei*,
   Words of Delivery and *Domine non sum dignus*: very rare at
   High mass)
Communion Psalm sung by choir
   Cleansing of chalice
   Collects *Quod ore sumpsimus* and *Corpus tuum Domine*
   Covering of Chalice
Salutation and Post-communion collects
Deacon's salutation and dismissal of people
Collect, *Placeat tibi*
Blessing of People, *Benedicat vos*
Last Gospel, John i. 1–14, and response *Deo gratias*

The service, like all others we have described up to this
point, is conducted from the altar, but during the medieval
period the Eastward position of the celebrant became universal, so that he now faced East for the prayers, turning to
the people only when addressing them. Most of the prayers
are said inaudibly,[1] and some secretly, but the ecphoneses
indicate the celebrant's progress. The choir sings the Introit, *Kyries*, *Gloria in excelsis*, Gradual, Tract or Sequence,
Nicene Creed, Offertory, responses to *Sursum corda*, *Sanctus*, *Benedictus qui venit*, *Agnus Dei*, Communion. The
ceremonial is too elaborate to be described in brief space
here,[2] but it is of immense importance, and is most carefully regulated by authority.

We now turn to the rites of the Churches of the Reformation.

---

[1] The three tones used by the celebrant at high mass are 'vox sonora', for
those parts sung aloud to the plain-chant melody, 'vox submissa', which can
be heard by those around but not loud enough to disturb the singing, and
'vox secreta', which can be heard by the celebrant alone (see III. 18, p. 127).
There are three corresponding tones used at low mass (ibid., p. 49).

[2] See III. 18. Popular descriptions of ritual and ceremonial may be bought
for a few pence at most Roman church doors. Or see Text 25.

IV

LITURGICAL FORMS IN THE CHURCHES OF THE REFORMATION *c.* 1520 TO THE PRESENT DAY

WE have seen that, at the beginning of the sixteenth century, the celebration of the Lord's Supper in the Western Church had become a dramatic spectacle, culminating not in communion but in the miracle of transubstantiation, and marked by adoration, not unmixed with superstition, at the elevation. Said inaudibly in an unknown tongue, and surrounded with ornate ceremonial and, if a sung mass, with elaborate musical accompaniment, the rite presented only meagre opportunity for popular participation. The people were not encouraged to communicate more often than once a year. The sermon had fallen into a grave decline, most parish priests being too illiterate to preach; and the place of the Scripture lections had been usurped on a great many days by passages from the lives and legends of the saints. The Scriptures were not fully accessible in the vernacular, and paid masses and indulgences were a source of simoniacal exploitation. Reformation was an urgent necessity.

The results of the Reformation movement, so far as the forms of worship were concerned, were imperfect. A tendency soon became evident for the pendulum to swing to the other extreme, resulting in services excessively didactic and inadequate in structure. Nor was the break with a legalistic theology complete, and legalism began to express itself in new ways.

The most serious defect lay in the fact that the continental Reformers were without any profound historical knowledge of the origins and principles of worship. Their acquaintance with liturgical forms appears to have been largely restricted to the contemporary Roman forms; of Gallican and Eastern worship they appear to have known almost nothing; and their knowledge of even the primitive worship that they wished to restore was rudimentary and incomplete. This meant that at a time of intense spiritual revival there was no leader on the Continent equipped to provide forms of worship fully adequate to express the new spirit. Spiritual fervour largely took the place of this lack during the first generations, but the result ultimately was a lamentable impoverishment of the worship in the Reformed Churches. The liturgical achievements of the Reformers, the Strasbourgers and Cranmer excepted, were largely negative. Both in the eucharist and the offices they simply omitted what they considered superfluous or incompatible with the new teaching; at other points they made drastic substitutions. Yet throughout, apart from the new psalmody and hymnody, there was little that was creative.

But if the forms were inadequate, the principles they were intended to express are living and imperishable. To those who inherit the Reformers' spirit the task yet remains to provide forms broad enough and deep enough for man's whole being to go out to God in adoration, praise, and prayer, and for God's grace to come to man without let or hindrance. To accomplish this requires a bringing forth from the Christian treasury of things both new and old.

Under the Reformation movement there were five distinct schools of liturgical revision, represented by Luther in Germany, Zwingli at Zürich, Bucer at Strasbourg, Calvin at Strasbourg and Geneva, and Cranmer in England. These we shall consider in that order, examining briefly their origins and development, and their distinctive principles.

§ 1. *The Lutheran Rites*

In Luther there is much that is sharply contradictory. He was the most conservative of all the Reformers in his theory of worship, yet in actual practice he made some drastic and far-reaching changes; at other times he could scarcely be persuaded to make any changes, and his theory far outstripped his practice; while in some particulars his theory and practice remained in permanent disagreement. But too much emphasis need not be laid upon this, since it is an experience common to all reformers.

Central to Luther's conception of the Lord's Supper was the fellowship of Christians in and with the living Lord. This idea is prominent in the New Testament, particularly in the early chapters of the Book of the Acts, but it had been largely lost in the teaching of the medieval Church. It fell to Luther to rediscover it, and in his early writings especially he gave it a conspicuous place. This recovery alone changed the whole aspect of worship. No longer could it remain merely a spectacle splendidly enacted as it were upon a stage; it must become a common action in which all shared. But if all were to share in it, the worship must be intelligible, and to be wholly intelligible it must contain didactic elements. This end, Luther held, could be achieved only by retaining the celebration of the Lord's Supper as the central service of the Church. Thus in 1520 he declared that the Lord's Supper ought 'to be celebrated daily throughout Christendom';[1] but three years later he modified this view when in another sermon he stated that in future the eucharist would be celebrated only on Sundays, unless there were those who wished to communicate more frequently.[2] The result was that a weekly celebration of the Lord's Supper, with sermon and communion, became the early Lutheran tradition.

Luther's idea of fellowship involved belief in the Real Presence, and his interpretation was conservative rather than creative. His doctrine of consubstantiation did not differ greatly from the medieval doctrine of transubstantiation, save that he insisted that the Real Presence could be

---

[1] *Sermon von den guten Werken.*
[2] See also his *Formula Missae*, 1523, Text 26, vol. xix; Text 36, pp. 127–32; and pp. 77–8 below.

completely realized only when the worshipper received communion.

Luther, however, sharply attacked the medieval view of the sacrifice of the mass, which taught that the mass was a repetition of the sacrificial death of Christ. But he did not make the mistake of discarding altogether the idea of sacrifice. He transformed it, giving it a truer interpretation. In the eucharist, he declared, we do not offer Christ; He was offered once for all on Calvary. But we enter into His sacrifice, 'offer ourselves up together with Christ; that is, we cast ourselves upon Christ with sure faith in His covenant'. We offer ourselves, our souls and bodies, in fellowship with Him; and we offer a sacrifice of praise and thanksgiving as we identify ourselves with Him. In this sense, the Lord's Supper is a sacrifice; but it is not a veritable re-enactment of our Lord's sacrificial death.

While Luther's criticism of the mass was often violently polemical, he was reluctant to make any hasty changes in its text and ceremonial, though he encouraged the people to receive communion at every celebration and insisted that the Words of Institution be said audibly. A vernacular mass was a logical inference from his idea of fellowship, and in 1520 he went so far as to declare himself openly in favour of this change. But he was slow to make it. Some of his more impulsive followers anticipated him, and several German masses appeared before his.[1] These are too numerous to describe in detail, but the general trend of the movement may be indicated.

At first both Luther and his followers were content to prepare private prayers to be said silently by the people while the celebrant said mass in Latin at the altar. But in 1520 his *Babylonish Captivity* appeared. In this aggressive work, he urged the need for a mass in the vernacular, repudiated the doctrine of transubstantiation, attacked the

---

[1] These are conveniently collected and edited in Text 27. They are not available in an English translation.

doctrine of the mass as a sacrifice, and declared the Last Supper to be the norm of all masses. This spurred his followers to action.

Carlstadt made the first experiment at Wittenberg on Christmas Day 1521. He celebrated in the vernacular without eucharistic vestments, omitted the Canon except the Words of Institution, and gave communion in both kinds. During Luther's absence from Wittenberg this use was established and followed for a short time.[1] But on his return, impatient of these changes, he insisted upon reversion to the old ways.

The oldest German mass[2] that has come down to us belongs to the year 1522; it was compiled for the Carmelite monks at Nördlingen by their prior, Kaspar Kantz.

It was said in German throughout, but only the second part, the liturgy of the faithful, remains. It was designed, apparently, to be celebrated as a low mass, music to fit the German words being not yet available. The offertory psalm therefore disappears, and a brief exhortation[3] relevant to communion, concluding with a general absolution, takes the place of the offertory prayers. The *Orate fratres* becomes a bidding to prayer for the celebrant alone, and a collect for him follows. He then repeats, in accordance with an old custom in that province, the *Veni Sancte Spiritus*. The Prayer of Consecration consists of Preface, *Sanctus, Benedictus qui venit*, a paraphrase of *Quam oblationem*, and the Words of Institution. The Lord's Prayer and the *Agnus Dei* follow. The collect, *Domine Jesu Christe Fili Dei vivi*, from the celebrant's private preparation, is cast into the plural as a prayer of preparation for all. The other private prayers disappear, an almost inevitable result when the whole rite is now said audibly. After communion the *Nunc dimittis* or *Te Deum* is said, followed by a paraphrase of the post-communion collect, *Placeat tibi*.

[1] He also forbade communion of the sick by means of the reserved elements, enjoining a separate celebration in the sick-room. This was not unknown in the medieval Church; but, on the whole, it was a practice to be deplored, and it soon spread far beyond Lutheranism. Communion of the sick by the reserved elements is as early as the second century. To hold a private celebration in the sick-room is to obscure the sense of fellowship.

[2] Text 27, pp. 73-8. For the sake of clarity the Latin designation of the prayers is retained, but it will be understood that the whole rite was said in German.

[3] Such an exhortation was commonly a part of the Prone in Germany.

During the next year other German masses compiled on similar lines appeared throughout Germany,[1] and many attempts were made to prepare a Canon that would accord with Lutheran opinions. Luther disagreed with much of this activity, and it compelled him to take the lead himself in liturgical reform. In the autumn of 1523 he published his *Formula missae*.[2] In the introduction he states that the time is ripe for the creation of new forms, and a return to primitive simplicity. This is to be attained by cleansing the old service of the human inventions and accretions that have perverted it out of all recognition. The Canon he describes as incoherent patchwork and an abomination; and he condemns the medieval ceremonial and over-elaborate music. But after all this protestant thunder, what he presents as a substitute is merely a truncated version of the Roman mass, retaining the Latin language, most of the ceremonial, lights, incense, and vestments.

In the Liturgy of the Word, lights and incense at the Gospel are made optional, the *Confiteor* is discarded, and the only sequences retained are those for Christmas and Pentecost.

The Liturgy of the Faithful is more ruthlessly treated. All that remains of the Offertory is the preparation of the elements, which may take place during the Creed. He allows the mixed cup, but prefers pure wine because of his notion that it was so used at the Last Supper. The *Sursum corda* and Prefaces remain, but his treatment of the Canon is negative, illogical, and subversive. By an indefensible innovation he attaches the Words of Institution to the Preface, then adds the *Sanctus* and *Benedictus qui venit*; these latter are sung by the choir, and during the *Benedictus qui venit* the elevation takes place. The remainder of the Canon is omitted,[3] so the rite contains neither intercessions nor a consecration prayer. After the elevation, the Lord's Prayer is said, with protocol but without the embolism; and the *Pax* is given. During communion, which follows,

[1] Edited in Text 27.

[2] In Text 28, i. 2 sqq.; Text 29, vol. i, i, pp. 4 sqq.; Text 26, vol. xix; Text 36, pp. 127–32; English translation in Text 30.

[3] Essentially a radical change, with the result that most Lutheran rites to this day consecrate not by prayer but by the formula of the Words of Institution. On the surface, however, the change was slight and would hardly be noticed by the people, since the Canon was always said silently.

the *Agnus Dei* and communion psalm are sung as formerly. The post-communion follows, but the dismissal is omitted, and the Aaronic Blessing (Num. vi. 24–6)[1] may be substituted, if so desired, for the *Benedicat vos*. The whole service was to be said audibly.

In the second part of his work he states that mass is not to be said if there are no communicants, that communicants must show a proper knowledge of the faith, and when they wish to communicate they are to inform the celebrant in advance. Private confession before communion is not to be compulsory, but Luther considers it as of high practical value and to be encouraged; communion is to be in both kinds; before communion there is to be private preparation, not confined merely to the formal fast. He also urges the need for new spiritual songs in the vernacular.

Unconstructive and negative as the *Formula missae* is, it became the norm of the best and most comprehensive of the later Lutheran liturgies, many of which, including the important liturgies of Strasbourg,[2] far surpass Luther's own work.

Those based upon his *Deutsche Messe*[3] were slighter in structure and content. Nevertheless, its appearance in the autumn of 1526 acted as a brake upon his more extreme followers. Luther did not publish his *Deutsche Messe* until he himself had used it for a year at Wittenberg; this enabled him to present it, with a musical accompaniment, as the embodiment of his considered opinion.

The introduction, if somewhat contradictory, is illuminating. He admits his reluctance to provide a German mass, and urges that the Latin mass should still be said on certain days. He retains vestments, lights, and altars 'for the time'; but states that the altar should be moved out from the east wall so that the celebrant might take his place behind it in the basilican posture, facing the people 'as without doubt Christ did at the Last Supper'. Strangely enough, however, in practice he seems to have clung to the eastward position.

As before, his work is negative, the only positive contribution being

---

[1] His preference for the Aaronic Blessing arose from his extravagant fancy that it was used by our Lord at His Ascension to bless His disciples. It enjoyed a wide popularity among the Reformers after it was introduced by Luther.   [2] See pp. 87–111 below.

[3] Text 28, vol. i, pp. 35 sqq.; Text 29, vol. I, i, pp. 10 sqq.; Text 26, vol. xix, pp. 14 sqq. English translation in Text 30.

the new German hymns. In the Liturgy of the Word, all the private and incidental prayers of the celebrant disappear, a development, as we have pointed out, which was more or less inevitable if the mass was to be said audibly. The old introits were translated into German, but German hymns are permitted as alternatives. The *Kyries* (still in Greek) are to be threefold instead of ninefold, and the *Gloria in excelsis* is deleted. The gradual and *Alleluia* are replaced by German hymns that the people could sing. The Apostles' Creed in German metre is substituted for the Nicene Creed.

He deals drastically with the Liturgy of the Faithful, sadly mutilating it beyond what the Lutheran teaching required, and providing a most inadequate vehicle of devotion. The Offertory has disappeared, and the preparation of the elements takes place while the Creed is being sung. In place of the old offertory there is a short paraphrase of the Lord's Prayer, followed by a short exhortation. These are both derived from the old German Prone, but they are now said at the altar, not from the pulpit as formerly. The whole of the Canon except the Words of Institution is abolished; and the rite contains no prayer of consecration, thanksgiving, or intercession. The elevation is retained, and consecration is effected by reading the Words of Institution over the elements; and Luther initiates and encourages the unfortunate departure, although he does not insist upon it, of consecrating and distributing each element separately. During communion, while the communicants go forward, the *Sanctus* is sung in German (Luther's *Jesaia dem Propheten*), or the *Agnus Dei*, likewise in German, or a German metrical hymn. After communion Luther's collect, *Wir danken dir almechtiger Herr Gott*, is said, and the service concludes with the Aaronic Blessing. The whole service is to be said in German, and examples are given of how the Epistle and Gospel may be sung.

A glance at the scheme of Luther's *Deutsche Messe* given below shows how extreme Luther's revision was, particularly in the second part of the rite.

Liturgy of the Word

Introit or German hymn
Kyrie eleison
Salutation and collect
Epistle
German hymn
Gospel
Apostles' Creed (Elements prepared now)
Sermon or homily

Liturgy of the Upper Room

Paraphrase of Lord's Prayer

Exhortation

Recitation of Words of Institution, accompanied by Fraction and Delivery

Communion, hymns sung meanwhile

Post-communion collect

Aaronic Blessing

As a form, Luther's German mass was defective in many parts. But he broadened and deepened the spirit of worship and gave the people a more intelligible part. They now knew at least what was being done, and could join in the common action; and communion was restored to its rightful place. The impetus given by Luther to the hymnody of the Church was to produce lasting and glorious benefits.

Not all of Luther's followers were so negative or extreme as he was in the preparation of new forms of worship, and some of the Lutheran liturgies are richer in content than those of Luther himself. Absolute liturgical uniformity was never a Lutheran ideal, and the rites in the various cities and provinces varied considerably, though all belonged unmistakably to the same family.[1]

Outside Germany Lutheranism was more creative liturgically. The Swedish, Norwegian, and American Lutheran rites are evidence of this.[2] In Germany recently there have been liturgical movements of great interest,[3] but in the present unsettlement between Church and State it is difficult to know what their future may be.

[1] The numerous texts are edited in Text 29. The modern rites will be found in such service books as those noted in Text 31.

[2] Swedish: Text 32; Norwegian and Danish: Text 33; American: Text 34.

[3] See, e.g., Rudolph Otto, who expounds his liturgical views in IV. 7, following it with prayers and lections for the Christian Year in IV. 8, and further prayers in IV. 9. A translation of his Order of Worship, with an admirable exposition is given in an article in *The Journal of Religion* (Chicago University), October 1931; see also I. 7, pp. 238–40; and Prof. H. R. Mackintosh's article in VI. 8, year 1931–2. Another movement is described by Heiler in his article, 'The Catholic Movement in German Lutheranism', in *Northern Catholicism*, London, 1933, ed. by Williams and Harris. See also Heiler's periodical, *Hochkirche* (Munich).

§ 2. The Zwinglian Rites

Zwingli's doctrine of the Lord's Supper is not to be simply branded as memorialism and so dismissed; it was more complex than that, and there is much with which to agree in Dr. Barclay's statement that 'in their essential teaching on the Holy Supper, Luther, Zwingli, and Calvin were as one'.[1] The striking difference between Zwingli and his two fellow Reformers lay in early training and consequent approach to theological doctrine. Calvin and Luther were scholastics, while Zwingli was a humanist. Consequently, Zwingli was more rationalistic in his theological outlook, less mystical, and more subjective and analytical; while his idea of God is characterized by an extreme transcendentalism difficult to reconcile with the necessary complement of immanence.

This had two effects upon his proposed forms of worship. His prayers tended to be precise theological definitions of belief rather than simple direct petitions and praise; they were didactic rather than devotional. While he speaks repeatedly of receiving Christ in the eucharist, his exposition of how this is achieved is unreal, an inevitable defect if the exposition attempts to be purely rationalistic.[2] A further effect was to obscure the idea of fellowship in the eucharist, for such fellowship ultimately depends upon the Real Presence.

One essentially fundamental difference between Zwingli and the other Reformers did, however, exist. Zwingli did not regard the Lord's Supper in itself as a means of grace, or as the norm of Christian worship. In theory and practice, therefore, he did not favour frequent communion. This difference from Luther and Calvin was decisive.

[1] See I. 19, an important contribution. See also V. 5, vol. v, pp. 351 sqq.
[2] This accounts for his being generally misunderstood by both his followers and his opponents. The task he undertook was too exacting for rationalism alone.

De canone missae epicheiresis,[1] Zwingli's first revision of the mass, appeared in 1523. As the title, *An Attack upon the Canon of the Mass*, indicates, his first assault was against the Canon, which he cannot consent to use because of its incoherence, contradictions, sacrificial ideas, and general inadequacy as a consecration prayer. At first, 'for the sake of the weaker brethren' he had thought of retaining it with a few modifications; but when he came to revise it, the incoherence of its content and the barbarity of its style defeated him. He therefore had to prepare a substitute, and, unlike Luther, he did not shirk the task. His pamphlet indicates what he proposes as a reformed rite, and it is written in graceful and classical Latin as befits the pen of a humanist. Here is a digest of its contents:

Most of the Liturgy of the Word is retained, but the lectionary is simplified, and the collects, lections, and sequences related to saints' days deleted. The musical settings are ruthlessly simplified. The lections and sermon are to be in the vernacular, but the remainder of the service in Latin.

In the Liturgy of the Faithful the offertory and *Sursum corda* are deleted, and the preparation of the èlements takes place, no doubt, during the singing of the Nicene Creed. The Preface and *Sanctus* are retained; but for the Canon are substituted four prayers, which, taken together, are about the same length as the original Canon, or slightly shorter.

The first prayer is a thanksgiving for creation, providence, and redemption; it concludes with the Lord's Prayer.

The second prayer is highly definitive and didactic. In essence, it is a prayer that the faithful may be fed with the true Bread of Heaven, which is the Word, 'the bread that giveth life to the world'; there is also a slight reference to the Passion; and a petition that the Spirit may quicken those who partake at this Table.

If there is an anamnesis, it is found in the third prayer. It begins with the affirmation that 'taught by Thy Word, we steadfastly believe, O Lord, that heaven and earth shall pass away rather than Thy Word', which moves into a confession of faith in our Lord's sacrifice upon the cross whereby He reconciled us to the Father, and in the validity

---

[1] Text in Text 35, vol. lxxxix, pp. 561 sqq., especially pp. 605 sqq.; Text 36, pp. 424–5 (in part only); Text 28, vol. i, pp. 342 sqq.; and Text 27, pp. 192 sqq.

of His sacrament wherein 'He offered himself to be the food of our souls under the forms of bread and wine, that the memory of His gracious deed might never be abolished'. Then follows a petition that our faith may be so increased as we eat our Lord's flesh and drink His blood, that we may be enabled to overcome the world. At the conclusion the note of fellowship is struck, in the petition that as many as shall partake in the nourishment of the Lord's Body and Blood may manifest and express one spirit, and be one in Him who is one with the Father.

The fourth prayer is one of humble access. It opens with a petition that when we cry, 'O Lamb of God that taketh away the sins of the world, have mercy upon us', God will graciously forgive our sins. It concludes with prayer for worthy communion at the banquet of our Lord, who Himself is both host and sumptuous feast.

The Words of Institution, which follow, are from 1 Cor. xi. 23–6, in their Scriptural form, and with one verse more than in the Roman rite. Our Lord's invitation is added: 'Come unto Me all ye that labour, &c.'. Communion follows, after which *Nunc dimittis* is sung; and a brief post-communion prayer concludes the service.

This digest shows how different from Luther's was Zwingli's approach to revision of the old worship. His radicalism was more unrestrainedly expressed two years later, when in April 1525, he published the first German rite to appear in Zürich. It was entitled *Action oder Bruch des Nachtmals*,[1] and became the norm of all later Zwinglian worship.

He prefaces his rite by a letter to the faithful and a foreword. In the letter he says that, while error has long reigned, God in His mercy has now disclosed the true way, and as the Israelitish kings Hezekiah and Josiah purified the Passover so that it had been rightly observed since their time, so by the help of God the Lord's Supper is now to be celebrated according to its proper use. In Zürich, cere-monies and ritual are reduced to their barest form;[2] only sufficient is retained for the remembrance of Christ's death in a spiritual way. But Zwingli does not venture to prescribe rules for other Churches; these are for each Church to determine for itself. The letter con-cludes with the statement that in Zürich it is held that the Church

---

[1] Text of *The Action or Use of the Lord's Supper* in Text 35; Text 36, pp. 443 sqq.; Text 28; Text 27, pp. 194 sqq.; Text 37, vol. iii, pp. 147–57.

[2] The use of eucharistic vestments and all music was now forbidden in the Zürich rite.

has the right to exclude from communion those who live in open sin, who thereby defile the Body of Christ.

The foreword is really a comprehensive rubric, giving certain directions for the service. Those who intend to communicate are to take their places in the choir, and the bread and wine is to be carried to them by deacons. The communicants are to remain in their places and receive sitting, each taking a small piece of bread in his hand off the large wooden plate that now does service as a paten; the wine is given in a large wooden cup. At reception all say, Amen. Unleavened bread is used. Communion is to be celebrated only four times in the year: at Easter (on which day several successive celebrations are permitted), Whitsun, autumn, and Christmas.

Two points of importance emerge from the foreword. First, we have here the origin of sitting communion;[1] and secondly, although Zwingli encouraged more frequent communion for the people than the medieval Church had done, he confines it to four times a year. In both these matters he stood alone among the continental Reformers in theory; though both Calvinists and Lutherans later came to adopt infrequent communion in practice. This, however, was in direct opposition to the teaching of both Luther and Calvin.[2] The structure of Zwingli's German rite was as follows:

Liturgy of the Word

Ordinary Morning Service (a form of mattins), concluding with
    Sermon and a Confession of sins
Offertory: preparation of elements
Invocation: 'In the Name of the Father, &c.'
Collect
Epistle
Gloria in excelsis (said antiphonally)
Gospel
Apostles' Creed

Liturgy of the Upper Room

Exhortation
Fencing of the Table
The Lord's Prayer

[1] See pp. 126, 140, 144, and 150 below.
[2] For Luther see pp. 74 sqq. above; for Calvin see pp. 112–19 below.

Prayer of humble access
Words of Institution, with:
  Fraction
  Ministers' communion
Delivery, and communion of the people
Post-communion psalm (said antiphonally)
Post-communion collect
Dismissal

The service was carried out in this manner:

The ordinary Sunday Morning Service, probably a much simplified form of Mattins, though in content more like the Prone, consisting mainly of reading, preaching, and a long prayer, preceded the eucharist. This first service was concluded by a confession of sins following the sermon, and the Holy Table was then made ready and the elements prepared for communion. Thereafter the celebrant and two assisting deacons, corresponding to the deacon and subdeacon at high mass, took their places at the Holy Table in the basilican posture. The whole service was said in a clearly audible voice in the vernacular.

The service proper began, as did the celebrant's part in the mass, with the Invocation, to which the assisting ministers replied, Amen, 'for the people'. A collect followed, to the intent that the service might be in accordance with our Lord's command to show forth His death, with a right and true faith; the people kneeling for prayer, and saying, Amen. Then one of the ministers read the Epistle, which like the Gospel was fixed. It consisted of the Words of Institution and subsequent verses (1 Cor. xi. 20-9); at its conclusion ministers and people said the old response in the vernacular, 'Praise be to God'. Then the celebrant said the opening clause of the *Gloria in excelsis*, and the men and women, who sat on opposite sides of the choir, took it up antiphonally. The senior deacon, standing at the north end of the Holy Table, then read the Gospel. He greeted the people with the familiar salutation, 'The Lord be with you', and they responded, 'And with thy spirit'; he then announced the passage, John vi. 47-63, the people responding, 'Praise be to God'. After the reading, he kissed the Gospel Book, and said, 'Praise and thanks be to God, who according to His Holy Word willeth to forgive us all our sins', the people responding, Amen. The Epistle and Gospel remained fixed until 1846; then the only change was to reduce the number of verses in the Gospel by five. After the Gospel the Apostles' Creed was recited in the same manner as the *Gloria in excelsis*.

The Liturgy of the Faithful began with a brief exhortation said by the celebrant, concluding with a fencing of the Table which forbade any to approach fraudulently. He then bade the people kneel, while he recited the Lord's Prayer (as in the old rite, without the Matthean doxology, which was not inserted in the Zürich rite until the next century), to which the people responded, Amen. The celebrant continued in a brief prayer of humble access, recapitulating God's mercy and loving-kindness in the gift of His only-begotten Son, for the fellowship and redemption that come through Him, confessing our unworthiness of so great a redemption, and beseeching forgiveness; the prayer ended on a note of self-oblation and was concluded with the traditional doxology to the Holy Trinity. The people responded, Amen, and having risen from their knees, sat while the celebrant consecrated, using the Words of Institution, during the repetition of which he performed the manual acts and communicated himself and the deacons. He then delivered the consecrated elements, one of the deacons bearing the bread and the other the wine to the people in their seats. The people might either be communicated by the deacons or else take the paten and cup into their own hands. After communion, Ps. cxiii, 'Praise ye the Lord; praise O ye servants . . .', was said in the same manner as the *Gloria in excelsis.* The *Gloria patri* was not said after the psalm. The service ended with the thanksgiving: 'We give Thee thanks, O Lord, for all Thy gifts and goodness; who livest and reignest, God for ever', the people responding, Amen. The celebrant then dismissed them with the words, 'Go in peace'.

Music had been abolished from the Zwinglian rite in 1525, and the antiphonal recitation of the psalms and canticles substituted; it is doubtful, however, if this innovation ever proved successful, and there is evidence in the later editions[1] that the actual recitation of the psalms and canticles was carried out by the two deacons 'for the people'. Zürich was the only centre of the Reformation movement where singing was abolished; elsewhere the more reasonable course was taken of substituting congregational singing for the elaborate music rendered in the old rite by choirs. Before the end of the sixteenth century, Zürich had abandoned the extreme view that led to the exclusion of music from worship, and introduced congregational song.

[1] Plainly stated in the rubrics of all editions of *Action oder Bruch* after 1525.

It is interesting to observe in this rite the survival of the two assisting ministers, their functions practically unchanged. They did not long remain in the other Churches of the Reformation, although the word 'deacon', in the old sense, was still used in some of them. In England deacons were retained as an order of the Holy Ministry.[1]

Though Zwingli retained many of the parts of the old rite, the actual content of his worship is bare. There is no prayer of consecration, and no prayer of intercession. While both Luther and Zwingli stressed fellowship as an essential aspect of the Lord's Supper, their rites strangely failed to give expression to it. In neither rite is there a sense of communion with the whole Church on earth and in heaven; and in Zwingli's rite, after the antiphonal recitation of the psalms had broken down, there was no point where there was a common action. In content, the Zwinglian rite must be regarded as the least adequate of all the Reformation liturgies.[2]

Its most tragic influence, however, was the beginning of the separation of the Lord's Supper from the Lord's Day, making it no longer the norm of Sunday worship, but a memorial feast infrequently celebrated.

§ 3. *The German Rites of Strasbourg*

In Strasbourg, until Bucer became the superintendent in 1530, Lutheran influence was dominant, though from the beginning the Reformers there acted independently of him. Bucer, however, brought Zwinglian influence to bear upon the Strasbourgian Reformers, especially on the humanist side, so that Strasbourg became the *via media* between Luther and Zwingli. Thus there sprang up in that city

---

[1] On Holy Orders, see J. W. Hunkin, *Episcopal Ordination*, &c., Cambridge, 1929; C. S. Carter, *Reformation and Reunion*, London, 1935: *Presbyterian Orders* (Scottish Church Society), Edinburgh, 1926.

[2] *Pace* Brilioth, III. 14, pp. 162-3, and Hislop, following him, III. 15, p. 187. For the connexion between Zwingli's rite and Knox's use at Berwick-on-Tweed see Dr. McMillan's paper in VI. 8, year 1934.

a family of rites of great importance to the study of the worship of the Reformed Churches.

Elsewhere[1] I have traced in detail and step by step the evolution of the Sunday morning worship at Strasbourg between the years 1525 and 1539. Here, therefore, it is necessary only to indicate the development in broad outline; but, by way of illustration, I shall include the two most important texts in translation, since these are not available in English.

The first revision of the mass in Strasbourg was carried out by Diebold Schwarz (Theobaldus Niger);[2] and, on February 16th, 1524, he celebrated in German for the first time in St. John's Chapel in the church of St. Laurence.

Schwarz's mass was much less radical yet essentially more creative than any revision Luther had either suggested or achieved. The new spirit was amply expressed, but the best in the old form was preserved. It was a translation into simple German of the old service, and as many as possible of the old familiar things were retained: the *asperges*, vestments, elevation, washing of the celebrant's hands, genuflexions, and most of the ceremonial. But all that pertained to the Roman doctrine of sacrifice was ruthlessly expunged. This was accomplished by slight omissions here and there, the paraphrasing of familiar words, and a creative, as opposed to a negative, treatment of the whole rite. The·whole rite was said in a clearly audible voice, and all invocations of the saints and the Virgin were excluded. The private prayers of the celebrant were, most of them, omitted; and, since music was not yet available for the German words, the parts ordinarily sung had either to be said or omitted. The *Confiteor* was modified slightly, and said aloud as a general confession of sins, though the first person singular was still retained.[3]

---

[1] See V. 7, pp. 24–32, 66–9; all the German liturgies of Strasbourg are edited and collated in Text 38, a most important and valuable volume.

[2] Text 38, pp. 57–75; and in Text 39

[3] When the first singular was replaced by the first plural, general con-

Of all these changes, the most important and far reaching was the saying of the rite audibly; for this meant that, although the traditional ceremonial remained, the people were no longer dependent upon it for following the service. That, at one stroke, relegated the ceremonial to a subordinate place; and what before had been of primary importance now became a mere enrichment of the rite.
The following is Schwarz's rite in outline:

Liturgy of the Word

Preparation at the altar steps:
Invocation: 'In the Name, &c.'
Confession of sins, the local *Confiteor* revised
Absolution: 1 Tim. i. 15
Scripture Sent. (Ps. cxxiv. 8: 'Our help, &c.') from celebrant's
    private preparation in old rite, said as he goes to altar
Salutation and response
Introit, said not sung
Kyries
Gloria in excelsis
Salutation and collect
Epistle
Gospel
Nicene Creed, said

Liturgy of the Upper Room

Offertory:
Preparation of elements
Exhortation[1]
Salutation and *Sursum corda*
Preface and proper preface
Sanctus and *Benedictus qui venit*
Lavabo and related collect
Canon (said standing, with upraised hands):
Intercessions
Prayer for quickened life

fessions appeared for the first time in the eucharist. Actually, it was the substitution for private confession of public and common confession.
[1] Derived at Strasbourg not from the Prone, but from the *Orate fratres*, clumsily changed to meet the new teaching; see pp. 94 and 105 below. Brightman fails to distinguish between the origins of the Lutheran and Strasbourg exhortations in Text 24.

Words of Institution, with ëlevation
Anamnesis
Lord's Prayer, with Matthean doxology
Pax
Agnus Dei
Communion collect, *Domine Jesu Christe fili Dei vivi*
Celebrant's communion
Delivery, and People's communion (in both kinds, if desired)
Two post-communion collects
Salutation and response
Blessing, *Benedicat vos*

The Latin names are retained in the above outline in order to indicate how closely Schwarz's rite followed the old. The actual text of Schwarz's rite is embedded in the translated text on pp. 91–7 below, and if this scheme above is compared with that text, Schwarz's can be easily distinguished from what has been added or altered.

The Strasbourgers were constructive in their treatment of the Canon, as we see also by the translated text on pp. 95–6 below. The text there differs only in the slightest degree from Schwarz's. By retaining the thanksgiving, intercessions, and anamnesis, they retained the essential content of a consecration prayer. Consecration was effected by the inclusion of the Words of Institution in the prayer, and no epiclesis was added. That may be regarded as a defect, but it was typical of contemporary Western use.

During the years 1524–5 nine or ten printed editions of the German mass appeared at Strasbourg, each differing slightly from the others, but all closely related in form and substance. The text printed below is the seventh in this series, but it represents the third step in the revisions of Strasbourg. The service book in which it is contained is entitled *Teutsch Kirchē ampt mit lobgsengen vñ götlichen psalmen wie es die gemein zu Straszburg singt vñ halt mit mer gantz Christlichē gebettē dañ vorgetruckt.*[1]

[1] Text 38, pp. 77–82, 57–75; and Text 27, pp. 126 sqq. These translations first appeared in VI. 8, year 1930–1; the aim has been to reproduce as far as possible in English the style of the German original.

By this time Bucer's influence was making itself felt, but not so strongly as was the case after 1530. The reforms had, however, been carried further than by Schwarz, and the principal differences may be briefly summarized. A choice begins to appear in the prayers; the Apostles' Creed is given as an alternative to the Nicene; the Aaronic Blessing may be said instead of the Roman Blessing; psalms and hymns in German metre appear, providing the people with opportunity to participate in the service; such phrases as, 'Lord's Supper', 'Minister', 'Holy Table' are beginning to replace 'Mass', 'Priest', 'Altar', though there is a good deal of interchanging for some time; the Latin titles for the parts of the service are gradually replaced by German titles; the Epistles and Gospels are no longer selected according to the old lectionaries, but are read in course and are of greater length; sermons are regularly preached, sometimes one on each lection; the ceremonial is much simplified, and the elevation discarded; and the worship is now conducted from behind the Holy Table, which has been moved forward to provide room for the celebrant. All this does not appear from the texts themselves, but there are contemporary accounts which describe the worship; these will follow the texts.

THE ORDER OF THE MASS, AS THE CHURCH AT STRASBOURG NOW CELEBRATES IT

In the Name of the Father, and of the Son, and of the Holy Ghost. Amen.

Kneeling—Make your confession to God the Lord, for He is good, and His mercy is everlasting. I said, I will confess my transgressions unto the Lord; and Thou forgavest the inquity of my sin.

And I, poor sinner, confess before God the Almighty, that I have sinned grievously through the transgression of His Law; that I have done much that I should not have done, and have left undone much that I should have done, through unbelief and distrust towards God; and that I am lacking in love towards my fellow-ministers and towards my neighbours. God knoweth how great is my guilt, and I repent. O God, be gracious unto me, a poor sinner; and be merciful, for my sins are many. Amen.

This is a faithful saying, and worthy of all acceptation, that Christ Jesus came into the world to save sinners, of whom I am the chief. Lord, I believe; help Thou my unbelief, and grant me salvation. Amen.[1]

Then, going to the altar,[2] *and facing the people, the Priest says:*

God be gracious and merciful unto us all. *Amen.*

Another Confession of Sins [to be used in place of the above.]

Seek ye the Lord while He may be found, call ye upon Him while He is near. Give unto God the glory, and confess your iniquity, and say:

Almighty God, everlasting and merciful Father, behold, in iniquity were we[3] shapen, and in sin did our mother conceive us. To Thee we confess and acknowledge all our sins and transgressions. We have not believed Thy Word; and we have gone aside from Thy way; our whole life is vain transgression. In Thy mercy and goodness remember, O Lord, these who are here gathered from the world; remember not the sins of our youth nor our transgressions; but in Thy mercy remember us yet for Thy goodness' sake and for Thy Name's sake. O Lord, forgive our sins, for they are very great, and be merciful unto us.

Now let us be comforted and be glad, and hear the good tidings of the Gospel:

Brethren, if any man hath sinned, we have an advocate with the Father, Jesus Christ the righteous; and He is a propitiation for our sins; and not for ours only, but also for the sins of the whole world. Believe the Gospel (*or* these words), and live in peace. *Amen.*

The Introit or the beginning of the Mass

I cried with my whole heart: hear me, O God, I will keep Thy commandments and Thy statutes. I cried unto Thee: save me, and I shall keep Thy testimonies (Ps. cxix. 145–6). Hear my voice according unto Thy loving-kindness: O God, quicken me according to Thy judgment (Ps. cxix. 149). Glory be to the Father, and to the Son, and to the Holy Ghost; as it was in the beginning, is now, and ever shall be, world without end. *Amen.*

---

[1] The confession and absolution are the same as those in Schwarz's mass.

[2] The first part of this rubric is from an earlier edition, but is here included to indicate the ceremonial, which remained the same in 1525.

[3] The first confession is in the singular, but this alternative becomes plural. It is the final step from a *Confiteor* to a general confession.

The Kyrieleison

Kyrieleison; Lord, have mercy. Christeleison; Christ, have mercy. Kyrieleison; Lord, have mercy upon us.

The Gloria in excelsis deo

Glory be to God on high, and on earth peace to men of good will. We praise Thee, we bless Thee, &c. [In the text a German translation of the whole canticle is given.]

The Priest, facing the people, says:

The Lord be with you.

The Collect or Congregational Prayer (gebet der gemein) *follows:*

Let us pray.

Ever merciful, eternal God and Father, who willest to lead us by a right and true faith to Thine only-begotten Son: Grant now to Thy people that they may never cleave to any created thing, but only seek and find an entrance into Thy favour; through Christ Jesus our Lord. *Amen.*

Or, in place of this, some other Collect proper to the time, or a prayer as the Spirit of God doth prompt.

Now, facing the people, a Minister reads the Epistle, which is chosen by the Priest.

Gal. iii. 3–14. [In the text a German version is given.]

The Alleluia

Alleluia, praise the Lord. O Lord, deal with Thy servant according to Thy mercy, and teach me Thy statutes. I am Thy servant; give me understanding, that I may know Thy testimonies (Ps. cxix. 124–5).

The Gospel (Euangelium) follows:

John vi. 41–58. [In the text a German version is given.]

It is to be noted here, however, that sometimes instead of the Gospel (Euangelium) (and the same applies to the Epistle), one of the Gospels (Evangelisten) may be chosen for itself and each Sunday a part of a chapter expounded to the people in such a way that the context is kept; and the passage chosen is not to be such a small and imperfect fragment as it has been the custom to have in the popish Church.

Afterwards, the Creed follows:

I believe in God, the Father Almighty, &c. [In the text a German version of the Apostles' Creed is given.]

[*Or*] *sometimes the Great Creed, which is called the Symbolum Nicaenum is sung:*

I believe in one God, &c. [In the text a German version of the Nicene Creed is given.]

Here the Priest prepares the chalice with bread and wine; after which he turns to the people and says[1] *this Exhortation:*[2]

Dearly beloved, pray God the Father, through Jesus Christ our Lord, that He will send us the Holy Ghost, the Comforter, to make our bodies a living sacrifice, holy, acceptable unto God, which is our reasonable service. May this happen to us all. *Amen.*
The Lord be with you.

The Preface of the Lord's Supper:
Lift up your hearts.
Give thanks unto the Lord our God.

It is indeed our duty, and is just, right, and salutary, that we should always in all places give thanks unto Thee, O Lord, holy, Almighty Father, eternal God, who hast procured our redemption by the Wood of the Cross, so that the life of those from whom death has been banished might spring up, and that the enemy might be controverted; for, if through the wood disobedience had overcome us all in Adam, so now by the Wood obedience is achieved again,[3] through Jesus Christ our Lord; through whose majesty and glory the angels and all the heavenly hosts praise Thee with exultant honour and praise, for evermore; and in the same, be willing, we beseech Thee, to unite our thanksgiving, as with humble confession we say:

The Sanctus
Sanctus, Holy, Holy, Lord God of Hosts; Heaven and earth are full of Thy glory; O God Most High, save us.

The Benedictus
Blessed is he that cometh in the Name of the Lord; O save us, God Most High.

[1] The rubric thus far is from an earlier edition, probably of the same year, and serves to illustrate the current practice in the Strasbourg churches. Except for the first post-communion prayer the remainder of the text is practically identical with Schwarz's mass. In Schwarz, however, the *Lavabo* with its accompanying prayer followed the *Benedictus qui venit*, apparently according to a local custom of long standing. In Schwarz there are no rubrics about communion, but in this case it is safe to argue from silence that the old order was followed.

[2] Derived from *Orate fratres* of Roman rite.   [3] A special preface.

The Canon follows:

Almighty and ever merciful Father, forasmuch as Thy Son, our Lord Jesus, hath promised that what we ask in His Name thou wilt grant unto us, and forasmuch also as Thy Spirit hath commanded us to pray for those in authority over us; we beseech Thee from our hearts that Thou wouldst move the hearts of the Emperor, the Princes and the Nobility, and especially of our Lords and Magistrates of the Council, to the knowledge of Thy goodness and of the Gospel; also that Thou wouldst subdue all peoples to Thy Son through the Holy Ghost, in order that they may willingly comprehend, receive, and guard His promises; and especially do we pray for this congregation that Thou wouldst grant them to increase in the knowledge of the Gospel and of its sweet yoke and comfortable burden. And forasmuch as, Almighty and eternal God, beloved and ever gracious Father, Thine only Son, our Lord Jesus, hath come into the world to heal the sick and not the sound, and to heal our blindness which dulls the shame of sin since it is not able to see or recognize even itself as sickness, for, alas, we are infected, and in our wandering and transgression we please ourselves, hate the commandments, and love vice: write Thy law, we beseech Thee, in our hearts through God the Holy Ghost; quicken the hidden sin within us; and thus grant us to prove and experience how impossible it is for us to do any good thing of ourselves, so that we may hunger and thirst for grace and righteousness which alone truly proceed from Thee, and which Thou hast given to the world through Thy well-beloved Son, our Lord Jesus Christ;

The Consecratio. *The beginning of the Mass proper and of the Lord's Supper:*

Who, on the day before His passion, took the bread into His holy hands, and gave thanks to Thee, O God, His heavenly Father; brake it; and gave it to His disciples, and said: Take ye and eat, this is My Body which is given for you.

Ad calicem:

In like manner, after supper, He took the cup into His holy hands, and gave thanks, and said: Take and drink ye all of it; this is the chalice of My Blood, the New and Eternal Testament, which was shed for you and for many for the forgiveness of sins. And as oft as ye do this, saith the Lord, do it in memory of Me, and show forth the Lord's death, till He come.

After which the Priest says:

How great is Thy goodness, that Thou hast merited for us and for all ours not only the forgiveness of our sins, but by Thy grace hast given Thy Son Jesus Christ unto death for a propitiation. Wherefore, we now have a great and unassailable safeguard in Thy grace, and know that we are Thy children, Thine heirs, and joint-heirs with Christ; and that we may freely pray, as Thine only-begotten Son hath taught us, and say:

Our Father, which art in heaven, &c. [In the text a German version is given in the Matthean form with the doxology.]

Turning to the people, he says:

The peace of the Lord be with you alway.

The Agnus Dei

O Lord Jesus Christ, Thou Lamb of God, that takest away the sins of the world, have mercy upon us. O Lord Jesus Christ, Thou Lamb of God, who remittest the sins of the world, grant us peace.

Let us pray. [Entitled 'The *Communicatio*' in a text of 1525.]

O Lord Jesu Christ, Thou Son of the living God, Thou eternal Word of the Father, Thou Saviour of the world, Thou true, living God and Man, Thou who according to the will of the Father and with the aid of the Holy Ghost didst through Thy death bring the world to life: By Thy bitter pains and death, deliver us, we beseech Thee, from all our unrighteousness and sins; and grant that we may alway be obedient to Thy commandments, and never be cut off from Thee eternally. *Amen.*

Here it is the custom to have a short and earnest Exhortation for those who wish to come to the Sacrament; this Exhortation is usually based upon the Epistle and Gospel.

Then he [the Celebrant] takes the Host in his hand, and says; Our Lord Jesus Christ said to His beloved disciples: Take ye and eat; this is My Body which is given for you. *And similarly also with the Cup, as it is described in the Gospels and in Paul. Then the Priest may himself partake of the Sacrament, though he is also permitted to have done so first, before he delivered it to the people. Then they kneel, and say the Nunc Dimittis:* O Lord, lettest now Thy servant depart in peace, &c. [In the text a German version is given in full, without the Gloria Patri.]

Or,

Let the congregation now sing the Anthem.[1]

The Communion Hymn (Commun), or the Congregational Thanksgiving, follows: Gott sey gelobet, &c. [This is a hymn of Luther's, and it is given in full in the text.]

[1] This hymn or anthem is sung during communion, and probably part of the communion hymn following is also sung during communion.

Then the Priest, facing the people, says:

The Lord be with you.

Let us pray.

O Lord Jesu Christ, who hast given Thy body unto death for us, and hast shed Thy blood for us and for many: Ordain us not unto damnation nor unto judgement, but according to Thy goodness may Thy Body and Blood be unto both our souls and bodies for a protection and medicine unto eternal life. *Amen.*

O Lord God, we beseech Thee also from our hearts to grant unto us, that what we have received with our lips we may receive also with a pure mind, that it may be unto us at this time a medicine unto eternal life; through Jesus Christ our Lord. *Amen.*

Facing the people, he says:

The Lord be with you.

Give thanks unto the Lord, and praise ye Him.

And then he says:

The Lord bless you and keep you; may He make His face to shine upon you, and be merciful unto you, and give you His peace. The blessing of God, the Father and the Son and the Holy Ghost, be with us, and remain with us always. *Amen.*

We may add to this text by way of commentary a contemporary account of this worship from a young French student's letter to his friend and patron, the Bishop of Meaux, written in December 1525.[1]

The writer first states that nothing is said or sung which is not intelligible to all and founded upon the Scriptures, and that the Scriptures themselves are expounded clearly and simply, without resort to allegory. He then proceeds to describe the Sunday worship:

'On the Lord's day, which is the only day they keep as a festival, . . . they celebrate the Lord's Supper in this manner: The Table is set well forward, in a place in full view of the church, so that it may be seen by all. They do not call it an altar, in order that they may not be thought to be in any way like those who make a sacrifice out of Christ's Supper, but the Table does not differ in any way from ordinary altars.[2] To this Table the minister comes, but in such a manner that he faces the people and does not turn his back upon them. . . . Standing at the Table, with his face towards the people,

---

[1] Text in V. 8, vol. i, Letter 168; relevant parts also in V. 7, p. 29.
[2] Later these tables, while still constructed like altars, were made of wood.

and while the eyes of all the people are upon him, he says first certain brief prayers . . ., and then psalms are sung by all. When this has been done and the minister has prayed again, he goes up to the pulpit and reads the Scripture which he wishes to expound, in such a way that it may be understood by all. . . . The sermon finished, he returns to the Table, and the Creed is sung by all. After this, he explains to the people why Christ left us His Supper, . . . then relates the words of Christ as they are written by the Evangelists or Paul. Thereupon, he gives bread and wine to those who wish to come forward (for no one is compelled, but all are bidden), true symbols of the body and blood of Christ, sealed in His death and left by Him to His apostles. While they are communicating and each one receives his portion of the Supper, *Kyrie eleison*[1] is sung by all, that by this hymn they may render thanks for the benefit received. And communion is so ordered that the minister may partake last, in order that he may consume all that remains.[2] When this is finished, each one returns to his home.'

We see from this account and from the texts themselves how the worship has become again a corporate action in which the two characteristics of the early worship as re- corded in Acts, fellowship and joy, are predominant. Con- temporary evidence of this fact is not lacking, as, for example, this letter[3] shows:

'No one remembers to have seen the benches of our churches filled by a people so zealous, resourceful, and eager for instruction. Before the minister has gone into the pulpit, one sees innumerable crowds discussing the Word of God, or listening to the reading of the passage that is to be expounded. The buzzing of the crowd as it arrives is such that one would have said a bishop was to be consecrated.'

Further changes in the services took place during the succeeding years as Bucer's influence became paramount. Some of these are to be welcomed, others to be deplored.

---

[1] Here this refers, as we see from the texts, to Luther's hymn, *Gott sei gelobet*, which has *Kyrie eleison* for its refrain.

[2] This contradicts most of the rubrics of the texts, which state that the minister communicated first; it is probable that he has confused the minister's communion, which preceded that of the people, with the practice of consuming what remained after the people's communion.

[3] Quoted in V. 5, p. 489.

Greater variety was introduced into the choice of the prayers: by 1537 there was a choice of three confessions of sin, three prayers of consecration, four post-communions, while other prayers were left to be framed by the celebrant. This accorded with the use of the Primitive Church, and variety may serve many useful purposes. It was unfortunate, however, that each prayer, as it was added, should be lengthier, more prolix and more didactic than its predecessor, and so influenced by the current theology that it lacked the timelessness and universality that should, generally speaking, characterize Christian prayer. This gain in variety, while it need not have done so, actually did in every case involve a loss of simplicity and directness. Many of the later prayers of the Reformed Churches were marred through failure to arrest this tendency. One cause of this fault was the laudable desire to make the worship completely intelligible to the worshippers and fully expressive of their needs; but the result was too often an undue focusing of attention upon the needs of man so that worship tended to lose its proper objectivity and direction.

Most of the versicles and responses disappeared, and the worship lost its antiphonal character. The proses also were gradually replaced by psalms and hymns in metre; these latter, together with the music to which they were set, proved to be an enduring enrichment of common worship; but we must regret the extremism that abolished all responses save the Amens, and which failed to use the prose psalms and canticles in worship. It would have been easy to simplify the traditional music without destroying its unique character.

Thus the *Gloria in excelsis* and the *Kyries* were supplanted by metrical psalms and hymns. It is to be deplored that words so fitting and so rooted in the worship of the Church as the *Sursum corda* should disappear from use. And to substitute for the Prefaces, the *Sanctus*, and the *Benedictus qui venit* a general thanksgiving for Christ's work and passion was a genuine impoverishment and an unnecessary departure from a tradition almost as old as the Church itself; for however excellently conceived such a substitute might be, it lacked the dignity and beauty, the variety and comprehensiveness and devotional grace of the historic forms; and in the end it achieved no more than a slight revision of them could have accomplished.

During this time also the lections disappeared, with the exception of those from the Gospels, which were now read in course. This again was a needless impoverishment. The preparation of a revised lectionary would have sufficed to remedy such abuses as had been common. And important as the sermon is in worship, to make it an hour in length was surely an excess of zeal.

All saints' days were abolished without discrimination, and only the chief festivals of the Christian Year were kept. Eucharistic vestments dropped out of use, and by 1537 the black gown and cassock alone were retained; these had previously been normally used for preaching and outdoor wear.

The exhortation, originally a brief revision of *Orate fratres*, was now extended to several paragraphs; and it was to become lengthier still in the Calvinian and Anglican rites. During this period also the practice of weekly communion declined; so that by 1537 communion was celebrated weekly only in the cathedral, and monthly in the parish churches and chapels-of-ease. But the eucharist still remained the norm, and if there was no communion, those parts were omitted which belonged directly to consecration and communion.

Bucer's own description[1] of the worship at Strasbourg between 1526 and 1539 indicates the direction taken by the successive revisions:

'When the congregation come together on Sunday, the minister

---

[1] In his *Grund und Ursach ausz gotlicher schrift der newerungen an dem nachtmal des Herren.* For German Text see V. 7, p. 43, n. 42.

exhorts the people to confess their sins and to pray for pardon; and on behalf of the whole congregation he makes confession to God, prays for pardon, and pronounces absolution to the believers. Thereupon, the whole congregation sing a few short psalms or hymns. Then the minister says a short prayer, reads to the congregation a passage from the writings of the Apostles, and, as briefly as possible, expounds the same. Then the congregation sing again, this time the Ten Commandments, or something else. After that, the minister reads the Gospel, and preaches the sermon proper. The sermon ended, the congregation sing the Articles of our Belief [i.e. the Apostles' Creed in metre]; and the minister says a prayer for the Magistrates and for all men, and specially for the congregation there present, beseeching an increase of faith, love, and grace to hold in reverence the memory of Christ's death. Then he admonishes those who wish to observe the Lord's Supper with him that they are to do so in memory of Christ, to die to their sins, and bear their cross willingly, and be strengthened in faith for what must come to pass when we contemplate with believing hearts what measureless grace and goodness Christ hath shown to us, in that for us He offered up to His Father His life and blood upon the Cross. After this exhortation, he reads the Gospel concerning the Lord's Supper, as the three Evangelists and Paul in 1 Corinthians xi have described it. Then the minister distributes the Bread and the Cup of the Lord among them, having partaken of them also himself. The congregation then sing again a hymn of praise; and afterwards the minister closes the Supper with a short prayer, blesses the people, and lets them go in the peace of the Lord. This is the manner and custom with which we now celebrate the Lord's Supper on Sundays only.'

This description represents the rite before the revision of 1537, when further changes were made. The rite of 1537–9 appears in the service book entitled *Psalter mit aller Kirchenübung*.[1] This rite is chiefly important because from it are derived the Calvinian[2] and Scottish rites and services; therefore the whole rite, with its many and prolix alternative prayers, is not reprinted here, but only the parts that later came to have a place in those rites.

[1] Edited in Text 38, pp. 90–113.
[2] See the scheme on pp. 114–15 below.

CONCERNING THE LORD'S SUPPER OR THE MASS AND THE SERMONS

[Standing before the Sunday Service is a long rubric treating of the daily services.[1] These are three in number, and are held approximately at 4 a.m., 8 a.m., and 5 p.m. in Summer and at 5 a.m., 8 a.m., and 3 p.m. in Winter. Normally they consist of a confession of sins, Scripture lection and sermon, a 'seemly space . . . for special private prayer', a collect or brief free prayer and the grace. The rubric also states that, because of the gross misuse of the holy days, Sunday only is to be kept as a festival for the whole day, and it is to be hallowed as the weekly rest to the service of God. The great festivals of the Christian Year—Christmas, Passion Week, Ascensiontide, Whitsun, and others—are to be observed in the sermons, but there is no provision for such an observance of the Saints' days. The 'memorial days of our Lord' are to have the central place. Generally speaking, there is to be no withdrawal from work on holy days falling on days other than Sunday, but Christmas, 'and a few other days also,' are exceptions to this rule.

The rubric then proceeds:]

On Sundays, the following services are held: first, early Morning Prayer in the Cathedral, as on other days. Then at six o'clock approximately, the Curates have a Sermon and Exhortation for domestic servants in the parish churches. Soon thereafter, when the congregation is assembled, the Pastor (Pfarrer) enters, and goes to the Holy Table (Altartisch) taking up such a position that he faces the people, and in order that every one may hear every word he stands upright, and begins the Common Worship, using approximately the following words; for he is able to lengthen or shorten them as opportunity or time affords:

The Confiteor

Make confession to God the Lord, and let each one acknowledge with me his sins and iniquity:

Almighty God, eternal Father, we acknowledge and confess unto Thee, that we were conceived in unrighteousness, and in all our life are full of sin and transgression, in that we have not gladly believed Thy Word nor followed Thy holy commandments. For Thy goodness' sake and for Thy Name's sake, be gracious unto us, we beseech Thee, and forgive us our iniquity, which is very great.

---

[1] The daily services are discussed on pp. 163 sqq. below.

Another Confiteor[1]

Almighty God and eternal Father, we confess and acknowledge that we, alas, were conceived and born in sin, and are therefore inclined to all evil and slow to all good; that we continually transgress Thy holy commandments, and more and more corrupt ourselves. But we repent us of the same, and beseech Thy grace and help. Wherefore, most merciful and most gracious God and Father, show Thy mercy upon us, through Thy Son our Lord Jesus Christ. Grant to us and increase in us Thy Holy Spirit, that we, acknowledging from the bottom of our hearts our sin and unrighteousness, may come to be repentant and sorry for it, die to it wholly and please Thee entirely by a new life blessed of God. *Amen.*

Another

[This third *Confiteor* we shall not reprint here. It is probably from Bucer's pen, and is based upon the Ten Commandments, each Commandment supplying a paragraph of confession, and it is much longer than the two Confessions translated above. In all likelihood this Confession played a part in influencing Calvin to use the Decalogue as the first singing in his service. Later the compilers of the *Book of Common Prayer* followed Calvin's use of the Decalogue in combination with the *Kyries*, but added 'upon us' and 'incline our hearts', &c.]

An Absolution or Comfortable Word: 1 Tim. i

This is a faithful saying, and worthy of all acceptation, that Christ Jesus is come into the world to save sinners.

Let each make confession in his heart with St. Paul in truth ['that I am the chief' in some editions], and believe in Christ. So in His Name do I pronounce forgiveness unto you of all your sins, and I declare you to be loosed of them in earth so that ye may be loosed of them also in heaven and in all eternity. *Amen.*

Sometimes he takes other Words which comfort us in the forgiveness of sins and in the ransom of Christ for our sins, such as St. John iii. 16, or iii. 35-6, or Acts x. 43, or 1 John ii. 1-2. [In the text these verses are given in full.]

Thereafter, the Church begins to sing a Psalm or hymn instead of the Introit; and sometimes the Kyrieleyson and the Gloria in excelsis follow.

[1] This *Confiteor* was the one translated by Calvin, and an enlarged English version of it was subsequently used in Knox's service 1556 onwards. Compare with the first part of Knox's Confession in Text 43, p. 81.

When this has been done, the Minister (Diener) says a.short prayer for grace and for a right spirit, in order that the Word of God and the Sermon which are to follow may be heard with fruitful effect. The content of this prayer is based upon those desires which a Christian ought to have, and is usually drawn from the Sermon which follows it. I will now take one of the sort to which I refer, which I have formerly allowed to be issued.

The Lord be with you.

Let us pray.

Almighty, ever gracious Father, forasmuch as all our salvation depends upon our having truly understood Thy holy Word: therefore grant us that our hearts be set free from worldly things, so that we may with all diligence and faith hear and apprehend Thy holy Word, that thereby we may rightly understand Thy gracious will, and in all sincerity live according to the same, to Thy praise and glory; through our Lord Jesus Christ. *Amen.*

Then the Church sings a Psalm or some verse, and the Minister (Diener) goes to the front of the chancel, and reads from one of the Gospels (Evangelisten), reading it in order, and selecting as much as he is minded to expound in a Sermon. And, forasmuch as the Gospels quite clearly depict the words and works of our Lord, it is the custom on Sunday Mornings generally to preach from them rather than from the other books: and this in their order, and not as formerly to select some small parts, often not specially suitable, inasmuch as all the rest of the Gospels is kept back from the congregation. In the afternoon, and at the other hours of worship, the other books of the Bible are also explained.

At the end of the Sermon the action of the Lord's Supper is explained, and the people are exhorted to take part with a right faith and true devotion. This said Exhortation usually contains four points.

The first: that, forasmuch as we wish here to share the Body and Blood of our Lord, we are to reflect upon the fact that our body and blood, that is, our whole nature, is wholly corrupted to evil and thus to eternal death, so that they of themselves could never share in the kingdom of God. 1 Cor. xv.

The second: that it is to deliver us from such corruption that the eternal Word of God became flesh, so that there might be a holy flesh and blood, that is, that He should be a really divine man, through whom our flesh and blood would be restored and sanctified. And this happens, as we eat and drink of His Body and Blood truly.

The third: that the Lord truly delivers and gives to us His holy and sanctifying Body and Blood in the holy Supper under visible things, bread and wine, through the service of the Church, as His holy Word declares: 'Take ye and eat, this is My Body which is given for you; drink ye all of it, this is My Blood, which is shed for you for the forgiveness of sins'; and this word of the Lord we must accept with simple faith, and not doubt that He, the Lord Himself, is within us through the external service of the Church, which He Himself hath ordained. This also He hath shown us in His Word, that as the bread which we break is to us truly the Communion of His Body, so the cup which we bless is also to us the Communion of His Blood. 1 Cor. x. Only, we must always diligently consider why the Lord thus communicates Himself in holy, sanctifying Communion in the holy Sacrament, namely, in order that He may live in us increasingly, and that we may live in Him as our Head, as we all there partake of the Bread. 1 Cor. x.

The fourth: that we in this action of the Lord's keep His memory and festival with true devotion and thankfulness, so that we always laud and praise Him in all our words and works, yea, with our whole life, for all His good deeds, for His incarnation and bitter death whereby He hath ransomed our sins, and for this blessed Communion of His Body and Blood, that is, of His whole self, true God and man, through which we may alone obtain the right, true, and blessed life, and live both here and evermore.

Where, however, the holy Supper is not celebrated (as in the case of the parish churches where it is now celebrated but once a month, though in the cathedral it is celebrated every Sunday), but children are there to be baptized, the mystery of Baptism is explained, and the people are exhorted to a right and sacred use of this holy Sacrament.

At the conclusion of the Sermon the people sing the Creed [the Apostles' Creed in a German metrical version]; *or otherwise according to the time, a Psalm or hymn. When this is ended, if the holy Supper is to be celebrated, the Minister speaks to the people from the Table (Tisch):*

Dearly beloved, let us beseech God the Father, through our Lord Jesus Christ, who is given unto death for the salvation of our souls, that He will send upon us the Holy Ghost, to teach us to offer, not Christ who Himself hath offered Himself for us and cannot be offered by any one, but the only true offering well-pleasing unto God, that of a contrite spirit and broken heart; and that we may render our body as a sacrifice, living, holy, and well-pleasing unto Him, which is our only reasonable service, in which we offer to God honour, thanks, and praise. May the Lord hearken unto you, and reveal His salvation.[1]

---

[1] This little exhortation is an expansion of the *Orate fratres*; cf. p. 89 above.

And as follows:

The Lord be with you.

Let us pray.

[Here follow three forms of Canon which include the Intercessions; I translate only the last,[1] which is somewhat longer than the first two.]

Almighty God and heavenly Father, Thou hast promised us through Thy dear Son our Lord Jesus Christ that what we ask in His Name Thou wouldst grant unto us. The same, Thy Son our Lord, hath by Himself and by His beloved Apostles taught us to assemble ourselves in His Name, and hath promised that He will be there in the midst of us, and by Thee will obtain and procure for us that which we agree on earth to ask of Thee; and in especial He hath commanded us to pray for those whom Thou hast set over us to rule and to reign, then for all things needful, both for Thy people and for all men. And forasmuch as we are all come together as before Thine eyes (to Thy praise!), and in the Name of Thy Son our Lord Jesu; we beseech Thee from our hearts, ever merciful God and Father, through the same Thy well-beloved Son our only Saviour, graciously to forgive us all our sins and offences, and so to lift up our hearts and minds unto Thee, that we may be able to ask and implore Thee with our whole heart, according to Thy righteous will and pleasure alone.

Wherefore, we beseech Thee, O heavenly Father, for our gracious rulers, Thy servants, our lord Emperor and King, and all the lords and nobles, and the magistracy of this city, that Thou wouldst grant unto them Thy holy and right sovereign Spirit, and always increase the same in them, that they may with a true faith acknowledge Thee as King of all kings and Lord of all lords, and Thy Son, our Lord Jesus, as him to whom Thou hast given all authority in heaven and in earth, and so to rule over their subjects, the work of Thy hands and the sheep of Thy pasture, according to all Thy good pleasure, that we here and everywhere may lead a quiet and peaceable life in all godliness and lowliness, and, being delivered from the fear of enemies, may serve Thee in all righteousness and holiness.

Furthermore, we beseech Thee, ever faithful Father and Saviour, for all those Thou hast appointed to the care of souls and to the shepherding of Thy faithful people, and to whom Thou hast entrusted the proclamation of Thy holy Gospel, that Thou wouldst give unto

[1] Calvin's Prayer of Consecration and Great Prayer are immediately derived from this prayer (cf. Text 35, vol. xxxiv, pp. 175–80, or parallels in Appendix C, in V. 7). This same prayer translated from the French was carried into the *Book of Common Order* in 1562 (cf. Text 43, pp. 92 sqq.).

them and increase in them Thy Holy Spirit, that they may be found faithful, and always so serve Thee that they may everywhere gather again Thy poor wandering sheep to Christ, Thy Son, their Shepherd and Bishop, and daily be built up in Him unto all righteousness and holiness, to the eternal praise of Thy Name. [An edition of the same year, or slightly earlier, adds: 'and deliver all Thy congregations from all wolves and hirelings, who seek their own profit, and not the salvation of Thy flock.']

Moreover, we pray Thee, ever merciful God and gracious Father, for all men in general (menschen), that as Thou willest to be known a Saviour to all the world,[1] even so draw to Thy Son our Lord Jesus those yet estranged from Him, and those also whom Thou hast taught and drawn to Him, that Thou wilt pardon their sins, and show grace to us through Him our only Mediator; grant that these may grow and increase in such knowledge daily, that they may be filled with the fruit of all good works, live without scandal to the betterment of their neighbour and to Thy praise, and await trustfully the future and the day of Thy Son our Lord; and especially [do we pray] for those whom Thou hast disciplined, those whom Thou hast visited and chastened with poverty, want, imprisonment, and other misfortunes: grant to them, O Father of mercies and Lord of all consolation, that they may recognize Thy gracious, fatherly hand, and turn to Thee with their whole hearts, who alone chastenest them, so that, trusting Thee as a Father, they may finally be released from all evil.

And to us all here gathered before Thee[2] in the Name of Thy Son and at Thy Table, grant, O God and Father, that we may right thoroughly acknowledge the sin and depravity in which we were born, and that we of ourselves are always falling more deeply into the same by our sinful life, and seeing that in our flesh there is nothing good, yea, inasmuch as our flesh and blood cannot inherit Thy kingdom, [grant also] that we may yield ourselves with whole hearts and a true faith to Thy Son, our only Redeemer and Saviour; and forasmuch as He hath not only offered His body and blood unto Thee upon the Cross for our sin, but willeth also to give it unto us for food and drink unto eternal life, [grant] that we, with our whole eager desire and all true devotion, may receive this His goodness and gift, and with true faith partake of and enjoy His true Body and true Blood,

---

[1] The text of the *Book of Common Order* (see Text 43, pp. 92–4) follows this prayer closely to this point, but greatly enlarges the remainder of the paragraph of general intercession.

[2] This paragraph is reminiscent of the 1564 text of the *Book of Common Order* (Text 43, pp. 108–9), but the English version has been greatly altered. Calvin, however, followed the German much more closely.

yea, Himself, our Saviour, true God and man, the only true Bread of Heaven, so that we may no more live to our sins and in depravity, but that He may live in us, and we in Him, to a holy, blessed, and eternal life; [and grant further, we beseech Thee,] that we may truly be partakers of the true and eternal Testament, the Covenant of grace, certain and confident that Thou wilt be our gracious Father for evermore, never again imputing unto us our sins, and in all things providing for us in body and in soul, as Thy dear children and heirs, so that we may at all times render thanks and praise unto Thee, and magnify Thy holy Name in all our words and works. To that end, grant, O heavenly Father, that we to-day may celebrate and keep the glorious and blessed memory of Thy beloved Son our Lord, and show forth His death, in such manner that we shall ever grow and increase in faith to Thee and in all goodness; and now and always deeply trusting in Thee, our God and Father, we do call upon Thee, and pray, as our Lord hath taught us to pray, saying:

Our Father, which art in heaven, &c. [In the text a complete German version is given, concluding with the Matthean doxology.]

At the conclusion of this prayer, the Minister (Diener) makes a short Exhortation, if he has not done so already at the end of the Sermon, to the effect that the holy Supper is to be observed with true faith and meet devotion; and he also explains the meaning of this Mystery.

After such an Exhortation and explanation, the Minister (Diener) reads the words of the Lord, as they are written in the holy Gospels and in Paul:

The Institution of the Lord's Supper

In the night in which the Lord Jesus was betrayed, while they were at supper, He took the bread, and brake it, and gave it to His disciples, and said: Take ye, eat ye, this is My Body which is given for you; do this in memory of Me. In the same manner also, He took the cup, after supper, gave thanks, and gave it to them, and said: Drink ye all of it; this is the new Testament in My Blood, which was shed for you and for many for the forgiveness of sins; this do ye, as oft as ye drink it, in memory of Me.

Further, the Minister (Diener) speaks in these words:

Believe in the Lord, and give eternal praise and thanks unto Him.

Herewith he distributes the Bread and the Cup of the Lord, saying first these words:

Meditate upon, believe, and show forth, that Christ the Lord has died for you.

Thereupon the Church sings: Gott sey gelobet, &c., *or some Psalm, as announced.*[1]

After such a singing, he says once again a prayer, in this wise.

The Lord be with you.

Let us pray.

Grant unto us, O heavenly Father, that this memorial of our salvation may nevermore depart from our hearts, and that we may walk in the Light of the world and in Christ, far removed from our dull undertakings and blind wills, which are vain and injurious darkness; through Jesus Christ our Lord. *Amen.*

Almighty God and heavenly Father,[2] we evermore give Thee praise and thanks that Thou hast been so gracious unto us poor sinners, and hast delivered up unto death Thy Son our Lord Jesus Christ, and given Him also for our food and nourishment unto everlasting life. Wherefore, we beseech Thee, that we may never be unmindful of these things, but that we may ever grow and increase in faith to Thee, who through love art active in all good works, and so may our whole life be [devoted] to Thy praise and to the betterment of our neighbour; through the same Thy Son, our Lord Jesus Christ. *Amen.*

Another Thanksgiving

Almighty, gracious, and heavenly Father, we give Thee eternal thanks and praise that Thou hast offered and given through Thy holy Gospel and Sacrament Thy precious treasure, the true Bread of Heaven and nourishment of everlasting life, our Lord Jesus Christ; and we heartily beseech Thee to grant that, receiving and partaking with true faith, we may now and for all eternity so be fed by His Body and Blood, to the end that we may be set free from all evil and increase daily in all good, to Thy glory; through the same our Lord Jesus Christ. *Amen.*

Another Thanksgiving

Heavenly Father, we give Thee eternal praise and thanks that Thou hast given up Thy beloved Son, our Lord Jesus Christ, for us

---

[1] This hymn is sung during communion. Knox's practice, derived from Calvin's Genevan practice, was to read aloud passages from Scripture during communion. At Strasbourg, Calvin has psalms or hymns sung at this point.

[2] Calvin's post-communion prayer is a very slightly enlarged French translation of this prayer (cf. Text 35, vol. xxxiv, p. 180). In the *Book of Common Order* a further expanded version is given (cf. Text 43, pp. 125–6).

poor sinners, and hast again shared with us His true Communion; and we beseech Thee, grant to us that this holy Communion may always be effective and strong in us, so that in true faith, purity, patience, and love we, sparing no diligence and putting off the flesh, may lead a new and heavenly life wholly pleasing unto Thee, to the betterment of our neighbour and to Thy praise and honour, through the same, &c.

The Conclusion

Give thanks unto the Lord.

The Blessing from Numbers vi: The Lord bless you and keep you; the Lord cause His face to shine upon you, and be gracious unto you; the Lord lift up His countenance upon you, and give you peace.[1]

Depart; [and] the Spirit of the Lord go with you unto life eternal.

[At the end of the service there is a rubric of moderate length relating to the other Sunday services. It directs that, immediately after the noon meal, a service is to be held in the Cathedral consisting of psalms, common prayers, and a sermon. At the conclusion of this service, except in the winter-time when it is too cold for the children to attend in comfort, a service of instruction for the children is held, to instruct them in the Ten Commandments, the Apostles' Creed, and the Lord's Prayer, and catechization also takes place.

After these two services, Vespers are held in the parish churches. Vespers consist of psalms and prayers, concluded by a collect. After Vespers, Baptism may be ministered.

Four times in the year also, in the parish churches, a service of general congregational catechization is held morning and afternoon concerning the central facts of the Christian faith, the Creed, the Ten Commandments, the Lord's Prayer, the Sacraments, and the issues of all these in daily life and works.]

Several points of interest may be noted in this rite. First, the intercessions stand at the beginning of the Consecration Prayer; this follows the Roman custom, not that represented by the primitive rites in which the intercessions normally followed consecration.

Secondly, the Words of Institution have been removed from the Prayer of Consecration, and now stand alone as a warrant. This was in keeping with early practice, and

---

[1] Knox's preference for the Aaronic Blessing (cf. Text 43, p. 91) is also derived through Calvin from the German use at Strasbourg.

does not affect the validity of consecration.[1] It may be argued that if the Words of Institution are included in the Consecration Prayer as part of the memorial made before God, it enriches the objective content of the rite. But it cannot be said that they are essential to consecration. Consecration is not by formula but by prayer; it may even be by intention.

Thirdly, communion at Strasbourg was received standing or kneeling, the people going forward to the Holy Table. The celebrant stood at the north end of the Holy Table to give the Bread, and the assisting minister stood at the south end to minister the Cup. The communicants formed a continuous line down the central passage of the nave, coming slowly forward to receive first the Bread then the Wine, and so returning to their places.

In conclusion, we may observe that in the German rites of Strasbourg there emerges, for the first time after the Reformation, the service that was to become the norm of Sunday Morning Worship in the Reformed Churches, namely, the eucharistic service with the offertory, consecration, and communion omitted. Like the eucharist, it was conducted from the Holy Table,[2] the minister adopting the basilican posture. Such a service lacks the centrality of the eucharist, but it is immensely richer in content and broader in scope than worship that takes a quire office[3] as its norm.

---

[1] See W. C. Bishop in *Church Quarterly Review*, 1908, p. 392, where, speaking of the primitive liturgies, he says, 'It would appear that the Words of Institution were not recited as of themselves effecting consecration, but rather as the authority in obedience to which the rite is performed.' See also I. 3, pp. 64–5: 'We have here [in the Roman rite] a conception of the act of consecration which was unknown to the Early Church, and also differs essentially from the view held in the Eastern Churches', where, he adds, the Words of Institution 'had merely the character of a "cultus-narrative", . . . showing the eucharist to be divinely instituted. By making the Words of Institution the central words of the whole mass, the great prayer of thanksgiving . . . was robbed of its pre-eminent significance, and the epiclesis was deprived of its place.'

[2] On the position of the celebrant at Ante-Communion see V. 7, pp. 36 sqq.

[3] See pp. 163–70 below.

§ 4. *Calvin's French Rites at Strasbourg and Geneva*

To imagine that Calvin wished to replace sacramental worship by a preaching service is completely to misunderstand his mind and work and to ignore all that he taught and did. His aim was twofold: to restore the eucharist in its primitive simplicity and true proportions—celebration *and* communion—as the central weekly service, and, within this service, to give the Holy Scriptures their authoritative place. The Lord's Supper, in all its completeness, was the norm he wished to establish.

Calvin's rite first took form when he was minister of the Congregation of French exiles at Strasbourg from 1538 to 1541. He had been banished from Geneva partly because of his sacramental views, and he had come to Strasbourg to teach theology and to minister to the exiles there, a little group harried out of France because of their allegiance to the Reformed teaching, who had found refuge and hospitality at Strasbourg since 1533.

Until Calvin came to Strasbourg, the German magistrates had not permitted the French to celebrate the Lord's Supper; and, unless they may have used Farel's *Maniere et Fasson*,[1] published at Neuchâtel in 1533, they had no formulary of worship. But shortly after Calvin's arrival they were granted permission to celebrate the Lord's Supper monthly, in accordance with what was now customary in the parish churches of Strasbourg which followed Bucer. It at once became imperative that the French Congregation should have a service book, and there may even have been some arrangement not recorded that the French services should closely approximate to the German; in any event, Calvin seems to have had a high opinion of the worship then established in Strasbourg, for he adopted it almost word for word.

[1] Edited in Text 40. This was an utterly barren rite, a result of Zwinglian influence and the extreme views of Farel. It had no influence whatever upon any succeeding rites, except that Calvin borrowed from it considerably for his Marriage Service (for texts see V. 7, pp. 53–4, 144–59).

Calvin detested what he called the 'monkeying' of the medieval mass,[1] and his standard was the corporate worship of the early Church. This fact appears often in his writings, and he sought to make his ideal perfectly clear by entitling his service book, *The Form of Prayers and Manner of Ministering the Sacraments according to the Use of the Ancient Church*. The worship he found at Strasbourg appeared to him to conform to this model; accordingly, as he himself said, 'As for the Sunday prayers, I took the form of Strasbourg, and borrowed the greater part of it.'[2] An examination and comparison of the texts of the French and German rites undoubtedly confirms the truth of this statement.[3]

Since Calvin did not read or speak German, he had recourse to the services of a friend to translate the German rite into Latin or French.[4] With this draft before him, he proceeded to render it into literary French. By the end of the year 1539, or early in 1540, his task was finished; and he was able to publish his first complete service book, which included several psalms in French metre, with the melodies, for congregational singing.[5] This first edition is now lost, but a copy of the second edition is in the University Library at Geneva. This Strasbourg edition (1542) is not to be confused with the Geneva edition of the same year.

A third edition of the Strasbourg rite was published in 1545, and in this form was used by Valèrand Pullain, one of those who succeeded Calvin as minister of the French exiles, and who with his congregation later took refuge in London. Several editions of Pullain's rite after 1551 exist, some in Latin and others in French.

The rite used by Calvin at Geneva, after he was recalled,

[1] See, e.g., his well-known letter, *De fugiendis impiorum illicitis sacris* (Text 35, vol. xxxiii, p. 239), written in the previous year, 1537. See also ibid., pp. 258, 455, &c.   [2] Text 35, vol. xxxvii, pp. 894.

[3] See V. 7, pp. 22 sqq., and 85–104, 124–43 for the evidence of the original texts.   [4] Text 35, vol. xlii, p. 533.

[5] Calvin had published a separate Psalter of 19 psalms and 3 paraphrases in 1539. See X. 16.

was first published in 1542, and many editions from 1547 onwards are extant. This was a slightly simplified form of his Strasbourg rite, but the matter is essentially the same.[1] The close structural[2] relationship is apparent if the schemes of the three rites are set out in parallel columns: Bucer's of 1537–9; Calvin's of 1540, 1542, 1545, at Strasbourg; and Calvin's at Geneva, 1542, 1547 onwards.

The Liturgy of the Word

Stras. German, 1537	*Stras. French, 1540, &c.*	*Geneva, 1542, &c.*
	Scripture Sentence: Ps. cxxiv. 8	Scripture Sentence: Ps. cxxiv. 8
Confession of sins	Confession of sins	Confession of sins
Scriptural words of pardon (1 Tim. i)	Scriptural words of pardon	Prayer for pardon
Absolution	Absolution	
Psalm, hymn, or Kyries and Gloria in excelsis	Metrical Decalogue sung with Kyrie eleison (Gr.) after each Law	Metrical Psalm
Collect for Illumination	Collect for Illumination	Collect for Illumination
Metrical Psalm		
Lection (Gospel)	Lection	Lection
Sermon	Sermon	Sermon

The Liturgy of the Upper Room

Collection of alms	Collection of alms	Collection of alms
Preparation of elements while Apostles' Creed sung		
Intercessions and Consecration Prayer	Intercessions	Intercessions
Lord's Prayer	Lord's Prayer in long paraphrase	Lord's Prayer in long paraphrase
	Preparation of elements while Apostles' Creed sung Consecration Prayer Lord's Prayer	Preparation of elements while Apostles' Creed sung
Exhortation	Words of Institution	Words of Institution

[1] The titles of these service books in order of their appearance, with notes of contents and references to where texts may be found (many of them unedited, and existing only in original editions), are given in V. 7, pp. 69–72. For Calvin's texts, see Text 35, vol. xxxiv, pp. 165 sqq.

[2] The footnotes to the texts on pp. 102–10 above indicate the relationship in content; or see V. 7, pp. 95–6, 188–98, where the original texts are collated.

Stras. German, 1537	Stras. French, 1540, &c.	Geneva, 1542, &c.
Words of Institution	Exhortation	Exhortation
		Consecration Prayer
Fraction	Fraction	Fraction
Delivery	Delivery	Delivery
Communion, while psalm or hymn sung	Communion, while psalm sung	Communion, while psalm or Scriptures read
Post-communion collect	Post-communion collect	Post-communion collect
	Nunc dimittis in metre	
Aaronic Blessing	Aaronic Blessing	Aaronic Blessing
Dismissal		

The principal changes Calvin made were: to reduce the number of variants, choosing as his confession of sins one modelled upon the second in Bucer's rite, and as his intercessions and consecration one modelled upon the last of these in Bucer's rite; he also added a long and tiresome paraphrase of the Lord's Prayer. The Decalogue in metre was introduced, the two tables divided by a short collect for grace to keep God's Law;[1] although this is the first time the Decalogue is mentioned in the texts, Bucer's description previously quoted[2] from his Grund und Ursach states that it was used at Strasbourg. Calvin also includes the Nunc dimittis after communion; but this too is mentioned in the early texts of Strasbourg, and though it disappears from the texts, it probably continued in use. His other changes are only slight alterations of order. We may observe, however, that the structure of his Geneva rite is more meagre; this was no doubt the result of the extreme opinions that prevailed there among the magistracy, who insisted that the rite be as 'simple' as possible. We may take the Strasbourg rites as being a better indication of Calvin's own mind. It is, accordingly, of interest to include here a part of the

---

[1] Calvin put the Decalogue into metrical form, adding Kyrie eleison at the end of each verse; and in the Book of Common Prayer, 1552, the Decalogue was collated with the Kyries. It is a collation that has little to recommend it, for it narrows the scope of the Kyries and stresses unduly the subjective aspect of worship.   [2] See pp. 100–1 above, and cf. p. 103.

description and *apologia* with which he prefaced his service book of 1545.[1]

'We begin', he writes, 'with confession of our sins, adding verses from the Law and the Gospel [i.e. words of absolution], . . . and after we are assured that, as Jesus Christ has righteousness and life in Himself, and that, as He lives for the sake of the Father, we are justified in Him and live in the new life through the same Jesus Christ, . . . we continue with psalms, hymns of praise, the reading of the Gospel, the confession of our faith [i.e. the Apostles' Creed], and the holy oblations and offerings. . . . And, . . . quickened and stirred by the reading and preaching of the Gospel and the confession of our faith, . . . it follows that we must pray for the salvation of all men, for the life of Christ should be greatly enkindled within us. Now, the life of Christ consists in this, namely, to seek and to save that which is lost; fittingly, then, we pray for all men. And, because we receive Jesus Christ truly in this Sacrament, . . . we worship Him in spirit and in truth; and receive the eucharist with great reverence, concluding the whole mystery with praise and thanksgiving. This, therefore, is the whole order and reason for its administration in this manner; and it agrees also with the administration in the ancient Church of the Apostles, martyrs, and holy Fathers.'

This makes it perfectly clear that it was Calvin's wish to restore the eucharist in its primitive simplicity and completeness as the weekly worship of the Church. The Holy Scriptures, read in course and expounded, were given their central place as in the ancient rites; but he was concerned to restore not the Scriptures alone,[2] but also weekly communion. To Calvin the 'means of grace' were twofold, consisting of *both* the Word and the Sacraments. The Ministry was a ministry of the Word *and* the Sacraments. A minister's task and office was not only to preach and instruct, but also to celebrate the Lord's Supper every week, and to teach and urge the people to communicate weekly. This Calvin himself strove to do all his life, and he set it up as an ideal for his followers who should come after him.

[1] Text 35, vol. xxxiv, pp. 194–6; or in V. 7, p. 35.
[2] The oft-repeated statement that the Reformers sought to replace the mass by the sermon is a misrepresentation: they sought to replace the mass by a celebration of the Lord's Supper with sermon (i.e. instruction and exhortation) and communion.

It is lamentably true that he was never permitted to realize his own ideal; the magistrates of Geneva, with their civil authority, intervened. They, not he, were responsible for the fact that the Zwinglian example of separating the eucharist from the regular Sunday worship was followed at Geneva.

Calvin first made his attitude clear in the *Institutes*, written before he came to Geneva, where he protested sharply against infrequent communion as prevalent in the old Church.

'Indeed', he writes, 'this custom that enjoins that men should communicate only once a year is certainly an invention of the devil. The Lord's Supper should be celebrated in the Christian congregation once a week at the very least.'[1]

Calvin never swerved from this position. Before 1538 he fought stoutly for it in Geneva, and the record of that struggle is preserved for us in the memoranda of the City Council.[2] The struggle ended when the magistrates banished him from Geneva in 1538. After a period in Strasbourg, he was invited to return to Geneva. This time, 'for the sake of peace', he gave way to the magistrates, who would not consent to celebrations more frequent than quarterly, though it is expressly stated in the minutes that this was to be only 'for the present'.[3] He sought to mitigate the stringency of these decrees by arranging that the dates of communion should vary in each church in the city, thus providing opportunity for more frequent communion for the people, who might communicate in a neighbouring parish.[4] But the magistrates would not consent to this, and the times finally fixed were Christmas, Easter, Pentecost, and Harvest-tide.

[1] Text 35, vol. xxxiv, pp. 1051–2.

[2] Even at this stage, although Calvin had suggested weekly communion in his first draft of the *Ordonnances*, the magistrates wished it less frequently. He then, against his principles, suggested monthly communion, but this does not appear to have been acceptable. *Ordonnances ecclésiastiques*, in Text 35, vol. xxxviii, i, p. 7.

[3] *Projet d'ordonnances*, 1541, in Text 35, vol. xxxviii, i, p. 25.

[4] This afterwards became an almost universal custom in Scotland; communion there was celebrated infrequently in each parish, but it was usual for the people to communicate in the neighbouring parish churches as well as in their own church.

But if Calvin was forced to acquiesce in practice, he never failed to express his dissatisfaction with things as they were in this respect. In edition after edition of the *Institutes* he asserted it, as also frequently in his correspondence. There is, for example, this letter to the Magistrates of Berne, written in 1555:[1]

'There is another matter, though not a new one [to which I would call your attention], namely, that we celebrate the Lord's Supper four times a year, and you three times. Please God, gentlemen, that both you and we may be able to establish a more frequent usage. For it is evident from St. Luke in the Book of Acts that communion was much more frequently celebrated in the primitive Church; and that continued for a long time in the ancient Church, until this abomination of the mass was set up by Satan, who so caused it that people received communion only once or twice a year. Wherefore, we must acknowledge that it is a defect in us that we do not follow the example of the Apostles.'

Calvin regarded the Holy Scriptures as the supreme authority in faith and life, and, unlike many of his followers then and later, he was not afraid to face the implications of his conviction. And he saw clearly that one of these implications was frequent communion. Instruction and exposition was another implication, but it was not the only one.

Six years later, in 1561, Calvin once more declared his disappointment with the practice at Geneva, lamenting that his hands were tied, but hoping for better things in the future; and he concluded:

'I have taken care to record publicly that our custom is defective, so that those who come after me may be able to correct it the more freely and easily.'[2]

Thus, as a result of civic interference, Calvin was forced into a practice that he abhorred,[3] and which he knew to be completely at variance with the teaching and practice of the New Testament and the early Church.

Two further matters may also be noted. The order of

[1] Text 35, vol. xliii, p. 538. [2] Text 35, vol. xxxviii, i, p. 213.
[3] This and further evidence is given from the original texts in V. 7, Appendix E.

receiving communion[1] in Calvin's rite was the normal order throughout the Church, the celebrant receiving first, then his ministers, and the people. Communion was received standing or kneeling, the people coming forward to the Holy Table, where, as at Strasbourg, they received the Bread from one minister and the Cup from another.

On the Sundays when communion was not celebrated, Calvin followed the practice that had become customary in Strasbourg in the parish churches after 1530. The order, structure, and content of the eucharistic service were largely retained, but such parts as belonged directly to consecration and communion were necessarily omitted. This practice was followed in Scotland after the Reformation, and also in England by Anglicans and Puritans alike.[2]

It is not necessary for our purpose to pursue further the history of Calvin's rite on the Continent. Suffice it to state that it became the norm of worship in the Calvinian Churches of France, Switzerland, South Germany, Holland, Denmark, and elsewhere. There were many local variants of the rite, but they were all closely related members of one family. And to-day, as the modern service books[3] show, their worship follows the same lines.

We conclude with Doumergue's estimate of Calvin's rite:

'Shall it be said that . . . the true Calvinian cultus was by nature cold and impoverished? Those who were present at the services have told us that often they could not keep back the tears of their emotion and joy. Singings and prayers, adoration and edification, confession and absolution of sins, acts both formal and spontaneous: all the essential elements of worship were there. And, perhaps not less important, they were united in an organism that was very simple, yet supple and strong. Calvin is, in fact, of all the Reformers the one who most steadfastly rejected the division of worship into two parts. . . . The Calvinian cultus is one.'[4]

---

[1] See Appendix F in V. 7.
[2] See pp. 64, 105, 111, 126, 130-1, 134, 138, 146, 150-1, 162, and 166-70 of this volume.   [3] See Text 41.
[4] In V. 5, p. 504. See his whole chapter, of which the words quoted above are the conclusion.

§ 5. *The Reformed Rites and their Successors in Scotland*

The Reforming party in Scotland during the decade that preceded the legalization of the Reformation in 1560 was not always wholly identical with the party that favoured an alliance with England instead of with France.[1] But there were many who desired to extend to Scotland the English revolt against the Papacy; and a formulary of worship in the tongue common to both countries was ready at hand in the Second Prayer Book of Edward VI. To use such a book based upon English medieval formularies was also a natural liturgical development, for the use of Sarum[2] had been generally followed in Scotland after the earlier Celtic use had been abandoned. Accordingly, the service book to which they now turned was not a continental formulary but the Second Prayer Book of Edward VI.[3] In this revision the influence of the Calvinians had been active, and the new book appears to have been particularly acceptable in the North. Knox, though he objected to kneeling at communion, had at this time on the whole a 'good opinion' of the book, and John Rough, Knox's co-pastor at St. Andrews, also approved of it, 'as agreeing in all points with the Word of God'. In 1557 the 'Lords of the Congregation', that is, the nobles and barons of the Reforming party, entered into a bond or covenant; and the first resolution they passed was one adopting the *Book of Common Prayer*, 1552:

'It is thought expedient, devised, and ordeaned, that in all parochines of this Realme the Common Prayeris be read owklie on Sonnday and other festuall dayis, publiclie in the Paroche Kirkis, with the Lessonis of the New and Old Testament, conform to the ordour of the Book of Common Prayeris: and yf the Curattis of the parochynes

[1] For the political oscillations of the Reformers in Scotland, see W. Law Mathieson's *Politics and Religion in Scotland*, Glasgow, 1902, vol. i, p. 51 *et passim*. See also VI. 10.

[2] See p. 145, note 1, below.

[3] For evidence of the use of this book in Scotland, see Text 42, pp. 33–56; and VI. 1, pp. 29–46. For an outline of the rite, see pp. 152–3 below, that of 1662, to which it closely approximated.

be qualified, to cause thame to reid the samyn; and yf thai be nott, or yf thai refuise, that maist qualified in the parish use and read the same.'[1]

This had not the force of law, but it had the consent of all the Reforming party, and there can be no doubt that the book, banned by Mary before it could come into general use in England, was used for a time in many parishes in Scotland.   It was officially superseded by the *Forme of Prayers* or *Book of Common Order*[2] in 1562 for ministration of the sacraments, and finally for all purposes in 1564.[3]   Yet, while these enactments were probably generally obeyed, it was some years before the English book quite disappeared from Scottish use.

We find the origins of the *Book of Common Order* at Frankfort-on-Main, where in 1554 a group of English exiles gathered, refugees from the Marian persecutions.   The majority of these exiles were Calvinians, but many of them, while following Calvin in doctrine, preferred the *Book of Common Prayer*.   Others, among them John Knox, were strongly attracted by Calvin's forms of worship as well as by his theological teaching.   Neither party would accept the other's view, nor could they agree upon a basis of compromise.   Eventually the Anglican party got the upper hand, with the result that in 1555 Knox, the acknowledged leader

---

[1] Knox's *Works* (Wodrow Soc.), i. 275.

[2] This book was known variously as *The Forme of Prayers, &c.* (its title proper), 'the Book of our Common Order', 'our Book of Common Order', the 'Book of Geneva', the 'Order of Geneva', and often it was called the 'Psalm Book'. Later, it was loosely designated as John Knox's Liturgy. It passed through seventy or eighty editions in Scotland: these are given in W. Cowan's *Bibliog. of the Book of Common Order, ... 1556–1644* (Edinburgh Bibliographical Soc., vol. x, 1913); and there were some fifteen or twenty editions printed in England or abroad for the use of the English Puritans. On the whole, and for the text of the first editions in Latin and English with the history and sources, see V. 7. For a symposium of all editions, with a valuable introduction, see Text 43.

[3] It was mentioned as the standard of worship for the Scottish Church in the First Book of Discipline, 1560, but this did not become law. It was first printed in Scotland in 1562. For its adoption by the General Assembly, see V. 7, p. 8, and VI. 1, pp. 42–3.

of the Calvinians, was banished from Frankfort.[1] Going to Geneva, he soon gathered about him a congregation of English exiles, and became their first minister. A Calvinian form of service in English had been drawn up at Frankfort in 1554, but it was never used there. Now, however, it was revived and perhaps revised; and, if not already in existence, orders for the celebration of Holy Communion, the solemnization of matrimony, and the ministration of baptism were added, together with injunctions concerning the ordination of ministers, visitation of the sick, and burial of the dead. A preface and long 'letter to the faithful' were composed as introductions, and Calvin's Catechism in English, a few metrical psalms in English, and some private prayers were placed at the end of the liturgical portions. Much of this work was done while Knox was absent from Geneva, and the leading spirit was probably William Whittingham, a lay member of the first committee at Frankfort, afterwards ordained at Geneva, who later became Dean of Durham.

This book, the first Reformed rite in English, was printed in Geneva in 1556 under the title, *The Forme of Prayers and Ministration of the Sacraments, &c., vsed in the Englishe Congregation at Geneua; and approued by the famous and godly learned man, Iohn Caluin.* The same year, a Latin edition entitled, *Ratio et forma publice orandi Deum,* &c.,[2] was issued for the perusal of such scholars as were unable to read English.

The Forme of Prayers passed through successive editions[2] in its English form. There was no change made in the orders themselves, but additional prayers were included as alternatives, many of them drawn from Huycke's English translation of Calvin's service book[3] after slight revision. In these later editions the metrical psalter was gradually

---

[1] Contemporary account of the *Troubles at Frankfort*, edited by Arber (London, 1908), or in Knox's *Works* (Wodrow Soc.), vol. iv. See V. 7 pp. 1–15; and also Text 44.

[2] See note 2, p. 121 above.   [3] See Text 45, pp. 71, 220.

extended until it was completed in Lekprevik's Edinburgh edition, 1564.

In my *John Knox's Genevan Service Book* extensive textual evidence is given to show that *The Forme of Prayers* is derived directly from Calvin's service book, *La Forme des Prieres*. At the same time, *The Forme of Prayers* is not a slavish translation, and evidence of an independent spirit is not lacking. In the Sunday Morning Order and in the form for the celebration of the Lord's Supper new intercessions and a new prayer of consecration appear; both of these are similar to Calvin's in spirit and doctrinal content, but there is no verbal agreement. After 1562 Calvin's intercessions and consecration prayer are included as alternatives. In other parts of *The Forme of Prayers* the influence of the *Book of Common Prayer*, 1552, may be detected, particularly in the marriage service and in the exhortation before communion.

Here is the scheme of the Order for the Celebration of the Lord's Supper:

The Liturgy of the Word

Confession of sins
Prayer for pardon
Psalm in metre
Prayer for illumination
Scripture Lection
Sermon

The Liturgy of the Upper Room

Collection of alms (?)
Thanksgiving and Intercessions
Lord's Prayer
Apostles' Creed (prose version)
Offertory: preparation or presentation of elements while a psalm in metre is sung
Words of Institution
Exhortation
Prayer of Consecration:
  Adoration
  Thanksgiving for creation and redemption
  Anamnesis
  Doxology

Fraction
Ministers' communion
Delivery
People's communion, while celebrant reads 'the whole historie of
the Passion'
Post-communion thanksgiving
Psalm ciii in metre
Aaronic or Apostolic Blessing

This is the eucharist reduced to its simplest elements, but, as this analysis of its structure shows, it is by no means an inadequate vehicle of devotion, and its composition is unmistakably catholic.

The Liturgy of the Word,[1] though its parts were few, was of considerable length, for the lection and sermon together normally occupied an hour or more. The Scriptures were read in course, the sermon being an exposition and exhortation based upon the lection.

From the liturgical point of view, the most serious omission in this rite was the epiclesis, though such an omission was common to the Roman, Anglican, and the other Reformed and Lutheran rites. The epiclesis, however, had been a part of the old Celtic rite; and there are grounds for believing that its use never quite died out in Scotland.[2] In any case, the lack of an epiclesis was soon generally felt, and though one does not appear in the texts until later, there is evidence that an epiclesis was comparatively early supplied in practice. For example, Row complains about a celebration of Holy Communion in St. Giles', Edinburgh, in 1622, where, although the minister 'kneeled and prayed', and 'read the prayer of consecration', there was in it 'not one word of "Lord bless the elements and action" ';[3] while

---

[1] In Scotland it was often enriched by a Reader's Service, consisting of psalms and lections from the Old and New Testaments, which preceded the Liturgy of the Word. See my V. 7, Appendix A. As in all the Reformed Liturgies, the approach through the confession of sins alone is too subjective, and lacks the element of praise with which the main diet of Christian worship should begin.

[2] See, e.g., V. 9.

[3] Row, *Historie of the Kirk of Scotland* (Wodrow Soc.), p. 331.

Calderwood, writing about 1620, says that it had been the custom in Scotland for sixty years, that is, since the first days of the Reformation, to 'bless' the Bread and Wine.[1] A proposed revision of 1629[2] indicates the form taken by the Scottish epiclesis:

'Mercifull Father wee beseech thee that wee receiving these thy creatures of bread and wine, according to thy sonne our Saviour his holy institution, may be made partakers of his most blissed body and blood. Send doune o Lord thy blissing upon this Sacrament that it may be unto us the effectual exhibitive instrument of the Lord Jesus.'

An epiclesis appears in most Scottish forms from 'Laud's Liturgy' and the Westminster *Directory* to the present day.

The elements used in Geneva were ordinary bread and wine, and these also were generally used in Scotland; in many parishes, however, wafer bread, or unleavened bread in some form, still continued in use; and the admixture of water to the wine was not unknown.[3]

At the English Church in Geneva, communion appears to have been celebrated monthly, and the rubric enjoining this custom was continued in the Scottish editions of *The Forme of Prayers*. But in actual practice, as an Act passed by the General Assembly in 1562 indicates,[4] communion was celebrated in Scotland only quarterly in the large towns, and less frequently in the country. The primary reason for these infrequent celebrations was the shortage of ministers,[5] making it impossible for all the parishes to be adequately served; a secondary, but forceful reason was the old pre-Reformation habit of communicating only once a year or

---

[1] *Altare Damascenum*, pp. 777–8; see Text 43 for further evidence from Henderson and Gillespie, pp. xxxvii sqq.; VI. 1, pp. 168 sqq.; and V. 7, p. 135.

[2] Edition in Text 46, p. 93. 'Exhibitive' is to be given its primary meaning here: f. *exhibeo*, to render, give, deliver.

[3] For much interesting evidence see, VI. 1, pp. 199 sqq.

[4] *Book of the Universal Kirk*, p. 13.

[5] In 1567, e.g., there were in the Church only 289 ministers and five superintendents; the bulk of the parishes were served by readers, of whom there were 715. See Story, *Apostolic Ministry in the Church of Scotland*, p. 242.

less frequently; and we may also believe that the practice at Geneva exercised some influence in this direction, in spite of Calvin's own remonstrances. By the time that every parish could be supplied with an ordained minister, infrequent communion had established itself, and it is still general in Scotland, although monthly communion is now common and weekly communion is not unknown.[1]

Communion was received sitting; but the Scottish practice differed from Zwinglian practice in that the people came forward and sat at a long Communion Table placed in the quire or nave. This ancient Scottish Reformed custom has almost disappeared; and the Bread and Wine are now taken by the elders to the people in their pews, which, however, in many churches are covered at Communion Seasons with white linen or 'houselling cloths'. This method of communicating the people in pews is first encountered in Zürich under Zwingli; it was not introduced into Scotland until the first quarter of the nineteenth century. Dr. Chalmers, then minister of St. John's Parish Church, Glasgow, appears to have been the first to discontinue the long Table and to communicate the people in their pews, thereby copying English Nonconformist practice.[2]

As with Calvin, the Lord's Supper was the norm of public worship in Scotland. When communion was not celebrated, as much as possible of the eucharist was retained, only that which pertained to consecration and communion being omitted. After the recitation of the Creed (see the tabular form on p. 123 above), a metrical psalm followed, and the service was concluded with the Blessing. Thus, Scottish

---

[1] On this, see VI. 2, pp. 342–9. This is the best account of the Ritual of the Church of Scotland. Unfortunately, it lacks notes and sources. It should be reprinted separately, and these supplied by an editor.

[2] See Text 47, p. xxxviii. Baillie describes English Nonconformist practice in the mid-seventeenth century: 'The unhappy Independents would mangle that Sacrament. . . . No coming up to any table, but a carrying of the elements to all in their seats athort the church'. (Baillie *Letters*, ii. 195, quoted by Dr. Leishman). The Scottish Assembly declared against this on repeated occasions (1825, 1827, &c.), see also VI. 8, pp. 38 sqq., year 1928–9.

Sunday Morning Worship was based upon the eucharist, and not upon the Hours' Offices.

The Church of Scotland alone of all the Reformed Churches formally abandoned the Christian Year; but this was an abandonment in theory rather than in practice, for in a large number of parishes the chief festivals continued to be observed.[1]

We must also remember that *The Forme of Prayers* or *Book of Common Order*, as it was variously called, was not a fixed and absolute formulary such as the *Book of Common Prayer*, but rather a standard of worship which left much to the minister's discretion. At the same time, it is a mistake to imagine either that it was a mere directory or that it was never in wide use. The Act of Assembly indicates that it is to be followed at the sacraments in especial; and the large number of editions through which it passed is clear evidence that the demand for it must have been both general and sustained, until in 1645 it was displaced by the Westminster *Directory*.

It was no doubt largely owing to Knox's championship that *The Forme of Prayers* was introduced in Scotland after 1560. He had been soured by his controversies in Frankfort with the Anglican party; while in Geneva he had found so much to his liking that he declared the Genevan Church to be[2] 'the maist perfyt schoole of Chryst that ever was in the erth since the dayis of the Apostillis', and 'maneris and religioun so sinceirlie reformat' he had 'not yit sene in any uther place'. This enthusiasm for Geneva, its worship and discipline, he carried back with him to Scotland; and in the end his counsel prevailed.

The Forme of Prayers or *Book of Common Order* continued to be the standard of worship in Scotland for over eighty years after the establishment of the Reformation. During this time, there were attempts at revision: the King desired

[1] For a full account, see VI. 1, pp. 299 sqq.
[2] Knox's *Works* (Wodrow Soc.), iv. 240.

to see the worship brought into closer uniformity with England; another party desired a closer approximation to the practice of English and Irish Nonconformity. Space forbids a close examination here of these divergences of opinion.[1] Suffice it to say that Charles I urged on the work that his father had begun, but failed to carry the Church of Scotland with him, largely owing to his obstinate Erastianism. This met with blunt opposition in Scotland, and the crisis came in 1637, when Charles attempted to enforce the use of the book prepared at his command by some Scottish bishops under the direction of Archbishop Laud. This Scottish *Book of Common Prayer* was in many ways an excellent production, but it failed to meet Scottish views at certain points. The crowning error, however, on the part of the King was his attempt to enforce its use by an Order in Council without consulting the Scottish Church.[2] The result was its instant rejection, and the whole country broke out in revolt. The National Covenant, a document asserting the religious liberty of the Church, was circulated and signed; and in 1638 at the General Assembly convened in Glasgow Cathedral the bishops were deposed (the Scottish Church had been under a constitutional episcopate since 1610), Presbyterianism was re-established, the King's book repudiated, and the *Book of Common Order* restored. The King sent his army against the Covenanters; but England too began to stir in rebellion against Charles, and in order to make peace with Scotland he agreed to the ratification of the Glasgow Assembly's proceedings.

Later, however, many of the Scottish people, under the leadership of the Church, and lured by the prospect of the establishment of a common Presbyterianism in England and Scotland, were drawn into an alliance with the English rebels. This alliance was ratified by the Solemn League and

---

[1] Accounts are given in VI. 2; and very fully in VI. 1. For texts, see Text 46.

[2] See pp. 154–5 below, where details are given; and pp. 155–6 for the scheme of rite of the Scottish *Book of Common Prayer*. See also VI. 11.

Covenant. The ensuing coalition of forces served to over-
throw the King, and soon afterwards Parliament set up a
commission of divines at Westminster to report upon a
form of ecclesiastical government, a confession of faith, and
forms of worship. Scottish representatives were present,
but had not the right to vote. Nevertheless, they exercised
a considerable influence upon the Assembly, whose work
proceeded rapidly and amicably, except for the diversions
of the 'five dissenting brethren'[1] who were irascible English
Independents. In the end, the Westminster *Confession of
Faith* was produced, together with *The Form of Presbyterial
Government* and a *Directory for Public Worship*.[2] In 1645
these were accepted by the Scottish Assembly, but in
England they had a short life except among the Presbyterians.

Our concern here is only with the *Directory*. The influence of the *Book of Common Prayer* and *The Forme of Prayers*
is discernible in the framing of the *Directory*, though this
pursued a course distinctive to itself. It contained no
prayers, but gave precise directions concerning the order
and content of every service. The verbal agreement with
The Forme of Prayers is extensive. The structure of the
Sunday Morning Order is a compromise between *The
Forme of Prayers*, Morning Prayer in the *Book of Common
Prayer*, and certain Independent practices.

The following is the scheme of the rite for the celebration
of the Lord's Supper:

The Liturgy of the Word

Call to worship—'Let us worship God'
Prayer of Approach:
  Adoration
  Supplication for worthiness
  Supplication for illumination

---

[1] There were actually ten or eleven 'dissenting' Independents out of an
Assembly of one hundred and twenty-one. See VII. 2. The Anglicans with-
drew at an early period. See A. Mitchell and Struthers, *Minutes of Westminster Assembly*. Edinburgh, 1874.

[2] Edited with Introduction and Notes in Text 47.

Lection from Old Testament—one chapter in course
Lection from New Testament—one chapter in course
Metrical psalms to be sung before and, or, between the lections
Prayer of confession and intercession:

An explicit and lengthy Confession of sins, with prayer for pardon and absolution, and for a sanctified life; intercessions for the whole world, the Reformed and British Churches, the King, Parliament, and all in authority; for pastors, teachers, schools, universities, city or town, the local congregation, all in distress; for seasonable weather and fruitful seasons; and for the sanctification of the Lord's Day; together with prayer for grace to enter into fuller fellowship with God; and for the minister in his office and life.

Sermon
General Prayer:

Thanksgiving, more especially for the Gospel and for redemption; supplications related to the heads of the sermon; self-oblation together with prayer for the acceptance of the spiritual sacrifice of worship; special prayer and intercession suited to the needs of the times. (In Scottish use, the whole of the intercessions might be included in this prayer.)

The Lord's Prayer; after which, if there was no celebration of Holy Communion, the service concluded with a Psalm of Praise and the solemn blessing of the people.

The Liturgy of the Upper Room

Offertory:

(No specific directions, but it may be inferred from the rubrics following that at this point the Holy Table was decently covered, the elements placed thereon in suitable vessels; during which, it may be supposed, the Psalm mentioned above was sung.)

Invitatory exhortation, and Fencing of Tables
Setting apart of elements from all common uses
Words of Institution
Exhortation
Prayer of Consecration:

Prayer of Access
Thanksgiving for Creation and Providence
Thanksgiving for Redemption
Thanksgiving for the Word and Sacraments
Anamnesis
Epiclesis

Fraction
Delivery
Communion (Celebrant receiving first)
Exhortation to a worthy life
Post-communion Prayer:
    Thanksgiving for benefits received in Communion
    Prayer for a worthy life
Metrical Psalm of praise
Solemn Blessing

This service is comprehensive, but so excessively minute in its detail as to be unpractical by reason of its great length. It was not accepted by the Scottish General Assembly without important reservations and revisions. It was specifically stated in the Act that approval of the *Directory* should 'be no prejudice to the order and practice of this Kirk', and that communicants were to receive seated at the Table, not remaining in the pews.[1] It also prescribed that the old custom of including the intercessions in the prayer after sermon should not be abandoned in Scotland, but should be continued as formerly. The Scots objected strongly to the English Independents' practice of placing the long prayer before the sermon.[2]

Even with this cautious approval, certain unhappy results followed. The Creed dropped out of use, a concession to extreme English Independent views, and with it the doxology formerly sung at the end of the psalms. The recital of the Lord's Prayer, though enjoined in the *Directory*, soon fell into disuse. At this time, too, many Readers were suppressed; and the result was, as Baillie had foretold in a 'paper to his colleagues', the discontinuance of daily prayers. 'For three or four years the ministers in Edinburgh had daily prayers with exposition, but they tired of it.'[3] Indeed, during the next century it became general not to read the

---

[1] VI. 2, p. 442; and Text 47, Appendix B, where the Acts of Assembly are reprinted.
[2] VI. 2, p. 383; Text 47, pp. 189–90.
[3] VI. 2, p. 383; Text 47, Appendix E, where Baillie's paper to his colleagues is reprinted.

Holy Scriptures in public worship, but merely to expound
them at great length. There are signs that this neglect of
Scripture lections began early, for, seven years after the
Directory had been approved in Scotland, we find an Interim
Act passed by the General Assembly in 1652, enjoining that
two chapters be read (with brief expositions) from the Old
and New Testaments.[1] But neglect crept in once more, to
be finally denounced by the Assembly of 1856 in response
to an overture, and ministers were enjoined to follow the
Directory in its injunctions 'respecting the reading of the
Holy Scriptures of the Old and New Testaments at each diet
of public worship'.[2]

It is not possible here to trace in detail the decline in the
due ordering of public worship which followed the Crom-
wellian period, and which lasted until the mid-nineteenth
century.[3] Communion was celebrated very infrequently,
the structure of the ordinary services was bare in the extreme, sometimes reduced to the singing of a metrical psalm,
followed by a long prayer, another psalm, the sermon, and
a long concluding prayer, after which another psalm was
sung, to be followed by the benediction. After 1650 the
metrical Psalter was that of Rous, as revised by the General
Assembly. The number of tunes in use was very limited
until the latter part of the eighteenth century.[4] The Paraphrases were first drafted in 1745, and were issued in
their present form in 1781, though never formally authorized by the Church. The practice whereby the precentor
repeated each line in a monotone, on the note to be taken
up by the people, also went far to degrade the music. This
was an innovation derived from England, where the standard
of general education was so low that few of the country

---

[1] Text 47, p. xxvi.   [2] Text 47, p. xxxi, quotes this Act.
[3] The best account is VI. 2. See also VI. 6, pp. 241–309; this letter must
be read with reserve as it contains many inaccuracies.
[4] VI. 2, pp. 406–7. On praise in the Reformed Churches, see accounts in
X. 4 and X. 5. Rous's Psalter was so drastically altered by the Scottish
revisers that Rous disowned it.

people and poorer classes in the towns could read; but it was speedily naturalized in Scotland in the eighteenth century, and was not generally departed from until the nineteenth.[1] Hymns were gradually admitted into public worship.[2]

During the last eighty years there has been a marked revival in the music of the Church.

After the *Book of Common Order* had fallen into disuse, the prayers were extemporaneous and often tediously didactic; in some places they are so still, but the general standard has vastly improved during the last seventy-five years. Dr. James Moffatt's words[3] are of interest in this connexion:

'The re-action against liturgies [in Scotland] was partly due to an honourable but exaggerated devotion to freedom and spirit in worship, as though this was incompatible with the use of any forms of prayer, and partly to the fact that, as in the case of Scotland, the King sought to impose a new liturgy upon it, and thereby created a distaste for liturgies in general. It is a pity when minds work by re-action; in a Church, as in individuals, it may sound strong, mainly because it goes readily into strong words, but it is a sign of weakness. Progress is not attained by recoiling as far as possible from what some other people hold, nor by discarding a practice incontinently either because it is being abused by contemporaries or because it has acquired some compromising associations. Unluckily, Presbyterians for a time parted with some precious elements in their heritage of worship, for reasons into which it is needless to enter here; and one of these was orderly liturgical prayer, which like good music acquired odium from its connexion with episcopacy. It was for a long time believed that spontaneous, unpremeditated prayer was more inspired than any carefully drawn up collect. Even the Lord's Prayer has been tabooed! These sad days are over. . . . It is at least becoming more and more recognized that we are as free to use forms of prayer as to do without them in our worship. As a result of this slow and difficult revival, there is now, at any rate in Scotland, a welcome variety and wealth of worship, from the simple, most impressive service of a small congregation, to the more elaborate worship in our cathedrals, abbeys, and larger churches.'

[1] VI. 2, p. 406.
[2] See Introduction of X. 8, pp. xiii sqq.; also X. 4, and X. 3, pp. 45 sqq
[3] *The Presbyterian Churches*, London, 1928, p. 140.

It is perhaps true, on the whole, to say with Principal Story that 'toward the close of the eighteenth century the public services of the Church of Scotland had become probably the baldest and rudest in Christendom'.[1] We should remember, however, that throughout the whole of the Reformed Churches, including the Lutheran and Anglican, worship during this period had sunk to a low level. The decline was not confined to Scotland alone.

The revival came in the last decades of the nineteenth century, principally fostered by a strong body of scholars and divines who formed the Church Service Society.[2]

In 1923 the General Assembly of the Church of Scotland authorized the publication of a service book entitled *Prayers for Divine Service*.[3] Its content was drawn largely from *Euchologion*,[3] a service book issued by the Church Service Society in 1867 which has passed through many editions. *Euchologion* brought a great enrichment to Scottish worship, its chief defect being that in successive editions the structure of the ordinary Sunday worship was assimilated to the structure of Anglican Morning Prayer, instead of following the ancient Reformed Church norm of Ante-Communion.[4] In this it was followed by *Prayers for Divine Service*. But both were a notable and praiseworthy advance upon what had prevailed before.

In 1928 the United Free Church of Scotland, just on the eve of union with the Church of Scotland, authorized the

[1] Quoted in VI. 12, p. 2. On p. 3 he adds: 'In the degradation of worship England was the predominant partner. . . . "The curse of Cromwell" was more felt in Scotland than ever it was in Ireland. English Independency and Puritanism were responsible for the graceless condition of Presbyterian worship. The pity of it was that this conglomerate of rant and vulgarity had come to be regarded as purity of worship.'

[2] The story of its founding (1865), work, and leaders is given in VI. 12; see VI. 8, year 1928-9, pp. 17-20. The Church Worship Association rendered a similar service to the United Free Church of Scotland; it was founded in 1882 by Ministers of the United Presbyterian Church. See VI. 8, year 1930-1, pp. 79-82.

[3] Blackwoods publish both these; and also published the important *Prayers for Social and Family Worship*, 1st. ed. 1859, by authority of the G.A.

[4] See p. 119 above, note 2, for full references.

publication of *The Book of Common Order*, 1928 (Oxford), less liturgical in style than *Prayers for Divine Service* but attaining a high standard representing the best tradition of its Church.

Re-union between these Churches was accomplished in 1929, and after due deliberation and experiment *The Book of Common Order*, 1940 (Oxford) appeared as the authorized standard of the Church of Scotland[1]. This book contains five Orders for the Celebration of Holy Communion. The first is normative; the second[2] is a slightly shortened form; the third an alternative Order, similar in content to the first but framed in language less traditionally liturgical; the fourth a very short Order, when required for the Sick, etc.; and the last for use with the Reserved Elements. The scheme of the rite is as follows:

The Liturgy of the Word

Introit: Psalm xliii. 3–5, in metre

Scripture Sentences: Psalm cxvi. 12–14 *et al.*; or others to suit season

Collect for Purity (*B.C.P.*)

Confession and Absolution (*P.D.S.*)

Collect (Sixth after Trinity (*B.C.P.*) or other to suit season)

Canticle (e.g., *Benedictus Dominus*), Psalm, or Hymn

Prophecy, or other lection from O.T.

Prose Psalm sung

Epistle and Gospel

Nicene Creed, if not said at Offertory

Intercessions and Commemoration of Departed

Psalm, Paraphrase, or Hymn

Banns of Marriage, and Intimations

Sermon, preceded by collect and followed by Ascription

---

[1] Preceded in 1931 by *An Ordinal and Service Book for the Use of Presbyteries* (Edinburgh), which contained an Order for Holy Communion. Presbyterian Churches outside Scotland have their own service books closely related to above; in Text 48 many are listed.

[2] Taken in its entirety from *Forms of Prayer for Use at Sea* (Edinburgh, 1936); in it the Intercessions and Commemoration of the Blessed Departed conclude the Consecration Prayer following traditional Scottish usage.

The Liturgy of the Upper Room

Offertory: Collection of Offerings
  Invitation with Comfortable Words
  Psalm xxiv. 7–10 or Para. xxxv, while Elements are brought to
    the Holy Table in solemn procession
  Nicene Creed, if not previously used
  Unveiling of Elements: Prayer of the Veil and Offertory Prayer
  Salutation, and Warrant (1 Cor. xi, 23–6)
  'Taking' of Elements
Salutation and *Sursum corda*
Prayer of Consecration:
  Preface, with Thanksgiving for Creation and Providence, and
    proper of the season
  Sanctus, Benedictus qui venit with *Hosanna*
  Vere sanctus (Thanksgiving for Redemption)
  Anamnesis, Oblation, Epiclesis
  Self-oblation, Oblation of Church, and brief Intercession for
    living and dead
  Doxology
The Lord's Prayer
Words of Institution accompanied by Manual Acts (Fraction, etc.)
Agnus Dei and Celebrant's Communion
Delivery and People's Communion, followed by the Peace
Post-communion Thanksgiving (*B.C.P.*) and Commemoration of
  Departed
Psalm ciii. 1–5 in metre, or other Psalm or Hymn of Praise
The Blessing (*B.C.P.*)

This noble and notable rite indicates the richness, centrality,
and uniqueness of the Scottish liturgical tradition, its catholicity
yet independence. It is not a creation *de novo*, but a long
tradition brought to its perfection. An action of the whole
company, it possesses a simple but solemn ceremonial chiefly
utilitarian rather than symbolic; and the celebrant normally
(but not invariably) adopts the basilican posture. In its dignity
of action, felicity of expression, and adequacy of content, it
provides a worthy vehicle of worship entitling it to a place
among the great rites of Christendom.

§ 6. *The Reformed Rites and their Successors in England*

The first nonconformist English rites were based, like the
Scottish rite, on the Genevan *Forme of Prayers*[1]. It was

[1] See pp. 121–4 above for details of this service book.

at Frankfort-on-Main that the distinction between the two types, later to be known as Anglican and Puritan, first sharply emerged.[1] And after the return of the Marian exiles Puritanism became a vital force in England and has so continued until the present day.

In English Puritanism there were two distinct schools, the Presbyterians and the Independents, known later as the Congregationalists. The chief differences between them lay in their views of Church polity: so far as worship was concerned they were, and generally speaking, in England have always been, not essentially dissimilar in practice.[2] But Congregationalism, as it later developed, has had greater freedom, since each local church is entirely free to frame its own standards.

Until the Westminster *Directory* was issued, the standard of worship favoured by the Puritans was the *Forme of Prayers*; but in England it was used only as a general standard, not as a prayer-book. Non-liturgical prayer was favoured, and among the Independents the general prayer came to be used before instead of after sermon. The structure of the services was simple, and the content varied.

The Westminster *Directory* serves as an indication of the English Presbyterian mind in the mid-seventeenth century. Sixteen years later we have a further indication of that mind in the work of Baxter, the Puritan[3] divine who, in 1661, hurriedly prepared and presented to the bishops at their request a document entitled the *Reformation of the*

[1] See Arber's ed. of *The Troubles at Frankfort* (London, 1908); Knox's *Works* (Wodrow Soc.), vol. iv; and the publication of the Parker Society (London). See also V. 7, for details of texts and notes on early Puritan practice. Texts 49 and 50 contain the most accessible texts of Puritan forms of worship. The first Congregational Churches were formed between 1567 and 1571.

[2] Both insisted generally upon a Scriptural warrant for all that was done in worship, and preferred worship that was simple and even bare. See VII. 2, pp. 260 sqq. On the two streams of English Nonconformity, the Presbyterian (the stronger) and Congregational, see ibid., pp. 296 sqq.

[3] His biographer, the Revd. F. J. Powicke, Ph.D., D.D., includes him among the 'moderate Episcopalians'; see VII. 2, p. 298.

Liturgy.[1] It was presented at the Savoy Conference held the year following the restoration of the monarchy, and it has been commonly known as the 'Savoy Liturgy'. It was never used, but it purported to conform to the opinions of the large body led by Baxter.[2] As an indication of what was proposed, the scheme of Baxter's Liturgy is of interest:

The Liturgy of the Word[3]

Prayer of Approach (long and short alternatives)

Apostles', Nicene, or Athanasian Creed, 'read by the Minister'

The Ten Commandments, read by the Minister

Scripture Sentences, 'moving the people to a penitent believing Confession'

Confession of sins and Prayer for Pardon (long or short)

Lord's Prayer, said by all

Scriptural Words of absolution and exhortation

Ps. xcv, c, or lxxxiv, followed by 'the Psalms in order for the day'

Old Testament lection (one chapter chosen by Minister)

Psalm 'may be sung, or the *Te Deum* said'

New Testament lection (one chapter)

'Prayer for the King and Magistrates' (example given)

Ps. lxvii or xcviii 'may be sung or said'; 'or the *Benedictus* or *Magnificat*' ('and the same order to be observed at the Evening worship, if time allow it.')

Prayer '(in the pulpit)' for the Church, especially those present, and 'according to the subject that he is to preach on'

Sermon

Prayer for 'a blessing on the Word'; and 'in his prayers (before or after Sermon) ordinarily he shall pray for the conversion of heathens, Jews, and other infidels; the subversion of idolatry, infidelity, Mahometanism, heresy, Papal tyranny, supersti-

---

[1] Text 49, vol. iv.

[2] The Independents had no sympathy with this proposal, and would not compromise in any way with the Anglicans. After this they 'eliminated everything liturgical . . . from their way of worship'. VII. 2, pp. 298 sqq.

[3] This is the ordinary 'Morning Service for the Lord's Day', containing elements derived both from Ante-Communion and Mattins in the *B.C.P.*; when Holy Communion was celebrated, the above served as the 'Liturgy of the Word'. Apparently it was contemplated to use the Psalms in prose and metre, and the metrical versions recommended for present use 'until a better can be made' were Wm. Barton's and that 'approved by the Church of Scotland' (Rous's), 'being the best that we have seen', printed together 'for grateful variety'.

tion', &c.; for increase of faith in all nations; for King's Majesty, Royal Family, Lords of Council, Judges, Magistrates, Ministers, Congregation; concluding with 'thanksgiving and praises to God, especially for Jesus Christ, and his benefits'.[1] (In addition to this rubric, a long General Prayer is given as an example, followed by a long thanksgiving and a 'hymn' in four parts compiled from praise in the psalms, Luke ii. 14, and Revelation, apparently to be recited by the people).

Blessing (Aaronic or Apostolic), if communion be not celebrated

The Liturgy of the Upper Room

'Explication of the nature, use, and benefits of this Sacrament' followed by an Exhortation (both lengthy)

Prayer of Access (lengthy)

Offertory: 'Here let the Bread be brought to the Minister, and received by him, and set upon the Table; and then the Wine in like manner: or if they be set there before, however let him bless them, praying in these or the like words.'[2]

Prayer of Consecration (very brief):[3]

Commemoration of Creation

Commemoration of Redemption (Anamnesis)

Consecration: 'Sanctify these thy creatures of Bread and Wine, which, according to thy institution and command, we set apart to this holy use, that they may be sacramentally the Body and Blood of thy Son Jesus Christ.'

Words of Institution: 'Then (or immediately before this Prayer) let the Minister read the words of Institution' (1 Cor. xi. 23-6)

Declaration that Elements have been consecrated, and 'are now no

---

[1] It will be observed that Baxter himself, as of Presbyterian leanings, preferred this 'Great Prayer' to follow the sermon; the Independents generally preferred it to come before the sermon. This order, designed to represent the moderates, permits either practice to be followed. The position of the Lord's Prayer early in the service was also peculiarly English, no doubt a result of its position in Anglican Morning and Evening Prayer. On the proper principles of the use of the Lord's Prayer in public worship, see VIII. 10, pp. 134 sqq.

[2] The Presbyterian custom, following Geneva, was to bring in the elements at this point. The Independent practice was to have the elements on the Table before the service began.

[3] Three usages are permitted: (1) that above, as in accordance with Baxter's own mind, (2) the bread and wine might be consecrated and delivered separately, in which event the consecration would be twice repeated; or, (3) the Prayer of Consecration might include that given above, together with the prayer pleading our Lord's sacrifice and intercession and the prayer to the Holy Spirit, the Words of Institution standing before this prayer.

common bread and wine, but sacramentally the Body and
Blood of Christ'.
Brief Prayer pleading our Lord's Intercession and Sacrifice
Fraction: 'The Body of Christ was broken for us . . . behold the
    sacrificed Lamb of God, that taketh away the sins of the world.'
Libation of the Wine: 'We were redeemed with the precious Blood
    of Christ, as of a Lamb without blemish and without spot.'
Prayer to the Holy Spirit for a sanctified life
Delivery (Words of Delivery as in *Westminster Directory*)
Communion ('first taking and eating of it himself as one of them
    . . . first drinking of it himself . . .')[1]
Post-communion Prayer (lengthy):
    Adoration
    Thanksgiving for Creation and Redemption
    Prayer for a holy life
    Oblation of self and worship
    Exhortation to a godly life
    Psalm of praise ('part of the Hymn in metre, or some other fit
        Psalm of praise, as the 23rd, 116th, 103rd, or 100th.')
    Blessing, 'Now the God of peace, which brought &c.'

During the eighteenth and nineteenth centuries, worship
in England among Presbyterians and Congregationalists
alike sank to a low level. The structure was meagre, the
prayers lengthy and didactic, with the sermon as the principal act of public worship. A general revival of orderly worship, however, beginning in the latter part of the nineteenth
century, has made itself widely felt.

The Directory of Public Worship,[2] a semi-liturgical compilation authorized by the General Assembly, is the present
service book of the Presbyterian Church of England. Its
use is not obligatory, except at ordinations, but it provides a standard to which worship throughout that Church
more or less approximates. It contains orders and prayers

[1] Delivery might be made to each communicant separately, at the Table
'in general', or 'in general to as many as are in each particular form.' It
appears that communicants might either come forward to receive, or remain
in their pews; 'and let none of the people be forced to sit, stand, or kneel in
the act of receiving, whose judgement is against it'.
[2] First edition, 1898. Revised edition, here quoted, 1921 Published by
Publications Committee, 21 Warwick Lane, London, E.C. 4.

for Sunday worship, with litanies and special prayers for the principal seasons of the Christian and the Natural Year; and orders for the celebration of the Sacraments and for the Occasional Services. The liturgical value of the prayers is not high, but the whole represents orderly worship. This is the scheme of the ordinary Sunday worship and the celebration of the Lord's Supper.

The Liturgy of the Word[1]

Sentences of Scripture, or Call to worship
Prayer of 'Invocation'
Hymn or Psalm in metre
Prayer: Adoration
         Confession of Sin and Prayer for Pardon
         Thanksgiving
         Supplication for Grace
Hymn or Psalm in metre
Old Testament lection
Psalm or Canticle, or Anthem
New Testament lection
(Address to Children)
Hymn for Children
(The Apostles' Creed)
Intercessions and the Lord's Prayer (which may follow Sermon)
Notices
Offerings (with dedication)
Hymn
Sermon (preceded and concluded by prayer)
Hymn of Praise or Doxology
Blessing (Apostolic)

The Liturgy of the Upper Room

Scriptural Words of Invitation
Collect for purity (as in *B.C.P.*), or another brief prayer, or a shortened and altered form of the Anglican Prayer of Humble Access
Hymn (may be sung)

[1] This is the structure of the ordinary Sunday Morning Worship. When Communion is celebrated (monthly or quarterly is the usual practice) the ordinary service precedes it as the Liturgy of the Word. The precise liturgical principles that guided the compilers are difficult to detect. It is based partly on common use, while the influence of the *B.C.P.* and the Westminster *Directory* may be discerned.

Words of Institution
Taking of the Bread and Wine (which are usually placed on
the Holy Table before the Service begins)
Consecration Prayer:
Adoration and Thanksgiving
A form of epiclesis
Self-oblation
(*Sanctus*)
Fraction
Communion (taken by Elders to the communicants in their pews:
Elements given separately, all first partaking of the Bread)
Comfortable Words
Post-communion:
Thanksgiving and prayer for grace
Commemoration of Departed
Brief Intercessions
Psalm, Hymn, or Doxology
Blessing (as in *B.C.P.*)

During recent years there have been also interesting
liturgical movements in the. Congregational churches in
England.[1] In these churches worship takes many and varied
forms, ranging from the simplest and most unliturgical
worship to that which is both liturgical in its ritual and
accompanied by elaborate ceremonial. Each local congregation is a law unto itself; and it is also a cardinal principle of
Congregationalism that any lay member of a congregation
may be invited to celebrate the Lord's Supper.

The worship is so diverse according to local practice
that it is not possible to describe it generally. There is no
commonly accepted standard of worship, but in 1920 the
Book of Congregational Worship[2] was issued by the Congregational Union of England and Wales. As this book has no real
authority, it is difficult to estimate how far it is representative
of Congregational practice, but it probably serves as a guide
to a large number of congregations. It is semi-liturgical
in form, and provides ten Orders of Divine Service all

---

[1] Space forbids that these be described here, but their wealth and variety
is seen by Texts 51, 52, 53, and 69.
[2] Text 54.

comparatively simple in structure, but because they differ, not possible to summarize here. It also provides orders for the Sacraments and Occasional Services. There are brief litanies and responses provided in several of the services, and the prayers are drawn from many sources, ancient and modern; on the whole, these are classical in form and language, brief yet comprehensive. It is a book that should be known, containing as it does, much of great value. The following is the scheme of the Liturgy of the Upper Room, entitled simply 'Holy Communion'. It is designed to follow the ordinary Sunday Service, which thus provides the Liturgy of the Word. Holy Communion is usually celebrated once a month.

The Liturgy of the Upper Room

Hymn
Comfortable Words
Invitation (as in *B.C.P.*)
Confession of sins (compiled from Psalms)
Sursum corda
Preface (as in *B.C.P.*; people repeat with Minister from 'Therefore
    with angels, &c.,' to end of *Sanctus*).
Words of Institution
Consecration Prayer (brief):
    Commemoration of Redemption
    Thanksgiving for benefits of passion
    Self-oblation (as in *B.C.P.*, 1549)
Silent prayer
Delivery and Communion
Post-communion:
    The Lord's Prayer
    Prayer for the Church: 'O God of unchangeable power, &c.'
        (from *Gelasian Sacramentary*, as in Bright's *Ancient Collects*);
        or, 'We thank thee, our Father, &c.' (from the *Didaché*)
    Commemoration of Departed: first part of collect at the Burial
        of the Dead combined with commemoration of departed in
        Communion intercessions of *B.C.P.*, 1662.
Hymn, or *Gloria in excelsis*
Scripture Lection (foot-washing, example given)
Collection of alms
Blessing: 'Now the God of peace, &c.'

This rite is defective in its content, lacks creativeness, and is too closely modelled upon the *B.C.P.* But it serves to indicate a growing liturgical sense in modern Congregationalism. Communion is usually received sitting, the Bread and Wine carried reverently to the people in their pews by the deacons; in some churches, however, the people go forward to receive at the Holy Table.

In the Methodist Communities in England, and throughout the English-speaking world, the worship varies considerably, ranging from the barest Puritan services to what might be described as an Anglican evangelical service.[1] In some Methodist churches Wesley's recension of the *B.C.P.*[2] is used both for Morning and Evening Prayer on Sundays, and Holy Communion is commonly celebrated monthly or quarterly.[3] The Order of Holy Communion as revised by Wesley (a very slight revision) is the normal form of celebration in all Methodist Churches throughout the world. The people come forward to the altar rail to communicate.

§ 7. *The English Rite in the Book of Common Prayer*

The Church of England, after the Reformation, inclined doctrinally to Calvinism, but in liturgical practice it was more closely related to Lutheranism. Yet the Anglican Church cannot be classified under either category, and its own contribution to both doctrine and worship is unique. As in the Church of Scotland, the only doctrines expressly repudiated were the two extremes of transubstantiation and sacramentarianism;[4] while the development of its worship followed a course peculiar to itself.

Under Henry VIII the Church of England broke with the papacy, but the mass remained for many years un-

---

[1] On Methodist worship, see I. 14.

[2] See Texts 55 and 56.

[3] Wesley's own teaching and practice were, however, in favour of weekly (or more frequent) communion. This is the more significant in an age when weekly communion was almost unknown in the Church of England. See I. 14, pp. 85 sqq. [4] That is, Zwingli's doctrine of the eucharist.

altered.[1] Steps were taken, however, in 1536 to further the instruction of the people in the meaning of the ritual and ceremonial; and in 1542 the Convocation of Canterbury ordered that every morning and evening a chapter from the Old Testament and one from the New should be read in English in all parish churches on Sundays and holy days. Two years later, in 1544, the litany first appeared in English form.

But it was after Henry's death, and during the reign of the youthful Edward VI, that the influence of the Reformation movement became paramount in England.

In 1547 the *First Book of Homilies*, containing twelve sermons in English was published; and later in that year a royal injunction ordered that, in addition to the lections prescribed to be read in English in 1542, the Epistle and Gospel should now also be read in English at high mass.

In March of the following year Cranmer's English *Order for Communion* was issued. It provided that communion should be given in both kinds, that the people should be informed in advance when mass was to be celebrated, and that they should also be instructed how to prepare for communion. The *Order* itself consisted of an exhortation, a fencing of the Table, invitation, general confession of sins and absolution, comfortable words, and a prayer of humble access. This Order was to be inserted in the mass, after the celebrant's communion; and was incorporated in the text of the first Prayer Book, 1549, the exhortation before the offertory, and the remainder immediately preceding the communion.

[1] There was no absolute uniformity in worship in England before the Reformation. It was Roman in character, and the dominating use was that of Sarum; but dioceses had their own local customs, and besides that of Sarum there were the uses of York, Bangor, and Hereford. The Roman Canon was, of course, common to all, and none of the differences were essentially important. See VIII. 11, 12, 13. Text 24 indicates minutely the sources of the *Book of Common Prayer* and what parts of it were compiled from the old rites. Sarum mass edited in Text 57; also conveniently accessible in VIII. 1, pp. 282 sqq.; ibid., p. xxi, gives information about the texts of the other English pre-Reformation rites.

The first *Book of Common Prayer*[1] was chiefly the work of Cranmer, although he was assisted by Ridley and others. It preserved a rich treasure of liturgical material, the whole rendered in an English style singularly felicitous, dignified, and chaste. The character of the collects was retained, the English style equalling the Latin, while the style of the Canon far surpassed that of the old rite. The achievement was unique in that the *Book of Common Prayer*, in contrast with the other vernacular rites of the sixteenth century, survives in use to this day.

Although as much as possible of the old rite was retained, its character was fundamentally changed by the revision of the Canon: an epiclesis, based upon St. Basil's, was inserted as part of the consecration preceding the Words of Institution, and the doctrine of sacrifice was expressed as a 'sacrifice of praise and thanksgiving' and the offering of 'ourselves, our souls and bodies, to be a reasonable, holy and lively sacrifice unto' God. The whole service was also to be said in a clear voice.

Communion was an essential part of the rite, and at every celebration some of the people were required to communicate. On Wednesdays and Fridays, if there were no communicants, all that followed the Offertory was omitted, and one or two collects were added to conclude the service. This service was known as Ante-Communion, and it was in accordance with the custom of the Reformed Churches on the Continent.[2] Communion was to be celebrated at least every Sunday and Holy Day, at which times also a sermon was to be preached or a homily read.

The other changes[3] are comparatively unimportant, but they all contributed to alter the character of the rite in

---

[1] Edited and exhaustively annotated in Text 24; an excellent text is also edited in Dent's Everyman series: this contains the rites of both 1549 and 1552.

[2] See p. 119, n. 2, for full references.

[3] The new and old rites are given in structural outline in parallel columns in VIII. 1, pp. 449–58, 469, the best account of the history of the *B.C.P.*

accordance with the Reformed theology. The old *Confiteor* was replaced by a general confession of sins, and its position was changed; the celebrant's preparation was reduced to the repetition of the Lord's Prayer and the collect for purity. The Introits became in most cases complete psalms; and in the prayers the mediation of the Virgin Mary and the Saints was rejected. The lectionary was revised, and the number of saints' days drastically reduced, while many changes were made in the collects. The intercessions remained in their old position at the beginning of the Canon, and with them were included the prayers for the departed. The celebrant's private prayers were omitted throughout, and the ceremonial simplified. The Fraction accompanied the Dominical Words in the Consecration Prayer.[1]

This appears in the scheme below. The new title was, 'The Supper of the Lorde and the holy Communion, commonly called the Masse'.

The Liturgy of the Word

Introit: 'a Psalme appointed for that daie' sung by clerks
Celebrant's Preparation:
   Lord's Prayer
   Collect for purity
   Repetition of the introit
Kyries, ninefold in English with 'upon us' added
Gloria in excelsis
Salutation and collect of the day
Collect for the King
Epistle
Gospel (with people's response)
Nicene Creed
Sermon or Homily

The Liturgy of the Upper Room

Exhortation to right communion; and, when necessary, to frequent
   communion
Offertory:
   Scripture sentences, said by celebrant or sung by clerks

---

[1] A position peculiar to all the Anglican rites, but to be deprecated. The Fraction should be a separate action, and not embedded in the Consecration.

Collection of alms and other offerings
Communicants go to choir, men on one side and women on other
Preparation of bread and wine, and admixture
Salutation and *Sursum corda*
Prayer of Consecration:
Preface, and Proper Preface (5 only)
Sanctus and *Benedictus qui venit*
Intercessions for the living and dead
Commemoration of Passion
Epiclesis
Words of Institution, and manual acts including Fraction
Anamnesis
Oblation:
Of 'this our sacrifice of praise and thanksgiving'
Of 'ourselves, our souls and bodies'
Petition that Angels may bear our prayers on high
Conclusion and Doxology
Lord's Prayer, with protocol and embolism, the latter reduced to
'But deliver us from evil'
The Peace
Christ our Pascall Lambe (Paraphrase of 1 Cor. v. 7, 8; 1 Pet. ii. 24;
and *Ecce Agnus Dei*, John i. 29)
Cranmer's 'Order for Communion':
Invitation
General Confession and Absolution
Comfortable Words
Prayer of humble access
Celebrant's, ministers' and people's communion[1] in both kinds,
while clerks sing *Agnus Dei*
Post-communion Scripture Sentences, said or sung
Salutation and Post-communion thanksgiving
Peace and Blessing

This rite, beautiful, adequate, reformed, never became, however, the accepted use of the Church of England. Bitter contention greeted its issue from the press, and from the beginning it was doomed. A body of extreme opinion had arisen, and was clamorously vocal. There was an attempt to meet this agitation in the next year, 1550, when a royal ordinance ordered that all altars be replaced by wooden

---

[1] In the Anglican Church the people go forward to the altar rail, where they kneel to receive communion.

Communion Tables. But more was demanded, and in 1552 a new prayer-book appeared, a drastic and impoverished revision of that of 1549.[1]

In the new book the word 'mass' was deleted from the title of the rite, eucharistic vestments were abolished, and the replacement of altars by Communion Tables confirmed. These new Communion Tables were to stand east and west, that is, at right angles to the position of the former altars, and the celebrant was to stand at the north *side*.[2] The necessity of there being communicants at every celebration was reaffirmed; and this time it was specifically stated that there must be three or four in addition to the celebrant. The introit disappeared, and the Decalogue was collated with the *Kyries*; thus was the preparation made entirely subjective, a grave fault; and this lack of praise and thanksgiving was further emphasized by the transference of the *Gloria in excelsis* to the end, and by the deletion of the *Glory be to thee, O Lord*, at the Gospel, though the response was continued in practice. Prayers for the departed were not admitted, and the intercessions were removed from the Canon and placed at the offertory. The *Peace*, the *Agnus Dei*, *Christ our Paschal Lamb*, and the *Benedictus qui venit* were all removed; and the Prayer of Humble Access was placed in a curious and indefensible position following the *Sanctus*. This was followed by the memorial of the Passion, and the Words of Institution by which consecration was effected, the epiclesis being deleted. Communion took place immediately after the recital of the Words of Institution. After communion the Lord's Prayer was said; and it was followed by the oblation of the Canon of 1549, or, if preferred, this might be omitted altogether, and the post-communion thanksgiving be used in its place. Thus was that noble canon mutilated and decimated; and at consecration once

[1] Texts 24 and 57.
[2] Hence the curious compromise which later ensued when the Holy Tables were restored to the original position of the altar, and the celebrant stood at the north *end*.

more, as in the medieval Church, the emphasis was laid upon formula rather than upon prayer.

The *Order for Communion*, having had its unity destroyed by the removal of the Prayer of Humble Access, was now placed before the Prayer of Consecration instead of before communion as formerly. The words of delivery were changed to the last half of the present formula.[1] But the new book did lay greater emphasis upon the more frequent communion of the people. The first book, while it insisted that every celebration must be accompanied by communion of the people, retained the old minimum of yearly communion for each individual. But the second book increased this minimum to three times a year, one of these to be at Easter. There is no mention of the admixture of water to the wine, and although unleavened bread is not forbidden, leavened bread is deemed sufficient. At the end of the rubrics placed after the service the famous 'black rubric' was added; this is believed to have been secured by pressure applied by John Knox[2] and others. Its purpose was to declare that to receive communion kneeling did not mean that thereby 'any adoracioun' was done to 'anye reall and essencial presence . . . of Christ's naturall fleshe and bloude', and it concluded with the remark that 'It is agaynst the trueth of Christes true natural bodye, to be in moe places than in one, at one tyme.'

Ante-Communion—i.e. the eucharistic service to the end of the intercessions, but without consecration and communion—is now to be said on all holy days, in addition to Wednesdays and Fridays, if there are no communicants.[3]

This book, however, was never used in England (although it was extensively used in Scotland),[4] for Mary came to the

---

[1] Yet how little such a change is essentially related to doctrine appears by the fact that nearly all the Reformed rites retained the Scriptural words: 'This is the Body of Christ, &c.' and 'This is the Blood of the New Covenant, &c.'

[2] For Knox's influence on the liturgy, Articles, &c., of the Church of England, see VIII. 14.

[3] See p. 146 above. [4] See pp. 120–1 above.

throne shortly after it was issued, and she restored the old Roman rite.

Under Elizabeth the *Book of Common Prayer*, as revised in 1559,[1] did come into common use in England: this use being established and enforced by law.[2] The revision was but a slight one. The principal changes were to restore the ornaments rubric permitting the use of eucharistic vestments, &c., and to restore the Words of Delivery of 1549, placing them before the words of 1552, thus combining them according to present form. The 'black rubric' was omitted.

No further revision, except for the interlude of the Westminster *Directory*, occurred until 1662, after the Restoration. The chief changes at this time were the reinsertion of the 'black rubric', with the wording altered from 'real and essential presence' to 'corporeal presence', and the addition to the intercessions of a commemoration of the departed. The rubrics also were made more explicit and precise, limiting the freedom of ceremonial. An important change was the extension of the scope of the rubric concerning Ante-Communion to include Sundays as well as holy days, if there were no communicants. The practical result was to make Ante-Communion the principal Sunday Service henceforward in most parishes, communion being celebrated only three or four times a year.[3]

There has been no official revision of the *Book of Common Prayer* since 1662,[4] until the ill-starred attempt of 1927-8. It is needless to recount here its melancholy history. In itself it was a praiseworthy attempt to restore the ancient unity and sequence of the English rite, but a controversy

[1] Texts 24 and 58.

[2] But for some time there was great diversity of practice. See, e.g., Strype, *Parker*, vol. i, p. 302 (Parker Society), describing 'varieties in the service and the administration used' about 1565.   [3] See p. 146, footnote 2.

[4] There have, of course, been revisions in the Dominions, but of these that of the South African Church is the only one of constructive importance, especially its revision of the Prayer of Consecration (published by S.P.C.K., 1927, as an alternative form). The American *Book of Common Prayer* is related rather to the Scottish *B.C.P.* than to the English; see p. 157 below. See III. 8, pp. 795-6.

over Reservation resulted in the rejection of the revised book[1] by Parliament. Since then, however, many diocesans have permitted the use of the revised Order for Communion as an alternative to that of 1662. The schemes of the two orders given in parallel columns makes comparison easy.

B.C.P., 1662	Proposed Book, 1928
The Liturgy of the Word	
Lord's Prayer, said by celebrant alone	Lord's Prayer, said by celebrant alone
Collect for purity	Collect for purity
Decalogue with English *Kyries* and *Incline our hearts*, &c.	Decalogue with English *Kyries* and *Incline our hearts*, &c., or, Christ's Summary of the Law, with threefold English *Kyries*, or, with *Kyries* and *Incline our hearts*, or, Threefold *Kyries* in English (without 'upon us') or in Greek
Collect for the King	
Collect of the day	Collect of the day, and others
Epistle	Epistle
Gospel	Gospel, with *Glory be to thee, O Lord* and *Praise be to thee, O Christ* ·
Nicene Creed	Nicene Creed
	Bidding Prayers, if desired
Sermon or Homily shall follow	Sermon or Homily may follow
	Exhortation, if used
The Liturgy of the Upper Room	
Offertory:	Offertory:
Scripture Sentences, said	Scripture Sentences, said or sung
Collection of alms, &c.	Collection of alms, &c.
Preparation of elements	Preparation of elements, and Admixture
	Special prayers or thanksgivings

[1] Published by the Oxford Press. With this should also be compared the various revisions suggested by the different schools in the Church of England. See Text 59. See also *Anglican Liturgies*, Oxford Press, 1939.

B.C.P., 1662	Proposed Book, 1928
Intercessions, with commemoration of departed	Intercessions, revised and enlarged; including prayer for departed and commemoration of the saints
Exhortation	Exhortation (shortened), if desired
Invitation	Invitation (alternative, shorter)
General Confession	General Confession (or, alternative based on Roman *Confiteor*)
General Absolution	General Absolution (or, alternative form based on Roman)
Comfortable Words	Comfortable Words
	Prayer of Humble Access
	Salutation
Sursum corda	*Sursum corda*
Prayer of Consecration:	Prayer of Consecration:
Preface and Propers (5)	Preface and Propers (11)
Sanctus	*Sanctus*
	Benedictus qui venit
Prayer of Humble Access	
Commemoration of Passion	Commemoration of Passion
Words of Institution with manual acts and Fraction	Words of Institution with manual acts and Fraction
	Anamnesis
	Epiclesis
	Oblation
	Conclusion and Doxology
	Lord's Prayer (Matt. doxology) with protocol
	The Peace
Communion	Communion
Lord's Prayer (Matt. doxology)	
Oblation or Post-communion Thanksgiving	Post-communion Thanksgiving
Gloria in excelsis	*Gloria in excelsis*
Peace and Blessing	Peace and Blessing

There is no mention of an introit, gradual, 'offertory', or 'communion' in the *Book of Common Prayer*, but in practice these are now supplied by the use of hymns or psalms at these points.

The ceremonial of the rite as presently celebrated differs widely in the Church of England, according to the party to which the celebrant belongs.[1]

§ 8. *The Scottish Liturgy in the Scottish Book of Common Prayer*

It was the hope of King Charles I and of his archbishop, William Laud, to unite the Churches of England and Scotland, as the crowns had been united in the person of his father; and, as a step towards that end, he had favoured the preparation of a service book similar to the *Book of Common Prayer* to replace the *Book of Common Order* then in use in the Church of Scotland. This book was at last completed in 1637,[2] after many years of careful preparation. It was not the work of Archbishop Laud, though, as he stated at his trial, 'If I were [the author of that book], I would neither deny nor be ashamed of it.' Two learned Scottish bishops, Wedderburn of Dunblane and Maxwell of Ross, compiled it, and Laud probably carried out the final revision of the manuscript. It was a noble liturgy, closely affiliated to the English rite of 1549, but containing many independent features, as well as some common to the rite of 1552. The lectionary was revised, and festivals related to the Scottish use were included; all the passages from Holy Scripture were from the Authorized Version; the Biblical term 'presbyter' replaced 'priest'; the Communion Table was designated throughout the 'Lord's Table' or the 'holy Table', the one exception being the use of the homely old term 'God's Board' in the rubric before the Prayer of Humble Access. These distinctive features, as Professor Cooper points out, were all a result of Scottish influence.[3]

Familiar to all is the story of the book's unhappy reception in Scotland. On the seventh Sunday after Trinity

[1] On the ceremonial of the English rite, see, among others, VIII. 3, 15, 16.
[2] Edited with introduction and notes in Text 60; and in Text 50, vol. v, which also contains Communion Offices subsequently used by the Nonjurors.   [3] Text 60, pp. xiii–xix.

in the year 1637 the Dean began to read the service in St.
Giles' Cathedral, Edinburgh, when a woman is said to
have flung her stool at his head, thereby precipitating a
riot. But the disturbance went further than Edinburgh.
The National Covenant was presently drawn up and signed,
repudiating not only the King's service book but also de-
manding the abolition of episcopacy. In the following year
the General Assembly met in Glasgow Cathedral and gave
effect to these demands.

The cause of the trouble was not objection to a read
liturgy: the people had long been accustomed to that, and
indeed that very morning the prayers had been read from
the *Book of Common Order*. The cause was twofold: first,
the book was regarded as an 'English book', expressing the
views of a high-handed monarch and a tactless archbishop;
and secondly—and here was the fundamental objection—
the Scottish Church and people regarded it as a breach of
their hereditary liberties that the King, 'without warrant'
from the Church, should attempt to impose the book solely
by royal authority. Such a course was unconstitutional in
Church and State alike.

This liturgy was, therefore, never used in Scotland except
by small groups of Episcopalian separatists early in the next
century, and then not in its entirety. It deserved a better
fate, combining as it did much of the best in the English
rites of 1549 and 1552, and using throughout the noble
version of the Bible first mooted by the General Assembly
at Burntisland in 1601. Nevertheless, because of both its
inherent excellence and its later influence, it is well to
examine the rite here; and this scheme will indicate its
order:

The Liturgy of the Word

The Lord's Prayer; by celebrant alone
Collect for purity
Decalogue with *Kyries* and *Incline our hearts*, &c.
Collect for the King

Collect of the day
Epistle
Gospel, with *Glory be to thee, O Lord,* and *Thanks be to thee, O Lord*
Nicene Creed
Sermon or Homily

The Liturgy of the Upper Room

Offertory:
  Scripture Sentences, said
  Collection of alms
  Preparation of elements
Intercessions, concluding with
  Commemoration of the departed and of the saints
Exhortation and Fencing of Table
Invitation (with an added clause, 'before this congregation', &c.)
General Confession and Absolution
Comfortable Words
Sursum corda
Prayer of Consecration:
  Preface and Propers (5)
  Sanctus
  Commemoration of Passion
  Epiclesis
  Words of Institution, with manual acts and Fraction
  Anamnesis
  Oblation
  Conclusion and Doxology
Lord's Prayer, with protocol
Prayer of Humble Access
Communion (Words of Delivery, 1549)
Post-communion Thanksgiving
Gloria in excelsis
Peace and Blessing

This book was not without influence upon the revisers of the English rite in 1662, but its chief influence was upon the Scottish Episcopalian rite, which began to take form in the eighteenth century.

In 1724 the Liturgy of the Faithful was printed in the 'wee bookies' (little booklets that could be used inserted in or alongside the Anglican *Book of Common Prayer*; it was not till 1912 that the Scottish Episcopalians possessed a prayer-book of their own) and was formally recognized by the Scottish Episcopalian bishops in 1731. The next step was the reordering of the Consecration Prayer with a view to bringing it into closer conformity with the Eastern and primitive rites. For some thirty years experiments in revision were conducted by individuals, but in 1764[1] the Nonjurors' Communion Office was accepted by the Episcopal Church in Scotland, and it remained the rite of that Church until 1912; while, through the influence of Bishop Seabury, it became and still remains, in a slightly revised form, the rite of the Episcopal Church in America.[2]

The Episcopal Church in Scotland, however, which in the nineteenth century was revitalized largely by Englishmen under the influence of the Oxford Movement, authorized the English rite of 1662 as an alternative to the Scottish liturgy; a canon of 1863 even gave the primacy to the English rite, and it was not until the last revision in 1929 that the Scottish liturgy was placed first in the Scottish Prayer Book.

An earlier revision had taken place in 1912. The most important changes were a somewhat clumsy revision of the epiclesis, and the legalizing of reservation and the mixed chalice. The last revision of 1929 has brought the rite to a high standard as a vehicle of devotion. The epiclesis has been again slightly revised, and alternatives to the Decalogue are permitted. The rite is unduly long and not free from a certain pedantry, but it undoubtedly surpasses all other rites in the Anglican Communion (except perhaps the South African) by its adequacy of content, naturalness of sequence, propriety of structure, and fidelity to primitive use. The following scheme, if compared with that on pp. 155–6, will indicate the main changes that have taken place since 1637.[3]

---

[1] This Office edited in Text 61. Its use is still permissible
[2] See American *Book of Common Prayer*.
[3] To compare the developing Scottish rites, see Text 62.

The Liturgy of the Word
Collect for purity
Decalogue in full or shortened form, or Christ's Summary of the
Law, with *Kyries* and *Incline our hearts*, &c.; or, alternatively,
or additionally, a threefold *Kyrie* in English, with 'upon us'.
Salutation and Collects
Epistle or Lection
Gospel, with *Glory be to thee, O Lord*, and *Thanks be to thee, O
Lord, for this thy glorious Gospel*
Nicene Creed
Sermon may be preached
Exhortation, and, or, special prayers and thanksgivings

Offertory: *The Liturgy of the Upper Room*
  Scripture Sentences
  Collection of alms, &c.
  Preparation of elements and admixture
  Blessed be thou, &c. (1 Chron. xxix. 10–12)
Salutation and *Sursum corda*
Prayer of Consecration:
  Preface and Propers (18)
  Sanctus and *Benedictus qui venit*
  Commemoration of Passion
  Words of Institution, with manual acts and Fraction
  Anamnesis and oblation of gifts
  Epiclesis
  Oblation (as in *B.C.P.*)
  Conclusion and Doxology
  Intercession for living and departed
  Commemoration of Saints
  Doxology
Lord's Prayer, with protocol
The Peace, and *Brethren let us love*, &c.
Invitation
General Confession and Absolution.
Comfortable Words
Prayer of Humble Access
Celebrant's and ministers' Communion, while *Agnus Dei* is sung
  People's Communion, recipients responding *Amen*
Little Exhortation, and, or, Post-communion Thanksgiving and
  Propers (12)
Gloria in excelsis
Peace and Blessing

As in the English rite, the introit, gradual, 'offertory', and 'communion' are supplied by psalms or hymns. If a second consecration is required, the epiclesis is said as well as the Words of Institution, not the Words of Institution alone as in the English rite.

§ 9. *Some Modern Liturgies: The Old Catholic, The Catholic Apostolic, and The United Church of Canada*

The Old Catholic Church began its separate existence as a schism from the Roman Church in Holland in 1724, an indirect result of Jansenism. It was further strengthened in 1870 by the accession of those in Germany and Switzerland who refused to accept the decrees of the Council of the Vatican concerning the infallibility and universal episcopate of the Pope. There are also a few Old Catholic communities in England and many more in America.

Its liturgy[1] is a slightly simplified form of the Roman rite, usually but not invariably celebrated in the vernacular. The ceremonial is simple, and hymns are used. In Germany the Canon is supplemented by an epiclesis and a general intercession.

The Catholic Apostolic Church originated in 1835 in England when twelve 'Apostles' were designated by certain prophets. In 1842 it adopted its present liturgy[2] of which Heiler says, 'It is undoubtedly one of the finest and fullest forms of Christian worship. Indeed, of all the liturgies of to-day it comes perhaps nearest to the Primitive Church.'[3] The liturgy, however, contains many elements not Primitive. On the whole the structure is Roman, but much of the content is drawn from the early Eastern liturgies as well as from the Roman rite, the remainder being the work of

---

[1] English edition, Text 63; German edition, Text 64. On doctrine of eucharist, see *Report of the Lambeth Conference* (S.P.C.K., 1930), pp. 142–4. A brief history of the Old Catholic Church is given in the Appendix of Williams and Harris, *Northern Catholicism* (S.P.C.K., 1933), pp. 531–50.

[2] Text 65.

[3] I. 3, p. 109.

the compilers themselves. The Catholic Apostolic liturgy has had a marked influence upon the rite authorized by the Church of Scotland in *Prayers for Divine Service*, an influence that may be traced through the rite compiled and used by the late Rev. Dr. John Macleod of Govan.[1]

The most recent rite, and one of great interest, is that authorized by the United Church of Canada in its *Book of Common Order*, 1932.[2] The United Church of Canada was formed in 1925 by the union of the Presbyterian Church in Canada, the Methodist Church of Canada, and the Congregational Church of Canada. Its eucharistic rite is drawn partly from Scottish (Presbyterian and Episcopalian) sources, and partly from the Anglican rite, derived through Methodist and Congregational usage. Representing as it does the common experience of the united Churches, it is a living rite;[3] and its compilers have been guided by a sound knowledge of liturgical principles. It is a rite that deserves to be widely known. This scheme indicates its structure and content:

The Liturgy of the Word

Psalm or Hymn of Praise as Introit
Collect for purity (*B.C.P.*)
Litany and threefold *Kyries*
Gloria in excelsis, *Benedictus Dominus*, or Hymn of praise and
    humble gratitude
Collect of the day
Lection from Old Testament, or Epistle, or both
Psalm (prose)
Gospel, with 'Thanks be to thee, O Lord, &c.' (Scot. *B.C.P.*)
Sermon
Apostles' or Nicene Creed, or *Te Deum*
Exhortation, brief (if desired)

[1] Privately printed.
[2] Published by the United Church Publishing House, Toronto.
[3] 'The aim of the Committee has been to set forth orders that are loyal to the experience of the Church of all ages and of all lands; orders that carry on the devotional usage of the three uniting Communions in their living integrity . . .'. From the Preface of *Common Order*.

The Liturgy of the Upper Room

Offertory: Collection of people's offerings
    Preparation of Elements
    Psalm, or Hymn sung meanwhile
Cranmer's *Order of Communion*,[1] or Prayer of the Veil
Salutation and *Sursum corda*
Prayer of Consecration:
 Preface and Propers (5)
 Sanctus
 Thanksgiving for Christ's work
 Words of Institution
 Anamnesis
 Epiclesis
 Oblation of worship and self
 Conclusion and Doxology
 Intercessions
 Commemoration of Departed
The Lord's Prayer, with protocol
Fraction
Pax
Celebrant's Communion, Delivery, and People's Communion
Post-communion:
 Thanksgiving and prayer for grace
 Brief Intercession
 Commemoration of Departed
Psalm or Hymn
Blessing, Anglican, or 'Now the God of peace, &c.'

This Order is flexible within proper limits: the hymns may be omitted; the Creed is not compulsory; the Intercessions may, if desired, be used in the Anglican position following the Offertory instead of being joined with the Consecration Prayer; the *Benedictus qui venit*, if used, may follow either the *Sanctus* or the Lord's Prayer; the *Agnus Dei* may be sung during communion; the Words of Institution, besides being used in the Consecration Prayer, may also be read as a warrant after the Offertory; the *Pax* may precede the Prayer of Consecration; and alternatives to Cranmer's *Order of Communion* are the Prayer of the Veil,

---

[1] See p. 145 above.

or a confession and absolution based upon the Roman *confiteor* and *misereatur*. An alternative Canon is also provided in a shorter order, the content of which is similar.

Collects and lections are provided for every Sunday in the year, as also for special seasons. These are drawn largely from the *B.C.P.*, with slight revisions, and a lection from the Old Testament is added for many Sundays, thus restoring the ancient Prophecy.

The litany at the beginning of the rite, adapted from St. Chrysostom, together with the threefold *Kyrie*, is of especial interest, felicitously combining Eastern and Western practice. The Prayer of Consecration is also enriched by including in the ordinary preface a brief thanksgiving for creation and providence, as in Primitive and Eastern use. The wording of the Consecration Prayer is drawn largely from the classical English form in the *B.C.P.*, 1549. The Intercessions and the epiclesis are from *Prayers for Divine Service*. The post-communion thanksgiving and prayer for grace is an English translation of Calvin's prayer; and the concluding intercession is a shortened revision of the celebrant's last prayer in St. Chrysostom's liturgy.

Holy Communion is celebrated monthly or quarterly in the United Church of Canada. The ordinary Sunday morning worship is set out in two directories, based respectively upon the structure of Anglican Morning Prayer and the Eucharist. Throughout, the book is of paramount liturgical interest.

V

THE CHRISTIAN CYCLE OF PRAYER

OUR study thus far has been limited to the central worship of the Church; but worship has a circumference as well as a centre, and piety early sanctified days, weeks, and year by a cycle of daily prayer and praise. This practice may now be briefly examined

§ 1. *The Quire Offices and their Modern Developments*

The origin of the Hours or Quire Offices is no doubt to be sought in Jewish practice; in the Book of Acts[1] the third, sixth, and ninth hours are mentioned as Christian hours of prayer. The *Didaché* states that the Lord's Prayer is to be said three times a day, presumably at the times specified in Acts; and from the third century onwards there is frequent mention of these hours in the Fathers. Prayer was also offered upon retiring and rising. These hours were probably first observed privately, but by the fourth century we find them established in the great churches.

Their early history is obscure, and it is evident that they were not universally observed, nor were they all of the same pattern. The earliest to emerge clearly is the office of Vigils (*vigilare*, 'to watch at night').[2] Its origin may be twofold: a weekly continuation by Jewish converts of the Sabbath services and the 'watching' service on Easter Eve, which St. Augustine declared to be 'the mother of all holy vigils'.[3]

These early services were not fixed by a uniform rule, but their form and content were defined largely by the local bishop. Generally speaking, they consisted of psalms (to which the *Gloria Patri* was early added, transforming the

---

[1] Acts ii. 1, 15; iii. 1; x. 3, 9, 30; cf. Dan. vi. 10.
[2] Cf. Matt. xxiv. 42; 1 Thess. v. 2; &c. Our Lord's many injunctions 'to watch', and St. Paul's metaphor may be the basis of the early belief that Christ would come again in the night.
[3] Sermon 219.

Jewish psalms into Christian hymns), hymns, Scripture lections from the Old and New Testaments, and prayers. They were based upon the Synagogue services, and the psalms were first recited by one voice, the people responding at the end of each verse by some such formula as *Misericordiam et judicium cantabo tibi, Domine*.[1] By the end of the fourth century six hours were widely observed as hours of prayer:[2] cock-crow, or nocturns; daybreak, or lauds; the three hours mentioned in Acts, terce, sext, and none; sunset, or vespers.

It was, however, in the monasteries that they began to take definite and fixed form; and by the sixth century in the West fixed systems emerge. The very multiplication of the services had for long prevented the people from attending them; and they became the chief duty (*officium*, hence 'offices') of the monastics, though they were observed in some measure by the secular clergy as well. By the seventh century they had assumed a generally accepted structure and content (with, of course, many local variations), closely related to the present offices of the Roman Church. Many revisions have taken place since then, and hymns have been added; but these details need not be examined here. The offices were by this time said antiphonally in the quire of the church or abbey (hence 'quire' offices). They existed principally 'for the purpose of the orderly recitation of the Psalter and reading of the Bible', and the sanctification of time, day and night, by prayer and praise. They comprised the antiphonal recitation of psalms, some fixed, others in course, lections from the Holy Scriptures and the Ancient Fathers, canticles, collects, versicles and responses, and, later, hymns. As they assumed fixed forms, they were so constructed that the Old Testament would be read through more or less in course once a year, and the New Testament

---

[1] See St. Augustine's *Confessions*, ix. 12.
[2] As St. John Chrysostom relates; see Homily xiv on 1 Tim. iv, in Migne, *Pat. Graec.* lxii, cols. 575–7.

twice; while the Psalter was recited once a week. By the addition of Prime and Complin, eight or nine services were recited during the twenty-four hours of each day; but later these were said in groups of twos or threes, the number of separate monastic daily services being thus reduced to three or four.[1]

By the time of the Reformation it had become customary for the secular clergy to say the Quire Offices in two groups, in the morning and evening. In accordance with this custom experiments were made by Luther and his followers in revising and modifying these services to fit them for daily use as public morning and evening services.[2] In the Calvinian Churches, however, the Quire Offices disappeared, there being substituted family prayers said morning and evening, meetings of clergy and people on certain days each week for the study of the Holy Scriptures, and Catechism on Sunday afternoons.[3] But the Lutheran device was adopted in the Church of England. During the reign of Henry VIII Cranmer had projected a revision of the Quire Offices, in which he reduced them to two daily services of a common pattern. These appeared in the first *Book of Common Prayer*, 1549, under the titles Mattins and Evensong. This scheme indicates their structure:

The Lord's Prayer, said aloud by the Priest, without doxology
Introduction:
    Versicles and responses (2)
    Gloria Patri, by Priest alone
    Praise ye the Lord, or Alleluia, from Easter to Trinity Sunday
    Venite exultemus (Ps. xcv) with *Gloria Patri*
Psalms for the day, with *Gloria Patri*
Lesson from Old Testament

---

[1] This is a very brief summary. For structure of Quire Offices, see VIII. 1, pp. 347–404. For general description, see III. 7, pp. 555–607, a scholarly summary; briefly and more popularly in III. 11, pp. 137–51; III. 5, pp. 446 sqq.; III. 8, pp. 130 sqq., 257 sqq.; VIII. 17, p. 12. See also interesting modern suggestions in Text 67. The authoritative work is III. 24. And see articles in standard liturgical dictionaries.
[2] Text 26; V. 7, p. 102, n. 13; and pp. 101 and 110 above
[3] V. 7, pp. 92, 102, 177–9.

Te Deum (*Benedicite* in Lent); *Magnificat* at Evensong
Lesson from New Testament
Benedictus Dominus; Nunc dimittis at Evensong
Threefold *Kyrie*, with 'upon us'
Apostles' Creed
Lord's Prayer, said by Priest, except last clause, 'But deliver us
   from evil. Amen', which is people's response
Suffrages: six versicles and responses
Salutation and response
Collect of the day
Collect for Peace
Collect for Grace; for Aid against all perils, at Evensong

The Psalter was to be sung in course each month; the Old
Testament was to be read through, chiefly in course, once
a year; and similarly the New Testament twice each year,
except Revelation, which was read only once. For Sundays
and holy days special courses were provided.

In 1552, at the next revision of the *B.C.P.*, Cranmer
altered the titles to Morning and Evening Prayer, and
framed a Confession of Sins and Absolution, which by a
bold innovation he placed at the beginning of the services,
before the Lord's Prayer, preceded by Scripture Sentences
and an Exhortation. He also added *Jubilate Deo* (Ps. c)
as an alternative to the *Benedictus*, and placed the Creed
immediately following. The salutation was placed before
the *Kyries*, with a bidding to prayer, and the Lord's Prayer
following was to be said by all. The Litany was also to be
used on Sundays, Wednesdays, and Fridays, and at such
other times as the bishop ordained.

In 1662 an anthem, four collects, a general thanksgiving,
and the Grace were added after the Collect for Grace;
or, instead of the collects and thanksgiving, the Litany
might be said or sung. Later, though this was never mentioned in the rubrics, it became customary in many parishes
to preach a sermon after Morning and Evening Prayer.

The importance of the order of Anglican Morning and
Evening Prayer lies in the influence that its structure, and

in part its content, have had upon the worship of the Reformed Churches, particularly in English-speaking countries,[1] during the last half century or more. What was designed and intended for services of daily prayer, a beautiful but subsidiary order, has been adopted, with certain alterations, as the norm of the weekly worship in many of the non-Anglican Churches. This development, at a time when the standard of worship had declined, brought with it many new enrichments; but worship that takes its structure from Morning Prayer must inevitably lack the centrality and objectiveness which characterize the eucharist or even Ante-Communion.

The reason for the adoption of Morning Prayer as the non-Anglican norm in the late nineteenth century is not difficult to discover. We may take the story in Scotland as typical.[2] For some two hundred years worship in Scotland had declined so far as form and order were concerned, until even the reading of the Holy Scriptures found little place in the worship. The sermon was the principal act, but it was preceded and followed by the singing of metrical psalms and by long 'conceived' prayers. During the nineteenth century, particularly during the latter half, there were movements to improve and enrich the worship of the Scottish Church. By this time, however, the true norm of worship in the Reformed Church had been all but forgotten, and was not recognized except by one or two scholars.[3] The attention, therefore, of those who desired to improve the Scottish services found itself, not unnaturally, focused upon

---

[1] But not only in English-speaking countries. Its influence is marked in the French Reformed Church since Bersier's time; cf. p. 119, n. 3, above.

[2] The history in the Congregational and English and Irish Presbyterian Churches is practically the same, save that the Irish have been ultra-conservative. In the Congregational Churches hymnody had an earlier place.

[3] Recognition of the eucharist as the Reformed norm was made difficult, not only by the long period of decadence, but also by the fact that the texts of the early Reformed services were not easily available. The first collation of the Strasbourg services was not made till 1900 when Hubert published Text 38; and in the same year Büchsenschütz (V. 2) was able to show these to be the parent-rites of Calvin's orders. On the whole, see V. 7.

the *Book of Common Prayer* (the only service book in use in the English tongue except that of the Catholic Apostolic Church), and particularly upon the services of Morning and Evening Prayer, which, at that time, were the best known services in the Church of England.

Upon examination, the structure of Morning (and Evening) Prayer was found to approximate to that of the Scottish services if the old Reader's Service[1] was restored to its original place before the Sunday morning service proper. Structurally the chief difference seemed to be only that, in the Scottish service, the great prayer of intercession and thanksgiving followed the sermon. An examination of the order of the Westminster *Directory* also showed that it was not unrelated structurally to Morning Prayer.[2] Once this similarity had become established in the minds of scholars, it was natural that they should turn more and more to Morning Prayer as the norm of Sunday worship; and, in Scotland, the successive editions of *Euchologion*[3] show an increasing conformity to this structure.[4] The content, however, differed considerably: there was greater scope in the Scottish services in the intercessions, which replaced the English collects; the prayers throughout were more varied; the Anglican exhortation was replaced by a prayer of 'invocation'; and, in Scotland, the metrical psalms and hymns were generally preferred to the prose psalms and canticles of the English book. But fundamentally the *structure* was the same, as it still is. It is not possible here to give the scheme of all the non-Anglican modern service books, but that of *Prayers for Divine Service*, 1929 (Church of Scotland) and the *Book of Common Order*, 1928 (former United Free

[1] See Appendix A of V. 7, for the derivation and origin of the Scottish Reader's Service. It is clearly derived from Anglican Morning Prayer as in the *B.C.P.*, 1552.

[2] See Sprott's introduction to Text 68; also compare the scheme on pp. 129–30 (Liturgy of the Word) above with those on p. 169 below.

[3] For *Euchologion*, see p. 134 above.

[4] This also applies to the structure of services in Texts 48, 51–3, 69; see p. 135 above, note 1, and p. 142 above, note 1.

Church of Scotland) may be taken as typical.[1] Their structural similarity is clearly evident when the schemes of the three services are placed in parallel columns. Those parts not mentioned in the texts, but which were later added in common practice to the service, are placed in brackets.

Book of Common Prayer, 1662	Prayers for Divine Service, 1929	Book of Common Order,[2] 1928
(Hymn)	Psalm or Hymn	Psalm or Hymn
Scripture Sentences	Scripture Sentences	Scripture Sentences
Exhortation	Prayer of 'Invocation'	Prayer of 'Invocation'
		Psalm or Hymn
Confession of sins	Confession of sins	Confession of sins
Absolution	Prayer for Pardon	Prayer for Pardon
	Supplications	Supplications
Lord's Prayer	Lord's Prayer	Lord's Prayer
Introduction[3]		
Prose Psalms and *Gloria*	Prose Psalm(s) and *Gloria*	
O.T. Lesson	O.T. Lesson	O.T. Lesson
Canticle	Psalm or Hymn	Hymn or Canticle
N.T. Lesson	N.T. Lesson	N.T. Lesson
Canticle		Hymn
Apostles' Creed	Apostles' Creed	
Kyries		
Lord's Prayer		
Suffrages		
Collects (including any for special occasions)	Intercessions	Thanksgiving
	Communion of Saints	Intercessions
Anthem		
Thanksgiving	Thanksgiving	Communion of Saints
Grace		
(Hymn)	Psalm or Hymn	Hymn or Anthem
(Invocation)	Prayer for Illumination	
(Sermon)	Sermon	Sermon
(Ascription of Praise)	Ascription of Praise	Ascription of Praise
	Collects	
(Collection)	Collection	Collection
(Presented with prayer)	(Presented with prayer)	Presented with prayer
	(Anthem)	
(Hymn)	Psalm or Hymn	Hymn
(Blessing)	Blessing	Blessing

As this table shows, the relationship in *structure* between

[1] An examination of any or of all the service books mentioned on p. 135 above, note 1, makes it apparent that in the structure of the Sunday morning worship they are closely related to these Scottish books, and also to Morning Prayer in the *B.C.P.*

[2] This scheme is taken from the Second Order in this book.

[3] See p. 165 above for the content of the Introduction.

Anglican Morning Prayer and the present Sunday morning worship of the Scottish Church is indisputable. Movements, however, have begun to correct this, and to return to the eucharistic norm.[1] This will provide greater objectivity in the part of the service which precedes the lections, the restoration of the ancient scheme of lections comprising those from the Old Testament, the Epistles, and the Gospels, and a sustained action of prayer after the sermon consisting of thanksgiving, intercession, and oblation.

The structure of the Quire Offices, either in their Anglican or non-Anglican form, should, however, be preserved for the order of Sunday evening worship. The structure of Complin is also specially suitable. By this means, useful variety would be obtained between the morning and evening worship; and these beautiful Offices would not be lost to the Reformed Churches. For daily services, now being widely restored, they are specially fitting; an example of how they can be so used is found in the Church Service Society's publication *Daily Offices*.[2]

§ 2. *The Christian Year*

In common experience certain days stand out from others; this is also true of Christian experience, and it explains how the Christian Year came to be formed. The process was a gradual one, extending over many centuries. It began with the observance of Easter, followed a little later by that of Pentecost or Whitsunday, fifty days after Easter. For long there was no general agreement upon the date of Easter, though the differences were small. The Eastern, Roman, and Gallican Churches had each its own method of arriving at the precise date, while there were also differences within some of these communions. General agreement was reached, however, by the seventh century; and thereafter Easter was

---

[1] See, e.g., the second Directory in the *Book of Common Order* (United Church of Canada), pp. 9–11.

[2] Blackwoods, Edinburgh, 1893. Now out of print; a new revision is urgently needed.

computed to fall on the first Sunday after the Full Moon happening upon or next after March 21st.

The season of Lent[1] early attached itself to Easter, as a time of preparation by confession, discipline or penance, fasting, and prayer. For a long period the precise span of Lent varied, but ultimately it came to be recognized as comprising the forty days preceding Easter, to symbolize the length of our Lord's fast in the wilderness before He began His life's work. In Jerusalem Palm Sunday began to be observed on the Sunday before Easter, and by the ninth century it was generally observed throughout Christendom. It was a natural step to celebrate our Lord's last days and Passion between these two Sundays, hence we have the origin of Holy Week.

Christianity is the Gospel of the Incarnation; it was inevitable that our Lord's birth should also have its special day, though this was fixed much later. In the East January 6th, the date of the Epiphany, was also the festival of the nativity.[2] But in the West, about the fourth century, December 25th was fixed as the day of Christ's birth. Why this date was chosen is now difficult to determine. Duchesne[3] regards the primary reason as being the belief then current that a perfect life must have perfect and unbroken years; and in the early Roman Church March 25th was held to be the date of our Lord's death. Thus, reckoning life as beginning from conception, December 25th would require to be the date of birth. It may have been related also to an attempt to Christianize the Roman *Saturnalia* (though the dates do not quite coincide); more likely, if outside influence played a part, it was chosen to displace the Mithraic feast (*Natalis invicti*) which celebrated the birth of the Sun, and fell on the winter solstice.

---

[1] On the origin of the Lenten fast, see VIII. 18, pp. 105 sqq.

[2] Also the festival of our Lord's Baptism in the East, where it was believed to have taken place twenty-nine years later upon the same day as His birth. On the origin of the festival of the Magi, see VIII. 18, pp. 29–37.

[3] On the whole, see III. 5, pp. 257–65.

Christmas, like Easter, soon had its preceding period of preparation, which embraced both the future and the past. It was known as Advent, and was related both to the first and to the second Coming. It finally settled down to a fixed period of the four Sundays before Christmas.

With Christmas as the celebration of the birth and Easter of the resurrection of our Lord, it is not surprising that the intervening period should be largely occupied with lesser days that celebrated the other events of our Lord's life: His presentation at the Temple, the visit of the Magi, His baptism and temptation, and so forth. After Easter, the events of His risen life were remembered, culminating in the Ascension. Thus we find roughly one-half of the year related primarily to the life and teaching of our Lord.

Ascensiontide was followed by Pentecost, to which, in England, Trinity Sunday succeeded. The period, roughly six months, between Pentecost and Advent came to be devoted to the building up of the Christian life through the empowering work of the Holy Spirit.

Saints' days were observed on special days throughout the year, unrelated to, and often at variance with, the general scheme. Their origin is as early as the second century, the anniversary of the martyrdom of St. Polycarp, instituted at Smyrna immediately after his death c. A.D. 155, being the most ancient known; and such anniversaries became general from the beginning of the third century. They were usually closely associated with the preservation of the saints' relics; and while in the earliest period, as we know from the writings of St. Cyprian, it was the martyr's 'birthday' (i.e. death day) that was kept, later it became customary to keep the day on which the saint's or martyr's relics were deposited in a church.[1] Throughout the Church there was general agreement concerning the festivals of the Apostles and the greater saints; but regarding the lesser saints there were many local differences. During the Middle Ages the multi-

[1] See VIII. 18, pp. 38–57.

plication of saints' days reached preposterous extremes, and they were drastically reduced in number or entirely abolished at the time of the Reformation movement.

The worship of the Church was organized round these days. They gave colour and variety to the Offices, but chiefly to the eucharist with its many 'propers'.[1] Kalendars and lectionaries[2] have not all agreed in detail.

There is need in the Reformed Churches to-day for revision of the existing lectionaries. The short weekly services do not provide time to read the Holy Scriptures in course, as the Reformers intended they should be read.[3] But we may agree with them that the old lectionaries needed to be revised; and that work should now be undertaken. For daily services the lectionary of the provisional B.C.P. (1927) could hardly be bettered, and that in the Scottish B.C.P., together with its selection of psalms for special days and seasons. Another course of Old Testament and New Testament lections should be compiled for Sunday evenings. For the Sunday morning worship, the lectionary should be designed to include generally a lection from the Old Testament, a second from the Epistles, Acts, or Revelation, and a third from the Gospels. Three lections need not be too long, if prudently chosen. This course might well extend over two or three years, with certain great repetitions. It should be so designed as to present the core of Holy Scripture in the Christian perspective.

§ 3. Some Forms of Prayer

In so general a study as this it has been possible only to suggest the wealth and variety of the forms of prayer which the Church has come to possess through the successive ages of her history. If the reader has been led to an examination

[1] For 'propers', see p. 44 above.

[2] On the whole, see III. 25; VIII. 19 and 20; III. 26; III. 8, pp. 201-44, 374-409; III. 7, pp. 611-93; and the dictionary articles.

[3] See pp. 91, 93, 98, 100, 104, 116, 124, 130 above; for modern Reformed lectionaries, see inter alia, Text 48, and for a lectionary for the eucharist or Sunday morning worship, see Text 66. These all require reconsideration.

of those texts to which reference has been made he will have discovered for himself a mine of devotion. It seems fitting, however, to conclude with a brief discussion of some of the historic forms which prayer in the Church has taken.

For those who are members of the Reformed Churches this is especially important; for in the drastic reformation of the old forms which took place in the sixteenth century much that was of permanent value was thoughtlessly discarded. One of the most serious limitations of the Reformed Churches has been their tendency until recently to confine themselves to one or two forms in the public ministry of prayer. This limitation is now beginning to make itself acutely felt; and recent service books have provided greater variety in accordance with the rich inheritance of the Church to-day. These forms may be briefly examined.

Eucharistic Prayer.

This is the most dignified and noble form of prayer. It emerged at an early period as the distinctive form of the Prayer of Consecration at the eucharist. Invariably introduced by the *Sursum corda*, it began by echoing the last response of this call to prayer, and moved into exalted thanksgiving.[1]

It should always be used for the eucharistic consecration; but the experience of the Church has shown that it may also fittingly be used for any high act of thanksgiving and consecration. Thus it is particularly appropriate at the ordination of ministers, at the consecration of a church, the solemnization of a marriage, the giving of thanks at a funeral service, and, in a simplified form, at the sanctification of water at baptism;[2] recently it was very suitably used at the giving of thanks for the twenty-five years' reign of King George V.

---

[1] The eucharistic form of prayer will be found in all the historic liturgies, and in most modern service books.

[2] For examples of these uses, see the Western sacramentaries and pontificals, the English and Scottish *B.C.P.*, and the *B.C.O.* (United Church of Canada).

Litanies.

The litany was probably derived and adapted from the Synagogue worship; in any event, it is one of the earliest forms of Christian prayer. It appears in all Eastern liturgies from the *Apostolic Constitutions* onwards, and is undoubtedly earlier. In the simplest form in which it first appears it comprises a series of intercessory clauses, each followed by the people's response, *Kyrie eleison.* Originally in Christian use it was a form of free prayer, though the petitions soon became traditional; the people knew when to respond by the tone of the leader's voice.

In the Western Church the litany gradually assumed a fixed structure, and was normally sung in procession. It began with a series of Invocations of the Trinity, the Virgin Mary, Saints and Martyrs, with the responses *Lord have mercy upon us, O Christ hear us*, and *Pray for us.* The Deprecations followed: 'From all sin, from all snares, &c.', with the response *O Lord deliver us.* After these came the Obsecrations: 'By the mystery of thy holy incarnation, by thy baptism and fasting, &c.', with the same response as that to the Deprecations. The Suffrages of intercession follow, with the response *We beseech thee to hear us.* The petitions throughout are very brief, consisting only of one clause, the responses following each clause. Examples of this type of litany abound.[1]

At the Reformation a German litany was compiled by Luther; it followed these general principles, but omitted the invocations of the saints, and collated several clauses in order to reduce the number of responses.[2] Cranmer's English litany, based upon the medieval, was formalized further and included certain versicles, the Lord's Prayer, a collect for times of peril, and St. Chrysostom's Prayer.[3]

---

[1] In medieval service books; also in modern Roman missals. See, too, the Dunkeld litany adapted by Dr. Cooper in Text 84; original in Text 85. See also Adamson's article in VI. 16, Aberdeen, 1890.

[2] Text 26.

[3] Contained in the *B.C.P.*

Between the two extremes of the highly formalized litany and the simple spontaneous form of the early Church there is a vast number of intermediate forms. Examples appear in many modern prayer-books;[1] and an examination of these will indicate the variety in corporate prayer of which the litany form admits. Further, litanies may be less formally worded than the stricter forms, and this permits a spontaneity denied to some forms of prayer.

Bidding Prayers.

In its simplest form, the Bidding Prayer is closely allied to the simple litany. It consists of a series of biddings, followed by silent prayer.

It may be varied in many ways. The bidding to prayer may be followed by a versicle and response, e.g.

O Lord, hear our prayer;
And let our cry come unto thee.

Or a collect may follow each bidding; and, if desired, the collect may be preceded by an appropriate versicle and response, or sentence from Holy Scripture. This form of prayer also admits of infinite variety, and is very useful for special prayers. The biddings should be invariably brief, containing only one idea; and, if followed by silent prayer, the silence should be short.[2] Such prayer is best led from the west end of the church, or from the pulpit. At special mission services, biddings may be contributed by the people and written on slips of paper. If used at ordinary services at special times, they should be said from the pulpit either immediately before or after the sermon.

Collects.

The collect is a brief, direct, concise form of prayer governed by strict laws of construction. It is a contribution to devotion peculiar to the Western Church, reaching the

---

[1] Such as Texts 51–4, 56, 59 ('Grey Book', Pt. III), 69–75, &c.
[2] See, e.g., Texts 70 and 59 ('Grey Book') for forms of bidding prayers. Usually they will be compiled privately for the special occasion for which they are required.

most exquisite perfection in the old Roman collects, and also in those of the *B.C.P.* Normally, it consists of five parts,[1] in this order: Invocation, Relative Clause, Petition, Statement of Purpose, Conclusion or Doxology. On occasion. some of these parts may be omitted or interchanged.

The origin of the collect is uncertain, but Dr. Wickham Legg[2] has observed both private and ritual prayers of the structure peculiar to the collect in the Apocrypha[3] and in the ancient Benedictions used at the Morning Service of the Synagogue. These may be nothing more than coincidences, as Burkitt's discovery of a parallel in Horace's *Carmen saeculare* almost certainly is;[4] but they are nevertheless significant. Certainly the structure and brevity of the collect is unmistakable, as Dr. Wickham Legg has shown, in the prayer of the Apostles before the election of St. Matthias:[5]

'*Thou*, Lord, *which* knowest the hearts of all men; *shew* whether of these two thou hast chosen, *that* he may take part of this ministry and apostleship, from which Judas by transgression fell.'

And he further shows how this has been adapted as a collect *pro ordinandis* at Soissons in 1745:[6]

'*Tu*, Domine, *qui* corda nosti omnium, *ostende* quos elegeris accipere locum sancti ministerii; et, *ut* sanctificaris in iis qui appropinquant ad te, *abundantes* gratiae tuae divitias super eos effunde; *per* Dominum, &c.'

That serves also to illustrate the classical form of the

---

[1] In the examples of collects which follow, the beginnings of these parts or clauses are italicized to make recognition easy.

[2] III. 27, pp. 9–21.   [3] 2 Maccabees i. 23–4; 1 Maccabees iv. 30–3.

[4] III. 22, p. 56, where he quotes this stanza (the clause of purpose and the doxology are missing):

> *Alme* Sol, curru nitido diem *qui*
> promis et celas aliusque et idem
> nasceris, *possis* nihil Urbe Roma
> uisere maius.

The fact that the collect was used only in the Western Church may indicate that its origin lay in old Latin pre-Christian prayers. But texts to verify such a conclusion are lacking.

[5] Acts i. 24–5.   [6] Quoted in III. 27, p. 10.

collect in Latin, its native vehicle of expression. An even simpler example is this[1] chosen at random from the Roman missal:

'*Deus, qui* conspicis, quia ex nostra pravitate affligimur; *concede* propitius, *ut* ex tua visitatione consolemur; *qui* vivis, &c.'

It is not possible to state when the collect was first used in Christian worship, but it must have developed early in the West, where it is common to every known liturgy. As early as the fourth century it may be detected in private manuals of devotion, as this example from the Acts of St. Theodora:[2]

'*Pater* Domini nostri Iesu Christi, *adiuua* me, et libera me de meritorio hoc, *qui* adiuuisti Petrum cum esset in carcere; *qui* eduxisti eum sine contumelia, *educ* me sine macula hinc: *ut* omnes uideant, quoniam tua sum ancilla.'

This prayer has two petitions and two modifying clauses, and the concluding doxology is lacking, but the structure is plainly that peculiar to the collect form.

It is not necessary to give further examples of Latin collects, but one[3] may be given from the *Book of Common Prayer*, to indicate how the collect form has been preserved in English through the superb literary and liturgical genius of Cranmer:

'*O Almighty* God, *who* alone canst order the unruly wills and affections of sinful men: *Grant* unto thy people, that they may love the thing which thou commandest, and desire that which thou dost promise; *that so*, among the sundry and manifold changes of the world, our hearts may surely there be fixed, where true joys are to be found; *through* Jesus Christ our Lord.'

Canon Dearmer, in his exposition of the collect,[4] points out that it must have rhythm, finality, conciseness, and

---

[1] Ember Saturday in Advent.
[2] Quoted in III. 27, p. 13. 'The Acts of Theodora', he states, 'claim to be of A.D. 304.'   [3] For the fourth Sunday after Easter.
[4] See the admirable chapter, 'The Art of Making Collects', in I. 9, a valuable study. Collects are found in all the Western liturgies and service books (not in the Eastern); the best in English are those in the *B.C.P.*; but see also Texts 51–6, 68–83, 48.

vigour of thought, and adds: 'We might indeed say that it must be one complete sentence, an epigram softened by feeling; it must be compact, expressing one thought, and enriching that thought so delicately that a word misplaced may destroy its whole beauty.'

Because of its brevity and vigour, the collect compels the attention and co-operation of worshippers. In common worship, collects may be said either singly or in a series, or after biddings and versicles. If used in series, each collect should be concluded with the people's *Amen*.

Suffrages.

These take the form of versicles and responses, chosen mainly from the Psalter. They derive from antiphonal psalmody, and are a constant part of the Quire Offices. An example of their felicitous use is found in this exquisite little litany embedded in the Anglican Morning Prayer.

'*Minister*. The Lord be with you.
Answer. And with thy spirit.
Minister. Let us pray.
Lord, have mercy upon us.
Christ, have mercy upon us.
Lord, have mercy upon us.

Then the Minister, Clerks, and people shall say the Lord's Prayer with a loud voice.

OUR Father which art in heaven, Hallowed be thy Name, Thy kingdom come, Thy will be done, in earth as it is in heaven. Give us this day our daily bread; And forgive us our trespasses, As we forgive them that trespass against us; And lead us not into temptation, But deliver us from evil. Amen.

Then the Minister standing up shall say,

O Lord, shew thy mercy upon us.
Answer. And grant us thy salvation.
Priest. O Lord, save the King.
Answer. And mercifully hear us when we call upon thee.
Priest. Endue thy Ministers with righteousness.
Answer. And make thy chosen people joyful.
Priest. O Lord, save thy people.
Answer. And bless thine inheritance.

Priest. Give peace in our time, O Lord.

Answer. Because there is none other that fighteth for us, but only thou, O God.

Priest. O God, make clean our hearts within us.

Answer. And take not thy Holy Spirit from us.

Then shall follow three Collects.'

Or, a conclusion such as this might fittingly be used at an evening service.

'*Minister.* Into thy hands, O Lord, we commend ourselves, and all whom we love.

Answer. For thou hast redeemed us, O Lord God of truth.

Minister. The eternal God is our refuge.

Answer. And underneath are the everlasting arms.

Minister. The Lord be with you.

Answer. And with thy spirit.

Minister. Let us bless the Lord.

Answer. Thanks be to God.

Minister. May the Almighty and Merciful Lord bless and preserve us.

Answer. Amen.'

The use of such antiphonal prayer would enrich the daily services and the Sunday evening services in the Reformed Churches, creating, as it does, an intimate fellowship of prayer between minister and people. Further examples will be found in the breviaries and in many·modern service books.

The People's Amen.

It is morose sacerdotalism of an acute sort to allow the minister alone to say the *Amen*. Meaning 'So be it', it is a latinized Hebrew word which from remote antiquity has been the people's assent to prayer and praise. It occurs throughout the Old Testament, and its use by the people in Christian worship is mentioned by St. Paul in the New Testament.[1]

It should be said not only at the end of a long prayer, but also at the end of the various parts that compose such a prayer, whether it be a series of collects, or thanksgiving,

[1] 1 Cor. xiv. 16.

intercessions, &c. Thus used, it not only links the worshippers closely with the prayers offered, but also keeps their attention fresh and eager.

The people's *Amen* was retained by all the Churches of the Reformation, but in many Reformed Churches to-day it has dropped out of popular use, and is said only by the minister as an indication that the prayer is ended. Such sacerdotalism has no defence in history or reason; it is not only an impoverishment but a perversion of worship which should cease.

Extemporaneous Prayer.

Extemporaneous or conceived prayer has been a preciously guarded heritage of the Reformed Church, and it should have a place in modern worship. This is now generally recognized, and in 'The Prayer Book as proposed in 1928', a new rubric appeared at the end of 'Occasional Prayers and Thanksgivings', as follows: 'Note, that subject to any direction which the Bishop may give, the Minister may, at his discretion, after the conclusion of Morning or Evening Prayer or of any Service in this Book, offer prayer in his own words.'

William Arthur in *The Tongue of Fire* has said, 'He who never uses a form in public prayer casts away the wisdom of the past; he who will only use forms casts away the hope of utterance to be given by the Spirit at present'. If by 'form' Arthur means prayers that have come down to us written by others, his words are timely and true. But if his apophthegm is meant to present an antithesis between 'using forms' and 'not using forms', it is superficial and untrue. Forms are inevitable in any act of public worship, unless it be a Quaker meeting; and the choice is never between forms and no forms, but always between good forms and bad forms. The leader of public worship cannot escape the use of forms, even when 'extemporizing', any more than can a musician. The problem is to choose and adapt forms for particular purposes. Worship in a mission church need not follow the same lines as that in a cathedral; yet the need for differentiation is easily exaggerated.

When extemporaneous prayer is used, care should be taken to safeguard it from crudity of expression; it should be ordered, brief, and simple. Fervency is not achieved by floridity. All homiletic propensities should be resolutely avoided;[1] didactic prayer is a crude degradation of worship.

Extemporaneous prayer makes exacting demands upon those who use it. It requires careful preparation of heart and mind by constant study of the devotional literature of the Church and of Holy Scripture. Such preparation will create a taste for simplicity and sobriety in prayer, and will prevent the shamelessness of eloquent or over-familiar prayer to Almighty God.

[1] 'I do observe', wrote Benjamin Whichcote in the seventeenth century, 'a great deal in conceived prayer which is good, but may do better in the sermon.' On style in prayer, see I. 9; VIII. 5, 6.

LAUS DEO

BIBLIOGRAPHY

[*In some sections a few of the more important English works are marked with an asterisk, in order to help any who may be approaching a study of the subject for the first time.*]

I. THE THEORY OF WORSHIP

1. WILL, R. *Le Culte.* 3 vols. Paris, 1926, &c.
2. HEILER, F. *Das Gebet.* Munich, 1918. (Eng. translation, without references, by McComb. Oxford, 1932).
3. HEILER, F. *The Spirit of Worship.* London, 1926.
4. *SIMPSON, R. S. *Ideas in Corporate Worship.* Edinburgh, 1927.
5. *UNDERHILL, E. *Worship.* London. 1936.
6. *MICKLEM, N. (Editor). *Christian Worship.* By Members of Mansfield College. Oxford, 1936.
7. MICKLEM, E. R. *Our Approach to God.* London, 1934.
8. DEARMER, P. *The Church at Prayer.* London, 1923.
9. *DEARMER, P. *The Art of Public Worship.* London, 1919.
10. SPERRY, W. L. *Reality in Worship.* New York, 1928.
11. BYINGTON, E. H. *The Quest for Experience in Worship.* New York, 1928.
12. VOGT, von Ogden. *Modern Worship.* Yale, 1927.
13. VOGT, von Ogden. *Art and Religion.* Yale, 1921.
14. *RATTENBURY, J. E. *Vital Elements of Public Worship.* London, 1936.
15. *STONE, D. *The History of the Doctrine of the Holy Eucharist.* 2 vols. London, 1909.
16. *WOTHERSPOON, H. J. *Religious Values in the Sacraments.* Edinburgh, 1928.
17. *BRASNETT, B. R. *God the Worshipful.* London, 1935.
18. *BARCLAY. A. *The Protestant Doctrine of the Lord's Supper.* Glasgow, 1927.
19. HARDY, R. *Worship and Intercession.* London, 1936.
20. PUGLISI, M. *Prayer.* New York, 1929. (Contains extensive bibliography.)

II. WORSHIP IN THE PRIMITIVE CHURCH

1. *OESTERLEY, W. O. E. *The Jewish Background of the Christian Liturgy.* Oxford, 1925.
2. OESTERLEY and BOX. *Religion and Worship of the Synagogue.* London, 2nd ed. 1911.
3. MOORE, G. F. *Religion and Worship of the Synagogue.*
4. *WOOLLEY, R. M. *The Liturgy of the Primitive Church.* Cambridge, 1910.
5. *SRAWLEY, J. H. *The Early History of the Liturgy.* Cambridge, 2nd ed. 1947.

6. WARREN, F. E. *The Liturgy and Ritual of the Ante-Nicene Church.* London, 2nd ed. 1912.
7. MACDONALD, A. B. *Christian Worship in the Primitive Church.* Edinburgh, 1934.
8. MACGREGOR, G. H. C. *Eucharistic Origins.* Glasgow, 1928.
9. *WELCH, A. C. *Prophet and Priest in Old Israel.* London, 1936.

III. EASTERN AND WESTERN WORSHIP

1. *FORTESCUE, A. K. *The Orthodox Eastern Church.* London, 1907.
2. FORTESCUE, A. K. *The Lesser Eastern Churches.* London, 1913.
3. FORTESCUE, A. K. *The Uniate Eastern Churches.* London, 1923.
4. *KIDD, B. J. *The Churches of Eastern Christendom from A.D. 451.* London, 1927.
5. *DUCHESNE, L. *Christian Worship, its Origin and Evolution.* London, 5th ed. 1920.
6. *FORTESCUE, A. K. *The Mass: A Study in the Roman Liturgy.* London, ed. 1922.
7. AIGRAIN, R. (Editor). *Liturgia.* Bloud and Gay, Paris, 1931.
8. *CLARKE, W. K. Lowther (Editor). *Liturgy and Worship.* London, 1932.
9. LIETZMANN, H. *Messe und Herrenmahl.* Bonn, 1926.
10. *CABROL, F. *The Mass of the Western Rites.* London, 1934.
11. CABROL, F. *Liturgical Prayer.* London, 1922.
12. WARREN, F. E. *The Liturgy and Ritual of the Celtic Church.* Oxford, 1881.
13. JAMES, E. O. *Christian Myth and Ritual.* London, 1933.
14. *BRILIOTH, Y. *Eucharistic Faith and Practice, Evangelical and Catholic.* London, 1930.
15. HISLOP, D. H. *Our Heritage in Public Worship.* Edinburgh, 1935.
16. *DRURY, T. W. *Elevation in the Eucharist, its History and Rationale.* Cambridge, 1907.
17. *FRERE, W. H. *The Principles of Religious Ceremonial.* London, rev. ed. 1928.
18. FORTESCUE, A. K. *The Ceremonies of the Roman Rite Described.* London, 3rd ed. 1930.
19. DREWS, P. *Studien zur Geschichte des Gottesdienstes.* Tübingen and Leipzig, 1902.
20. ATCHLEY, E. G. C. F. *On the Epiclesis of the Eucharistic Liturgy.* Alcuin Club, 1935.
21. BISHOP, E. *Liturgica Historica.* Oxford, 1918.
22. *BURKITT, F. C. *Christian Worship.* Cambridge, 1930.
23. *LEGG, J. Wickham. *Three Chapters in Recent Liturgical Research.* London, 1903.
24. BATIFFOL, P. *History of the Roman Breviary.* London, 1912.

25. Guéranger, P. *The Liturgical Year.* 15 vols. London, 1901.
26. Frere, W. H. Studies in the Early Roman Liturgy: I. *The Calendar*; II. *The Roman Gospel-Lectionary.* Alcuin Club, 1930, 1934.
27. Legg, J. Wickham. *Essays Liturgical and Historical.* London, 1917.

IV. LUTHERAN WORSHIP

English works on Lutheran worship are lacking, but chapters will be found in III, 14, 15 and in I, 2, 3. See also Texts 32-4. The following are some of the principal German works.

1. Graff, P. *Geschichte der Auflösung der alten gottesdienstlichen Formen.* Göttingen, 1921.
2. Heiler, F. *Katholische und evangelische Gottesdienstordnungen.* Munich, 1925.
3. Rendtorff, F. *Geschichte des christlichen Gottesdienstes unter dem Gesichtspunkt der liturgischen Erbfolge.* Giessen, 1924.
4. Drews, P. *Beiträge zu Luthers liturgischen Reformen.* Tübingen, 1910.
5. Waldsmaier, H. *Die Entstehung der evangelischen Gottesdienstordnungen Süddeutschlands im Zeitalter der Reformation.* Leipzig, 1916.
6. Fendt, L. *Der lutherische Gottesdienst des 16ten Jahrhunderts.* Munich, 1923.
7. Otto, R. *Zur Erneuerung und Ausgestaltung des Gottesdienstes.* Giessen, 1925.
8. Otto, R. *Das Jahr der Kirche.* Gotha, 1927.
9. Otto, R. *Chorgebete.* Giessen, 1928.

V. CONTINENTAL REFORMED WORSHIP

1. Erichson, A. *Die calvinische und die altstraßburgische Gottesdienstordnung.* Strasbourg, 1894.
2. Büchsenschütz, L. *Histoire des liturgies en langue allemande dans l'Église de Strasbourg au seizième siècle.* Cahors, 1900.
3. Smend, J. *Der erste evangelische Gottesdienst in Straßburg.* Strasbourg, 1897.
4. Doumergue, E. *Essai sur l'histoire du culte réformé.* Lausanne, 1890.
5. Doumergue, E. *Jean Calvin*, vol. ii. Lausanne, 1902.
6. Doumergue, E. *La Genève Calviniste.* Lausanne, 1905.
7. *Maxwell, W. D. *John Knox's Genevan Service Book, 1556.* Edinburgh, 1931.
8. Herminjard, A. L. *Correspondance des Réformateurs dans les pays de la langue française.* Geneva and Paris, 1866-97.
9. Douen, O. *Clément Marot et le Psautier Huguenot.* Paris, 1878-9.
See also chapters in III. 14.

VI. WORSHIP IN THE CHURCH OF SCOTLAND

For the origins of Scottish Reformed worship, see *V. 7.

1. *McMILLAN, W. *The Worship of the Scottish Reformed Church, 1550-1638.* London, 1931
2. *LEISHMAN, T. *The Ritual of the Church of Scotland.* Contained in Principal Story's *The Church of Scotland, Past and Present,* vol. iv. London, N.D.
3. *SPROTT, G. W. *Worship and Offices of the Church of Scotland.* Edinburgh, 1882.
4. LEE, R. *The Reform of the Church of Scotland.* Edinburgh, 1864.
5. *WOTHERSPOON, H. J., and KIRKPATRICK, J. M. *A Manual of Church Doctrine.* London, 1919.
6. M'CRIE, C. G. *Public Worship in Presbyterian Scotland.* Edinburgh, 1892.
7. BANNERMAN, D. D. *The Worship of the Presbyterian Church.* London, 1884.
8. The Church Service Society *Annuals.* Edinburgh, 1928 &c.
9. MACGREGOR, D. *Early Scottish Worship.* Lee Lecture. Edinburgh, 1896.
10. LEISHMAN, T. *The Moulding of the Scottish Reformation.* Lee Lecture. Edinburgh, 1897.
11. SPROTT, G. W. *The Worship of the Church of Scotland during the Covenanting Period, 1638-61.* Lee Lecture. Edinburgh, 1893. (See also W. McMillan's *John Hepburn and the Hebronites.* London, 1934.)
12. KERR, J. *The Renascence of Worship.* Edinburgh, 1909.
13. DUNCAN, Andrew. *The Scottish Sanctuary.* Edinburgh, N.D.
14. GIBSON, James. *The Public Worship of God.* Edinburgh, 1869.
15. 'The Liturgy of the Church of Scotland'. Article in the *Edinburgh Review,* January-April, 1852.
16. *Transactions of the Scottish Ecclesiological Society.*

*See also the important introductions to the texts published by the Church Service Society (Texts 42-4, 46-7, 60), and the works mentioned in Text 48.

VII. ENGLISH PURITAN WORSHIP

1. BAIRD, C. W. *Eutaxia, or, a Chapter on Liturgies.* London, 1856.
2. PEEL, A. (Editor). *Essays Congregational and Catholic.* London, 1931.

For the origins of English Puritan worship, see *V. 7. See also the Publications of the Parker Society, London; I. 6; and Texts 49-54, 66.

VIII. ANGLICAN WORSHIP

1. *PROCTER and FRERE. *A New History of the Book of Common Prayer.* London, ed. 1925.

2. *GASQUET and BISHOP. *Edward VI and the Book of Common Prayer.* London, 1890.
3. *DEARMER, P. *The Parson's Handbook.* Oxford, 10th ed. 1921.
4. DEARMER, P. *The Story of the Prayer Book.* Oxford, 1933.
5. *DOWDEN, J. *The Workmanship of the Prayer Book.* London, 2nd ed. 1904.
6. *DOWDEN, J. *Further Studies in the Prayer Book.* London, 1908.
7. *DOWDEN, J. *The Scottish Communion Office, 1764.* Oxford, 1922.
8. PERRY, W. *The Scottish Liturgy.* London and Edinburgh, 1922.
9. *PERRY, W. *The Scottish Prayer Book, its Value and History.* Cambridge, 1929.
10. *FRERE, W. H. *Some Principles of Liturgical Reform.* London, 1914.
11. SWETE, H. B. *Services and Service-Books before the Reformation.* London, 1896.
12. WORDSWORTH, C. *Medieval Services in England.* London, 1898.
13. WORDSWORTH and LITTLEHALES. *The Old Service Books of the Reformation.* London, 1904.
14. LORIMER, P. *John Knox and the Church of England.* London, 1875.
15. DEARMER, P. *The Server's Handbook.* Oxford, 1932.
16. *A Directory of Ceremonial.* Alcuin Club, 1924.
17. HOSKINS, E. *Primers, Sarum, York, and Roman.* London, 1901.
18. *STALEY, V. *Liturgical Studies.* London, 1907.
19. DOWDEN, J. *The Church Year and Calendar.* Cambridge, 1910.
20. STALEY, V. *The Liturgical Year.* London, 1907.
21. *EELES, F. C. *Traditional Ceremonial and Customs connected with the Scottish Liturgy.* Alcuin Club, 1910.

IX. WORKS ON CHURCH ARCHITECTURE

1. *SHORT, E. H. *The House of God.* London, 1925. (See also new and revised edition, 1936, entitled *A History of Religious Architecture.*)
2. TYRRELL-GREEN, E. *Parish Church Architecture.* London, 1924.
3. *DRUMMOND, A. L. *The Church Architecture of Protestantism.* Edinburgh, 1934.
4. *HANNAH, I. C. *The Story of Scotland in Stone.* Edinburgh, 1934.
5. *MACGIBBON and ROSS. *The Ecclesiastical Architecture of Scotland.* 3 vols. Edinburgh, 1896-7.
6. COX and FORD. *The Parish Churches of England.* London, 1935.
7. BATSFORD and FRY. *The Cathedrals of England.* London, 2nd ed. 1935.
8. CROSSLEY, F. H. *The English Abbeys.* London, 1935.
9. *POWYS, A. R. *The English Parish Church.* London, 1930.
10. THOMPSON, A. H. *The Historical Growth of the English Parish Church.* Cambridge, 1911.
11. THOMPSON, A. H. *The Ground Plan of the English Parish Church.* Cambridge, 1911.

12. Cox and Harvey. *English Church Furniture*. London, 2nd ed. 1908.
13. Cox, J. C. *Pulpits, Lecterns, and Organs*. Oxford, 1915.
14. Lamborn, E. A. G. *The Parish Church*. Oxford, 1929.
15. Jones, R. P. *Nonconformist Church Architecture*. London, 1914.

X. WORKS ON CHURCH PRAISE

The recent valuable book, *Music and Worship*, by Walford Davies and Harvey Grace, London, 1935, contains an excellent bibliography, which it is unnecessary to repeat here. The following additions may be found useful.

1. *Aigrain, R. *Religious Music*. Translated by C. Mulcahy. London, Sands & Co. N.D.
2. *Gardner and Nicholson. *Manual of English Church Music*. London, 1923.
3. *Manual of Church Praise*. Church of Scotland. Edinburgh, 1932.
4. Patrick, Millar. *The Story of the Church's Song*. Edinburgh, 1927.
5. Stewart, G. Wauchope. *Music in Church Worship*. London, 1926.
6. Stewart, G. Wauchope. *Music in the Church*. London, 1914.
7. Moffatt, J., and Patrick, Millar. *Handbook to the Church Hymnary, with Supplement*. Oxford, 1935.
8. Macmillan, A. *Hymns of the Church*. Toronto, 1934.
9. Longford, W. W. *Music and Religion*. London, N.D.
10. Fleming, G. T. *The Music of the Congregation*. London, 1923.
11. Hadow, W. H. *Church Music*. London, 1926.
12. Nicholson, S. H. *Church Music*. London, N.D.
13. Duncan-Jones, A. S. *Church Music*. London, 1920.
14. Richardson, A. M. *Church Music*. London, 2nd ed. 1905.
15. Livingston, Neil. *The Scottish Psalter of 1635, with Dissertations*. Glasgow, 1864.
16. Terry, R. R. *Calvin's First Psalter (1539)*. London, 1932.
17. Terry, R. R. *A Forgotten Psalter*. Oxford, 1929.
18. Terry, R. R. *The Scottish Psalter of 1635*. London, 1935.
19. Macmeeken, J. W. *History of the Scottish Metrical Psalms*. Glasgow, 1872.
   Maclagan, D. J. *The Scottish Paraphrases*. Edinburgh, 1889.
20. *Nicholson, S. H. *Quires and Places where they sing*. London, 1932.
21. Dickinson, E. *Music in the History of the Western Church*. London, 1902.

XI. LITURGICAL TEXTS AND COMPILATIONS

1. Linton, A. *Twenty-five Consecration Prayers*. London, 1921.
2. Cresswell, R. H. *The Liturgy of the VIIIth Book of the Apostolic Constitutions*. London, ed. 1934.

3. WORDSWORTH, J. *Bishop Sarapion's Prayer Book*. London, ed. 1923.

4. EASTON, B. Scott. *The Apostolic Tradition of Hippolytus*, translated with Introduction and Notes. Cambridge, 1934.

5. BRIGHTMAN, F. E. *Liturgies, Eastern and Western*, vol. i. Oxford. 1896.

6. NEALE and LITTLEDALE. *Translations of the Primitive Liturgies*. London, 2nd ed. 1869. See also *Liturgies and other Documents of the Ante-Nicene Period*. Edinburgh, 1872.

7. HAPGOOD, I. F. *The Service Book of the Holy Orthodox-Catholic Apostolic (Graeco-Russian) Church*, compiled, translated, and arranged from old Church-Slavonic Service Books of the Russian . . . and Greek Church. Cambridge, U.S.A., 1906.

8. MAUGHAN, H. H. *The Liturgy of the Eastern Orthodox Church*. London, 1916.

9. PULLAN, Leighton. *A Guide to the Holy Liturgy of St. John Chrysostom*. London, 1921.

10. RILEY, A. *A Guide to the Divine Liturgy in the East*. London, 1922.

11. KUVOCHINSKY, P. *The Divine Liturgy of the Holy Orthodox Catholic Apostolic Graeco-Russian Church*. London, Cope & Fenwick, 1909.

12. JOHN, MARQUIS OF BUTE. *The Coptic Morning Service for the Lord's Day*. London, Cope & Fenwick, 1908.

13. TWO ARMENIAN PRIESTS. *The Armenian Liturgy*. London, Cope & Fenwick, 1908.

14. HARDEN, J. M. *The Anaphoras of the Ethiopic Liturgy*. London, 1928. With this compare Prof. Mercer's *The Ethiopic Liturgy*, Chicago, 1915, a transcription and translation, the translation unfortunately inaccurate at many points. See also VI. 8, year 1936–7.

15. NEALE and FORBES. *Gallican Liturgies*. London, 1855.

15 a. LIETZMANN, H. *Liturgiegeschichtliche Quellen*. 1918 *sqq*.

16. HAMMOND, C. E. *Liturgies, Eastern and Western*. Oxford, 1878.

17. ATCHLEY, E. G. C. F. *The Ambrosian Liturgy*. London, Cope & Fenwick, 1909.
    EELES, F. C. *The Mozarabic Liturgy*. London, Cope & Fenwick, 1909.

18. WARNER, G. F. *The Stowe Missal* (Facsimile and transcription). Henry Bradshaw Society, 1906–15.

19. PLUMMER, C. *Irish Litanies*. Henry Bradshaw Society, 1925.

20. FELTOE, C. L. *Sacramentarium Leonianum*. Cambridge, 1896.

21. WILSON, H. A. *Gelasian Sacramentary*. Oxford, 1894.

22. MURATORI. *Liturgia romana vetus*, ii. Venice, 1748.

23. ATCHLEY, E. G. C. F. *Ordo romanus primus*. London, 1905.

24. BRIGHTMAN, F. E. *The English Rite*. 2 vols. London, 1915.

25. RILEY, A. *A Guide to High Mass Abroad*. London, 1908.

26. LUTHER, M. *Werke*. Weimar ed.

190   BIBLIOGRAPHY

27. SMEND, J. *Die evangelischen deutschen Messen bis zu Luthers deutscher Messe.* Göttingen, 1896.
28. RICHTER, A. L. *Die evangelischen Kirchenordnungen.*
29. SEHLING, E. *Die evangelischen Kirchenordnungen des XVI Jahrhunderts.* 5 vols. Leipzig, 1902 &c.
30. WACE and BUCHHEIM. *Luther's Primary Works.* London, 1896.
31. Modern Lutheran Service Books: Those in Germany in present use obtainable through Berlin Booksellers. For English translations, &c., see Texts 32–4.
32. YELVERTON, E. E. *The Swedish Rite.* London, 1921.
33. HOLLOWAY, H. *The Norwegian (and Danish) Rite.* London, 1934.
34. American Service Books of the Lutheran Church in English: *The Common Service Book of the Lutheran Church.* New York, 1917; *The Evangelical Book of Worship*, compiled by the German Evangelical Synod of N.A. Eden Publishing House. New York, 1916.
35. BRETSCHNEIDER. *Corpus Reformatorum.* Brunswick, 1834 &c.
36. KIDD, B. J. *Documents illustrative of the Continental Reformation.* Oxford, 1911.
37. DANIEL. *Codex liturgicus.*
38. HUBERT, F. *Die Straßburger liturgischen Ordnungen im Zeitalter der Reformation.* Göttingen, 1900.
39. SMEND, J. *Der erste evangelische Gottesdienst in Straßburg.* Strasbourg, 1897.
40. BAUM, J. G. *La manière et fasson quon tient es lieux que Dieu, de sa grace a visités.* The first liturgy of the Reformed Churches of France, transcribed from the original. Strasbourg and Paris, 1859.
41. There are numerous French forms, and, while printed by authority, they are standards of worship rather than compulsory service books. Each Swiss canton has its own Church and service book: Vaud, Bern, Zürich, Bâle, Neuchâtel, &c. Of these, that of Neuchâtel is of special interest, for the influence of the famous divine, Osterwald, is marked in its compilation. Three others may be mentioned: *La Liturgie de l'Église de Genève*, last ed., Geneva, 1892; *La liturgie des Églises réformées évangéliques de France*, Paris, rue de Clichy, 4; and *La Liturgie d'Eugène Bersier*, Paris, Avenue de la grande Armée, 54. This last was compiled by M. Bersier for use in his own congregation in Paris, the first edition appearing in 1874, but followed by many successive editions; in it the influence of Morning Prayer in the Anglican *Book of Common Prayer* is marked, and the book itself has had a wide influence upon the worship of the French Reformed Church.
42. WOTHERSPOON, H. J. *The Second Prayer Book of Edward VI.* Edinburgh, 1905.
43. SPROTT, G. W. *The Book of Common Order.* Edinburgh, 1901.
44. SPROTT, G. W. *The Liturgy of Compromise.* (Bound with Text 42). Edinburgh, 1905.

45. HUYCKE, W. *The forme of common praiers vsed in the churches of Geneua . . . translated out of the frenche into Englyshe.* London . . . June, 1550. (There is no modern edition of this important source, but copies of the original are in the British Museum. See also V. 7, pp. 71, 220; in this work (V. 7) all the passages relevant to the Scottish *Book of Common Order* are quoted.)

46. SPROTT, G. W. *Scottish Liturgies of James VI.* Edinburgh, 1901.

47. LEISHMAN, T. *The Westminster Directory.* Edinburgh, 1901.

48. The following are the principal Service Books, official and unofficial, used in Presbyterian Churches throughout the world; together with books containing collections of prayers:

Prayers for Divine Service (Church of Scotland). Edinburgh, best ed. 1923; rev. ed. 1929.

The Book of Common Order (United Free Church of Scotland) Oxford, 1928.

Ordinal and Service Book for the Use of Presbyteries (Church of Scotland). Edinburgh and Glasgow, 1931.

The Scotch Minister's Assistant. Inverness, 1802. A second and revised ed. was published in Aberdeen, 1822, entitled *The Presbyterian Minister's Assistant.*

ANDERSON, James. *The Minister's Directory.* Edinburgh, 1856. Revised ed., 1862.

LISTON, W. *The Service of God's House.* Glasgow, 1866.

A. K. H. B. *A Scotch Communion Sunday.* London, 1873.

MILROY, W. *A Scottish Communion.* Paisley, 1882.

MILNE, Robt. *Directory and Guide to the Ministerial Office of the Church of Scotland.* Edinburgh, 1888.

Euchologion (Church Service Society). Edinburgh, 1867. Many successive editions, the last being 1929 and the most important the edition annotated by G. W. Sprott, 1905, which contains a historical introduction.

Presbyterian Forms of Service (Church Worship Assoc. of United Presbyterian Church). Edinburgh, 1891, 1894.

Directory and Forms for Public Worship (Church Worship Assoc. of United Free Church). Edinburgh, 1920.

Anthology of Prayers (do.). Edinburgh, 1920.

Directory of Public Worship (Presbyterian Church of England). London, 1898, 1921.

Book of Common Order (United Church of Canada). Toronto, 1932.

Book of Common Order (Presbyterian Church in Canada). Oxford, 1922.

Book of Common Worship (Presbyterian Church in U.S.A.). Philadelphia, 1905, 1906, &c. Revised in 1932.

Service Book and Ordinal (Presbyterian Church of South Africa). Glasgow, 1921, 1928.

Book of Common Order, Part I, Sacraments and other Offices (Presbyterian Church of Australia). Sydney, 1921.

The Liturgy of the Reformed Church in America. New York, 1924; see introduction for earlier editions from 1770 onwards.

Order of Worship for the Reformed Church in U.S.A. Philadelphia, 1866.

HODGE, A. A. *A Manual of Forms.* Philadelphia, 1882.

Prayers for the Christian Year (Church of Scotland). Oxford, 1935.

A Book of Common Order (St. Giles' Cathedral). Edinburgh, 1884.

MACLEAN, Norman. *Services for Holy Week and Easter, as used in St. Cuthbert's Parish Church.* Edinburgh, 1929.

PATRICK, Millar. *The Scottish Collects of 1595.* Edinburgh, 1933.

McMILLAN, W. *One Hundred Scottish Prayers* (Church of Scotland). Edinburgh, 1933. Contains references to many other Scottish Service Books.

Daily Offices of the Book of Common Order (Church Service Society). Edinburgh, 1893.

Home Prayers (Church Service Society). Edinburgh, 1882.

MACLEOD, W. H. *Offices for Occasional Use.* Gibson & Sons, Glasgow, N.D.

Presbyterian Liturgies with Specimens of Forms of Prayer used in the Continental, Reformed, and American Churches, by a Minister of the Church of Scotland. London and Edinburgh, 1858.

WOTHERSPOON, H. J. *The Divine Service.* London, 2nd ed. revised, 1929.

Form and Order for the Celebration of the Lord's Supper or Holy Communion used by the Moderator at the General Assembly. Edinburgh, 1936.

Forms of Prayer for Use at Sea. Edinburgh, 1936.

49. HALL, P. *Reliquiae liturgicae.* 5 vols. Bath, 1847.

50. HALL, P. *Fragmenta liturgica.* 7 vols. Bath, 1848.

51. HUNTER, J. *Devotional Services for Public Worship.* Last revision, Glasgow, 1901.

52. ORCHARD, W. E. *Divine Service.* Oxford, 1919. Revised ed. 1926.

53. *A Free Church Book of Common Prayer.* London, 1929.

54. *Book of Congregational Worship.* London, 1920.

55. *The Book of Public Prayers and Services for the use of the People called Methodists.* Epworth Press, London.

The Ritual of the Methodist Episcopal Church. New York, 1916.

The Doctrine and Discipline of the Methodist Church of Canada. Ryerson Press, Toronto, 1922.

56. *Divine Worship.* Published by Authority of the Methodist Conference. Epworth Press, London, 1936.

57. FRERE, W. H. *Use of Sarum.* Cambridge, 1898.

LEGG, J. Wickham. *The Sarum Missal.* Oxford, 1916.

58. BENHAM, E. *The Prayer Book of Queen Elizabeth.* Edinburgh, 1909.
59. Suggested revisions of the *Book of Common Prayer* before 1928: The 'Grey Book', and the 'Green Book', published by the Oxford Press; the 'Orange Book', published by the Faith Press, London. See also the 'Book proposed to be annexed to the Prayer Book Measure 192–', London, 1927.
60. COOPER, J. *The Book of Common Prayer for the use of the Church of Scotland, commonly known as Laud's Liturgy.* Edinburgh, 1904.
61. DOWDEN, J. *The Scottish Communion Office, 1764.* Oxford, 1922.
62. LEMPRIÈRE, P. A. *Scottish Communion Offices of 1637, 1735, 1755, 1764, 1889, together with the English Liturgy of 1549, arranged to show their variations.* Edinburgh, 1909.
63. DE VOIL and WYNNE BENNETT. *Old Catholic Eucharistic Worship.* London, 1936.
    MATHEW, A. H. *The Old Catholic Missal and Ritual.* Cope & Fenwick, London, 1909.
64. *Gebetbuch der christkatholischen Kirche der Schweiz.* Solothurn, 1917.
65. *The Liturgy and other Divine Offices of the Church.* London, 1899.
66. *The Book of Common Order,* 1932. United Church of Canada. Toronto, 1932.
67. HEILER, F., *Evangelisch-katholisches Brevier.* Munich, 1932.
68. *Euchologion.* Annotated by G. W. Sprott. Edinburgh, 1905.
69. *The Rodborough Bede Book.* Privately printed for the Revd. C. E. Watson, Rodborough, Stroud.
70. MILNER-WHITE and SMITH. *Cambridge Offices and Orisons.* London, 1921.
71. DEARMER and BARRY. *Westminster Prayers.* Oxford, 1936.
72. *Book of Prayers.* S.C.M. London.
73. FOX, S. F. *A Chain of Prayer across the Ages.* London, 3rd ed. 1923.
74. SKRINE, J. H. *Hymns, Litanies, and Prayers for a Village.* London, 1910.
75. BENSON, E. W. *Prayers, Public and Private.* London, 1899.
76. MILNER-WHITE, E. *A Cambridge Bede Book.* London, 1936. *Memorials upon Several Occasions.* London, 1930.
77. MILNER-WHITE, E. *Occasional Prayers of the 1928 Book reconsidered.* London, 1930.
78. SHEPPARD, H. R. L. *This Day. A collection of simple Prayers, made from those used at the Daily Broadcast Service.* London.
79. BRIGHT, W. *Ancient Collects.* Oxford, 6th ed. 1887.
    PLUMMER, C. *Devotions from Ancient and Mediaeval Sources.* Oxford, 1916.
80. WOTHERSPOON, H. J. *Kyrie Eleison. A Manual of Private Prayers.* Edinburgh, 1899.

81. MᶜMILLAN, W. *One Hundred Scottish Prayers.* Edinburgh, 1933.
    PATRICK, Millar. *The Scottish Collects of 1595.* Edinburgh, 1933.
82. HIND, L. *One Hundred Best Prayers.* London, 1927.
83. ROBINSON, A. W. *Prayers, New and Old.* S.C.M., London, 1932.
84. COOPER, J. *Reliques of Ancient Scottish Devotion.* Edinburgh, 1913.
85. FORBES, A. P. *Kalendars of Scottish Saints.* 1872.

XII. SOME ADDITIONAL BOOKS

1. *FRERE, W. H. *The Anaphora or Great Eucharistic Prayer.* London, 1938.
2. *CIRLOT, F. L. *The Early Eucharist.* London, 1939.
3. BATIFFOL, P. *Les Leçons sur la Messe.* Paris, 1927.
4. *The Book of Common Order* (Church of Scotland). Oxford, 1940.
5. SALAVILLE, S. *An Introduction to the Study of Eastern Liturgies.* London, 1938.
6. DIX, Gregory. *The Apostolic Tradition of St. Hippolytus.* London, 1937.
7. *DIX, Gregory. *The Shape of the Liturgy.* Westminster, 1945.
8. LADD, W. P. *Prayer Book Interleaves.* New York, 1942.
9. NORMAN, James. *Handbook to the Christian Liturgy.* London, 1944.
10. *ADDLESHAW, G. W. O. and ETCHELLS, F. *The Architectural Setting of Anglican Worship.* London, 1948.
11. *DAVIES, H. *The Worship of the English Puritans.* London, 1948.
12. *A Book of Public Worship.* Compiled for the use of Congregationalists by J. Huxtable, etc. London, 1948.
13. DAVIES, Horton. *Worship and Theology in England,* vol. iv, 1850–1900. Princeton and London, 1962.
14. REED, L. D. *The Lutheran Liturgy.* Philadelphia, rev. ed. 1960.
15. REED, L. D. *Worship.* Philadelphia, 1959.
16. BURNET, G. B. *The Holy Communion in the Reformed Church of Scotland,* 1560–1960. Edinburgh, 1960.
17. EDWALL, HAYMAN, and MAXWELL. *Ways of Worship.* S.C.M., London, 1951.
18. VISMANS and BRINKHOFF. *Critical Bibliography of Liturgical Literature.* Nijmegen, 1961.
19. KING, A. A. *Liturgies of the Primatial Sees.* London, 1957.
    —— *The Liturgy of the Roman Church.* London, 1957.
    —— *Liturgies of the Religious Orders.* London, 1955.
    —— *Liturgies of the Past.* London, 1959.
20. JUNGMANN, J. A. (tr. F. A. Brunner). *Early Liturgy to the Time of Gregory the Great.* London, 1960.
21. BAUMSTARK, A. (tr. F. L. Cross). *Comparative Liturgy.* London, 1958.

22. BOUYER, L. *The Paschal Liturgy*. London, 1951.
23. NICHOLAS CABASILAS (tr. Hussey and McNully). *A Commentary on the Divine Liturgy*. S.P.C.K., London, 1960.
24. WIGAN, B. *The Liturgy in English*. London, 1962.
25. GOGOL, N. V. *The Divine Liturgy of the Orthodox Church*. London, 1960.
26. BENOIT, J. D. *Liturgical Renewal*. S.C.M., London, 1958.
27. PAQUIER, R. *Traité de Liturgie*. Neuchâtel, 1954.
28. *Liturgie de l'Eglise de Genève*. Geneva, 1945.
29. COPE, G., DAVIES, J. G., and TYTLER, D. A. *An Experimental Liturgy*. London, 1958.
30. DAVIES, J. G. *Origin and Development of Early Christian Church Architecture*. S.C.M., London, 1952.
31. HAMMOND, P. *Liturgy and Architecture*. London, 1958.
32. HAY, G. *The Architecture of Scottish Post-Reformation Churches*. Oxford, 1957.
33. EVERY, G. *Basic Liturgy*. London, 1961.
34. DELLING, G. *Worship in the New Testament* (tr. P. Scott). London, 1961.
35. MICHELL, G. A. *Landmarks in Liturgy*. London, 1961.
36. PARRINDER, G. *Worship in the World's Religions*. London, 1961.
37. CUMMING, G. J. *The Durham Book*. London, 1961.
38. GARRETT, T. S. *Christian Worship: An Introductory Outline*. London, 1961.
39. VAN DIJK and WALKER. *Origin of the Modern Roman Liturgy*. London, 1960.
40. ROBINSON, J. A. T. *Liturgy Coming to Life*. London, 1960.
41. GARRETT, T. S. *Worship in the Church of South India*. London, 1958.
42. DANIEL, K. N. *A Critical Study of Primitive Liturgies*. Tiruvala, 1949.
43. SHEPHERD, M. H. *Reform of Liturgical Worship*. New York and London, 1961.
44. BOWMER, J. C. *Sacrament of the Lord's Supper in Early Methodism* London, 1951.
45. MAXWELL, W. D. *The Book of Common Prayer and the Worship of the Non-Anglican Churches* (Dr. Williams Lecture). London, 1950.
46. AULEN, G. *Eucharist and Sacrifice*. Edinburgh, 1962.
47. HINCHLIFF, P. *The South African Liturgy*. Cape Town and London, 1959.
48. ADDLESHAW, G. W. O. *The High Church Tradition*. London, 1941.
49. MCARTHUR, A. A. *The Evolution of the Christian Year*. S.C.M., London, 1953.
50. FLETCHER, B. *A History of Architecture*. London, rev. ed. 1954.
Studia Liturgica, Circulation Office, Postbus 2, NIEUWENDAM, HOLLAND, for current, past, and future Liturgical Bibliography.

INDEX

264
M46
1982

200

LINCOLN CHRISTIAN COLLEGE

INDEX

N.B. *The matter contained in the Schemes, being there sufficiently accessible, has not been included in the above index.*